Race Riot at East St. Louis
July 2, 1917

BLACKS IN THE NEW WORLD: *August Meier, Series Editor*

A list of books in the series appears at the end of this book.

Race Riot at East St. Louis
July 2, 1917

Elliott Rudwick

Foreword by William Julius Wilson

University of Illinois Press

Urbana   Chicago   London

Illini Books edition, 1982

Copyright © 1964 by Southern Illinois University Press
Reprinted by arrangement with Southern Illinois University Press

Manufactured in the United States of America

This book is printed on acid-free paper.

Library of Congress Cataloging in Publication Data

Rudwick, Elliott M.
  Race riot at East St. Louis, July 2, 1917.

  (Blacks in the New World)
  Reprint. Originally published: Carbondale : Southern
Illinois University Press, 1964.
  Bibliography: p.
  1. East St. Louis (Ill.)—Riot, 1917. 2. Afro-
Americans—Illinois—East St. Louis—History. 3. East
St. Louis (Ill.)—Race relations.   I. Title.   II. Series.
F549.E2R8   1982   305.8'96073'077389   82-1940
ISBN 0-252-00951-7   AACR2

*For Dorothy L. Rudwick
and Edward B. Groff*

THIS landmark study of urban racial violence is more than a historical analysis of one of the most serious intergroup riots in American history; it is also an insightful, imaginative, and sensitive sociological discussion of collective racial violence. With exceptional clarity, Rudwick captures the developments preceding, during, and following the cataclysmic and unforgettable upheaval in East St. Louis on July 2, 1917. Readers of this book are able to follow the chronology of events in graphic detail and understand in comprehensive terms the social and historical forces that gave rise to and molded them.

Making great use of various sources of data (including newspaper files, official and unofficial investigations of the riot, records of East St. Louis organizations, personal interviews, and transcripts of court trials), Rudwick portrays the racial anxieties, motivations, biases, orientations, and selective perceptions not only of the riot participants but also of others who were directly and indirectly implicated in the riot. He provides a comprehensive analysis of the institutions (business organizations, political parties, labor unions, and law enforcement agencies) that contributed to the social climate of heightened racial tension preceding the riot. Furthermore, he provides a brilliant account of the post-riot reactions in the court trials, local and national press, and congressional hearings—reactions which reveal local and national racial atmospheres and systems of racial justice in the first half of the twentieth century. Finally, Rudwick draws systematic comparisons between the East St. Louis riot, the Chicago riot of 1919, and the Detroit riot of 1943. He shows how shifts in population, increased economic conflict, overloaded public transportation systems, perceptions of changes in the racial order, fears of increased black participation in politics, and the spread of rumors were all antecedent conditions of each of these major racial flareups.

Rudwick's remarkable study should be read and re-read for many decades. It provides a rich description and analysis of an important event in American history, and it serves as a reminder of what could happen in the interracial arena in the future if the proper conditions are present. Although American cities have recently experienced spectacular ghetto revolts, the Detroit riot of 1943 was the last major interracial urban eruption. I use the word "interracial" because these violent outbreaks were qualitatively different from the ghetto revolts of the 1960s. The earlier interracial riots, as Rudwick's study clearly shows, involved groups of black citizens being attacked by and retaliating against groups of white citizens, whereas the later ghetto revolts involved groups of blacks attacking symbols of white power and authority (businesses and law enforcement officials) located or stationed in the ghetto. Unlike the interracial melees up to 1943, the white citizenry were not identified as combatants in the later ghetto revolts.

Because interracial riots are symptomatic of extreme hostility and bitterness between the races, it can be argued that they indicate an even more serious form of racial antagonism than that symbolized by ghetto revolts. We can only hope, therefore, that our nation can learn from this important volume and work to ensure that the East St. Louis riot is a prototype of an earlier, not a contemporary, form of racial violence.

William Julius Wilson

Center for Advanced Study in the Behavioral Sciences
September 30, 1981

IN the fall of 1960 I joined the Department of Sociology at Southern Illinois University, Edwardsville Campus. On the first or second day of class in East St. Louis, a student mentioned the 1917 race riot which had occurred here. I cannot recall my exact reply, but it was very brief. I knew almost nothing about the subject.

Since the professional literature on race relations almost completely ignored the East St. Louis riot, I began collecting local data about it. Through a faculty research grant from Southern Illinois University, materials were also located in Springfield, Chicago, Washington, and New York City. The volume which resulted is based on newspaper files, official and unofficial investigations made after the riot, correspondence and board minutes of various local organizations, transcripts of court trials, and personal interviews.

Because the riot occurred more than four decades ago, many records of the period have long since been lost or destroyed. The police files are gone, as are voter registrations and county tax assessment files. However, a considerable amount of primary data has been preserved; as a result of patience, sheer good luck, and the generosity of many East St. Louisans, these records were made available for this study.

Originally, I had planned to make greater use of personal interviews with old residents, but it became apparent that interesting interviews are not always illuminating ones. It was one thing to have lived through a riot and witnessed scenes of violence, but memory distorts events as well as effaces them. Still, conversations with "old-timers" provided leads and background information, as well as some insights.

One of the most fascinating informants was Bartley E. Schmitt, a retired but far from retiring linotype operator at the *East St. Louis Journal,* with whom I enjoyed countless talks in the newspaper library. Another octogenarian with a keen memory and a sense of humor was James A. Gladden, a Negro schoolteacher at the time of the riot and a witness in subsequent court trials of the Negro defendants. To them and the other East St. Louisans, a large debt is acknowledged.

There are many other people to whom I owe a great deal in the projection and completion of this volume, but, because of space limitations, not all are mentioned here. For counsel and advice I should like to express thanks to my colleague Jane Schusky of the Sociology Department at Southern Illinois University, Edwardsville Campus. Mrs. Schusky was particularly helpful in the planning of the chapter on Negro migration to East St. Louis. Mr. Virgil Seymour, Assistant to the Vice President on the Edwardsville Campus, offered encouragement especially during the bleaker moments and opened many doors in East St. Louis.

I am also indebted to Dr. August Meier, Associate Professor of History, Morgan State College. Dr. Meier, an esteemed friend who has contributed much to the study of Negro history, incisively criticized an earlier draft of this manuscript.

I am grateful for the courtesy shown by John M, Karns, Jr., St. Clair County State's Attorney and Robert Erd, Monroe County State's Attorney; Albert Bott, Chief of Detectives, East St. Louis Police Department; Dan P. O'Brien, City Clerk of East St. Louis; John Steuernagel, East St. Louis Superintendent of Schools; Clifford Basfield, Principal of the Lincoln School; George J. Walsh and Cecile C. Coombs in the office of the Board of Education.

Others who were helpful were Leo Bohanon, St. Louis Urban League; William Boyne, Editor of the St. Clair and Madison Counties *Evening Journal;* Mary T. Biggerstaff, East St. Louis YWCA; Raymond R. Sonnenberg, East St. Louis YMCA, Henry Lee Moon, Director of Public Relations at N.A.A.C.P., and Herbert Hill, National Labor Secretary, N.A.A.C.P. Among the librarians who were generous with their time far beyond the call of duty were Ollie Mae Williams, Southern Illinois University Library, Edwardsville Campus; Mrs. Edna James and Mrs. Eugenia McClinton, East St. Louis Public Library; Helen Key, the *Journal* library; Joseph Houston, St. Louis Public Library; and José D. Lizardo, Legislative Branch of the National Archives. I am grateful for the use of the following libraries besides the ones already mentioned: St. Louis University, Washington University, Missouri Historical Society, Chicago Historical Society, Illinois State Library at Springfield, Belleville Public Library, Chicago Public Library, New York City Public Library (especially the Schomburg Branch at Harlem), and Library of Congress.

Since my investigations began several years ago, the positions listed above may have changed.

Three of my students who typed the manuscript in its various drafts are Joy A. Montanaro, Janet Vaughn, and Janet Schroeder.

My largest debt is to Dorothy L. Rudwick, who encouraged and edited this manuscript. I, of course, assume complete responsibility for any errors.

Elliott M. Rudwick

East St. Louis, Illinois
Sept. 27, 1963

CONTENTS

LIST OF ILLUSTRATIONS

LIST OF TABLES

Race Riot at East St. Louis
July 2, 1917

1
An Introduction

IN his monograph on race riots, the sociologist Allen Grimshaw [1] identified thirty-three "major interracial disturbances" in the United States between 1900 and 1949; eighteen of these occurred between 1915 and 1919. Besides the East St. Louis riot of 1917, there were outbreaks of violence that year at Chester, Pennsylvania; Philadelphia, Pennsylvania; and Houston, Texas. The period, 1940-1944, had the second highest number of disorders. Five were listed but none of them, with the exception of the Detroit riot of 1943, ranked in seriousness with the inter-racial violence of the World War I era.

There were similarities but also significant differences between the World War I and World War II periods. In both periods a substantial Negro exodus from the South occurred and Negroes organized campaigns to challenge not only the concept of white supremacy but also the discriminatory practices resulting from it. However, the period of World War I was a greater upheaval because, for the first time, a large number of Northern Negroes aggressively and unconditionally claimed equal rights. For many whites it was their first encounter with Negro migrants who competed for jobs and seemed to be making unlimited demands on limited housing, transportation, and recreation facilities.

By the 1940's whites had learned to accept the presence of Negroes as a permanent part of the Northern scene. Between the two wars, the whites gradually became conditioned to accept a limited number of structured contacts with Negroes. Residential "invasion" was still a source of resentment, but job conflicts were not as acute as a generation earlier—partly because the CIO admitted lower-skilled Negroes. Civic-minded whites and Negroes in various cities took measures to prevent race violence. Under public and private auspices, they organized interracial committees to develop a moral climate stressing the peaceful race relations so vital to a democratic society fighting a second world war for its survival. Their efforts received encouragement from governmental leaders in Washington who were also paying some attention to Negro rights, in contrast to the racism of the Woodrow Wilson Administration. Painstakingly, a number of local agencies established "barometers" by which to gauge the level of social tensions in their communities, and municipal officials ordered police departments to take all necessary measures guaranteeing the preservation of law and order.

Undoubtedly, the memories of earlier riots in the World War I era helped to stimulate the later efforts to avoid a repetition of these tragedies. And, of all the race riots in that first period—or even in subsequent decades of American history—by far the most serious was the violence in East St. Louis, Illinois, on July 2, 1917, when nine whites and about thirty-nine Negroes were killed.

Before World War I, East St. Louis was known as "the Pittsburgh of the West." Located in Southern Illinois on the banks of the Mississippi River, the community was also variously called the "industrial offshoot of St.

Louis" and the "Hoboken of St. Louis." Twenty-seven railroads radiated from East St. Louis, and local residents boasted that "more trunk line railroads pass through it than through any other town of its size in America." In addition to transportation facilities, many heavy industries were attracted because of cheap land, low taxes, and access to inexpensive fuel. (There were over three hundred coal mines nearby.) For these reasons the city was a great commercial gateway between East and West.[2]

In 1917, the year of the race riot, thousands of workers were employed in the large stockyards and packing plants of the Swift, Armour, and Morris Companies. Other manufacturing plants with large payrolls were the Aluminum Ore Company and the Missouri Malleable Iron Company. Such industries created soot, dirt, odors, and noises, and, of course, large sections of the city were very unattractive in appearance. Workers crowded together in neighborhoods close to the factories, and a substantial portion of the population lived in small wooden shacks. It was commonly said that only those who must, live in East St. Louis; many business and professional men earned a living there but built homes elsewhere—often in St. Louis. Civic responsibility often began and ended with a membership card in the East St. Louis Chamber of Commerce. In looks, tone, and particularly attitudes, much of the community was an industrial slum, and a social worker in 1917 charitably called it "a satellite city . . . not a city of homes in the American acceptance of that term."[3]

Until the World War I period, Negroes were not regarded as a serious problem in East St. Louis. Few whites thought much about them since there was general agreement that Negroes were the South's problem. Little concern seemed to be evidenced when the local Negro population tripled between 1900 and 1910, and, as the city entered the second decade of the twentieth century, one in ten of its nearly 59,000 citizens was colored. Negro residents, occupationally at the lowest rung of the ladder, learned to accommodate themselves to a subordinated and segregated status. Although Illinois was the "land of Lincoln," white East St. Louisans liked to think of themselves as being in the Southern part of that "land."

Negroes were expected to conform to a rigorous system of racial segregation. For example, in the large factories, they had separate washrooms and dressing rooms, usually worked in segregated labor gangs, and ate meals in "the colored section" of the lunchrooms.[4] They lived in black ghettoes and, when the indigent among them were sick, they were treated by the colored assistant county physician. Their children went to "Negro schools," despite the fact that an 1874 Illinois law prohibited racially separate school systems.[5]

Although the Illinois legislature in 1885 had also passed one of the first public accommodation acts, theaters, eating places, and hotels in East St. Louis ignored it. Even when Negroes ran afoul of the law, they were locked away in a segregated section of the city and county jails. As long as they continued to accept a subordinate status and made no demands to challenge it, and, as long as they remained a relatively small minority, they constituted no threat to the whites. However, this pre-World War I system of accommodation was disrupted by the migration of a considerable number of Southern Negroes, and by the adoption of the racial equality doctrine among some long-time Negro residents.

2
The Colonization Conspiracy

IN East St. Louis organized hostility against Negroes first occurred in the fall of 1916 when Democratic leaders employed race prejudice to win a closely contested election. They charged the Republican party with the colonization of Negroes, i.e., importing them from the South where they could not vote and bringing them to the North shortly before the election for the purpose of illegally increasing the power of the G.O.P. East St. Louis Democrats had hurled similar accusations in 1912 but the attacks lacked organization and were not influential in that campaign.[1]

In national politics the partisan rallying cry of Negro colonization had had an earlier history and was employed in connection with the exodus of freedmen from the South during the late 1870's.[2] An even larger migration occurred in 1915-1917, but both population movements stemmed from essentially economic causes. The Republican party was not responsible for the migration; although major employers (who were Republicans) actually imported Negroes in some cases, the motivation was to obtain a cheap labor supply, not to recruit voters. Since obvious benefits accrued to the Republican party, the political opposition capitalized upon race prejudice. Particularly in 1916, the Democrats, conceiving the Negro influx as a threat, overestimated its size and for political purposes misrepresented the reasons behind the population movement. By injecting enough steam into attacks against colonization, the Democrats hoped not only to insure a large turnout of supporters at the polls and gain extra white supremacy votes, but in addition the strategy was to intimidate Negro migrants from casting ballots. Although the battle was fought at the local level, support and encouragement came directly from the National Democratic Committee.

East St. Louis Democrats were determined to defeat Republican Congressman William Rodenberg. In the latter's campaign to keep his Congressional seat, the steadily-increasing numbers of Negro voters played an important role. Rodenberg scattered a few political jobs in exchange for support, and although the Negroes were often dissatisfied,[3] they believed his opponents would give them less. In 1916, the Democrats charged that local Republicans were buying Negro votes and that "Rodenberg's Black Belt" contained some 2,000 migrants "imported" in late September to steal the election. East St. Louisans were reminded that newly-arrived Negroes could not legally vote since they were unable to meet the one-year residence requirement in Illinois. Notice was served that the Republican "colonization scheme" would be crushed by Democratic checkers who planned to examine registration lists in precincts which Rodenberg had previously carried. Beginning in October, the *East St. Louis Journal* (supporting the Democrats) aroused and reflected public opinion against the "Black Belters" who allegedly came into the community to plunder an election from the people.[4]

A month before the election, Democratic politicians charged that the "Rodenberg Black Belt Colonists" were committing many crimes in the city, and the *Journal* printed an item about Tennessee and Georgia Negroes breaking into local freight cars.[5] On October 10, the *Journal* announced that a railroad watchman was "Killed by Unknown Negro." The chief of police, a member of the Democratic machine, told of receiving a letter from Tennessee lawmen warning that "bad niggers" had migrated to East St. Louis. The *St. Louis Argus*, a Negro weekly, considered that the letter was a bald attempt to stop the exodus of colored people from the South.[6] Although the police chief spoke of a crime wave in the two weeks preceding October 10th, a search of the local newspaper for the previous month revealed that other than the watchman's murder, three crimes were attributed to Negroes: a Negro stabbed another; a Negro was charged with "taking money from a St. Louis man;" and a Negro was shot while allegedly attempting to steal a sack of flour from a railroad yard.[7]

Three weeks before the election, the *Journal* carried an account of a "Mississippi Negro Shot When He Resists Arrest." Several hours prior to the shooting, the Negro had allegedly asked a white man for street directions and the latter replied, "I don't know, but you can inquire at the police station, but when you do, be careful that they don't keep you there." The Negro supposedly took out a gun and retorted, ". . . so long as I have this with me, Mr. Copper will not fool around." [8] It is doubtful that this dialogue actually transpired, but it made good reading and conformed to the view that Congressman Rodenberg was teaching migrants they could do whatever they pleased in East St. Louis.

About this time, a newspaper in Belleville, the county seat, published a story which did not seem to substantiate the crime wave. According to the *Belleville News-Democrat*, East St. Louis Negroes "must be behaving very well this fall" since the county jail population for 1916 was smaller than in previous years. The editor declared that the crime rate would increase when local Negroes needed money after spending election year payoffs.[9] In attacking vote selling, most newspapers did not suggest that the practice existed among some whites as well as some Negroes. Only colored people were accused; race and vote fraud appeared synonymous. For example, a local resident asked, "Why do the colored voters sell their votes so cheap? Two dollars is not enough. Each colored voter should demand five dollars." [10]

As election day approached, the *Journal*, reporting that Negro colonization was state-wide, announced that the *Chicago Daily News* had sent investigators to East St. Louis to expose the Republican-inspired plot.[11] Furthermore, the residents of Rodenberg's "Black Belt" had supposedly established an "Early Morning Club" whose members made a pact to stop "legitimate voters" (i.e., Democrats) from casting ballots on election day. In this baseless and inflammatory newspaper comment, after Negroes had voted early in the morning they planned to form a bottleneck, preventing white Democrats from voting.[12]

The *Journal* also published an article linking Dr. Le Roy Bundy, an East St. Louis Negro Republican leader, with a plan "to vote" 1500 colonized Negroes in Southern Illinois during the morning and transport them to Chicago where they were to cast ballots later that night.[13] En route, a luncheon stop was scheduled, with time out for another round of balloting. In this account, another regiment was to leave Chicago and vote its way to East St. Louis. The editor never explained how these large movements of Negroes could descend upon various cities without detection.

In late October, the *Journal* declared that fifteen hundred Negroes had arrived during the preceding afternoon aboard a special train from Tuscaloosa, Alabama. Their purpose was "to swell Rodenberg's Black Belt vote." Actually, politicians and journalists had no idea how many migrants were in East St. Louis. The Tuscaloosa train contained fifteen hundred migrants in one news account and two thousand in another version.[14] According to one politician the entire Tuscaloosa group remained in the county, although federal attorney Charles Karch, who was a Democrat, guessed that only five hundred to eight hundred stayed in St. Clair County. The inventive *Journal* [15] noted that on the outskirts of the city were over three thousand Negroes—"driven out of East St. Louis"—who registered and would try to vote in Brooklyn, a Negro village whose total population of men, women, and children was considerably under two thousand.

The Democratic City Central Committee again warned that checkers were being sent to examine registration lists in Negro precincts, and on October 22, six hundred illegal registrants were allegedly found in "Rodenberg's Black Belt." U.S. Attorney Karch stated that his investigators were accumulating a considerable amount of evidence on the conspiracy and the men higher up would be prosecuted.[16] In view of all the accusations, the Board of Election Commissioners, with the cooperation of Republican and Democratic observers, summoned hundreds of Negroes and whites to determine which names should be stricken from the registration lists.[17]

The *Journal* was infuriated that any whites should be questioned: "One of the most damnable things that could have been perpetrated on the citizens of East St. Louis." The *Journal* also complained that at a meeting of the Board newsmen were barred by Thomas Green, a Negro: "The black has been in the employ of the Election Commissioners at the rate of $4 a day and took precedence over Chief Clerk Dan Wuersch and told the persons what should be done. 'I am messenger for the board,' he said." A short time earlier the *Journal* had accused the Board of involvement in the colonization conspiracy, and on that occasion the editor wondered about the employment of Green: "Was he hunting up illegal colored voters, and if so, was it to keep them off the registry books?" [18] Time and again, Negroes were depicted as bumptious or dishonest, or both.

William E. Trautman, the local Republican campaign manager, presenting his case to the public in a paid advertisement, charged that U.S. Attorney Karch knew Department of Justice investigators found no evidence of Republican colonization of Negroes. Trautman asserted that Karch's accusations were designed only "to intimidate colored voters . . . and to prejudice the white voters." East St. Louis police officers were condemned for trying to frighten Negroes from voting. Trautman checked the names of Negroes whom the Democrats challenged. He reported that many of these people resided in the city for over five years—in some cases twenty-five or thirty years.[19]

The *Journal* noted that according to a Democratic member of the Board of Election Commissioners, all the Negro registrants had perjured themselves and their cases would be submitted to a federal grand jury. Actually the Board scratched eighty-six Negroes from the registration rolls for not responding to suspect notices. The members of the local Democratic Campaign Committee were not satisfied since they thought that 720 names would be stricken.[20] Even this inflated figure was a far cry from the "thousands of illegally colonized Negroes." The *St. Louis Globe-Democrat* pointed out that not even all of the eighty-six Negroes were guilty of having registered fraudulently: "The talk of wholesale colonization failed to be proven and among the 86 were several who have lived in East St. Louis since Collinsville Avenue was an Indian trail but who were intimidated by a Democratic city administration and did not respond to notices and claim the right to vote."[21]

The colonization controversy in East St. Louis was a local manifestation of the jitters experienced by Woodrow Wilson's campaign managers as the 1916 election approached. Several midwestern states were placed in the "somewhat doubtful" column and Illinois in particular, with its increasing Negro population since 1912, was considered absolutely doubtful. In 1912 Wilson received over 400,000 votes in Illinois, but Taft and Roosevelt polled a combined vote of more than 640,000.[22] Democratic advisers evidently decided that necessity demanded rough tactics, and that the Republicans were vulnerable to the charge of vote fraud among Negroes, whose historical affiliation with the G.O.P. exposed them to the accusation of political enslavement caused by superstitious ignorance or brazen venality.[23] Since the public believed that only Republicans made political profit as a result of increasing migrations of Negroes from the South, the Democrats went into the 1916 battle with the cry, "Colonization."

President Wilson personally warned of vote frauds perpetrated by "conscienceless agents of the sinister forces," [24] and Attorney General Thomas W. Gregory announced that since Negro migration was motivated by political as well as economic forces, election law violations would be mercilessly prosecuted.[25] Shortly before the elections, Gregory placed Assistant Attorney General Frank Dailey in charge of a well-publicized colonization investigation which was particularly concentrated in Illinois, Indiana, and Ohio. Dailey captured headlines with the statement that over 300,000 Negroes of voting age had been colonized in those states since 1915.[26] Newspapers also quoted a Department of Justice statement that 60,000 Negroes were brought from the South since August 1916 and transported mainly to Ohio, Indiana, and Illinois. The *Chicago Herald* headlined the story, "60,000 Bogus Votes for Hughes; Plot to Steal Doubtful States." [27] Dailey announced that he had uncovered a gigantic vote fraud conspiracy, but he presented no evidence. In early November a strategy session was held at Chicago with federal attorneys of the state, and following the conference there was an announcement that wholesale arrests were expected.[28]

Agents of the Department of Justice interrogated many "colonized" Negroes in Chicago, East St. Louis, Cairo, and Danville, but in most instances the migrants insisted they were encouraged to leave the South because of higher paying jobs in Illinois. However, investigators told news-

men that some Negroes were promised railroad mainte-
nance jobs that never materialized or even existed. (It was
probably true that some railroads, in order to reduce wage
costs, did encourage more migrants than were actually
needed.) The Department of Justice agents read a political
plot in this lesson of old-fashioned capitalist economics,
and reporters were told that unscrupulous Republican politicians in Northern Kentucky had given labor contractors
the names of Negroes who were to be duped. Other federal
investigators seemed to accept the economic motive for
migration, but charged that Negroes registered without
fulfilling the Illinois residence requirement and were intimidated by employers to vote Republican.[29]

William R. Willcox, chairman of the Republican National Committee—like his local counterpart in East St.
Louis—angrily told newsmen that the colonization controversy was "a bold attempt to disfranchise negro voters by
the Democrats who have long been expert in the disfran-
chisement of negroes in the South." Willcox stated that
Northern Democratic political bosses and Democratic federal attorneys knew very well that the Negro vote was anti-
Wilson.[30]

On Election Day, the mass invasion of "colonized" Negroes did not materialize.[31] Despite this fact, Administration leaders announced that they would ask the United
States Senate to investigate Negro colonization and other
kinds of vote fraud. The Democrats blamed "colonization"
for defeats in a few states; for example, in Indiana they
talked of contesting the election of a Republican senator.[32]
Although Department of Justice officials had threatened
prosecutions, colonization cases were not brought to court,
and Republican newspapers in Illinois jeered at the "Investigation That Fizzled." [33]

The Attorney General was mockingly commended for
his interest in Illinois Negro voters and he was asked to
show a similiar measure of solicitude for the denial of Negro suffrage in the South. The *Chicago Tribune* snickered

at the Department of Justice's unproven discovery of a voting conspiracy in the Midwest: [34]

> We can imagine no assault, except one, upon the purity of our institutions more likely to shock the sensibilities of our present Department of Justice. There might be one worse offense. It is heinous to vote 300,000 colored Americans in the north. It would be unspeakable to vote them in the south, where they have been colonized for somewhat more than eighteen months. However, we congratulate the head of Mr. Wilson's Department of Justice, Mr. Gregory of Texas, on his opportune discovery and we suggest that he let us hear of the measures he has taken to assure the free vote of the several million colored Americans not yet colonized in the north.

In 1916 Illinois went Republican, as did Representative Rodenberg's Congressional district, but the Democrats captured East St. Louis and St. Clair County. In the Democrats' efforts to win Illinois for Wilson, race prejudice had been pressed into service for political ends. The embattled election left scars in East St. Louis, as whites believed the colonization charges, and the unwelcome Negroes were regarded as a threat to the very foundations of the democratic process. During the months after the election local labor leaders, who had supported Wilson, took a leaf from the Democratic party's campaign handbook, and anti-Negro propaganda emanated from the economic as well as the political front.

3
The Importation Crisis

MOST East St. Louisans did not belong to recognized labor unions and feared that job competition with the migrants would result in the denial of wage increases as well as the right of collective bargaining. As long as the whites believed they could obtain union recognition and job security, their hostility toward Negroes was held in check. However, the white labor leaders, like politicians in the 1916 presidential election, were prepared to use racist propaganda when, in their view, legitimate goals were jeopardized. Such a situation occurred during the spring of 1917 when a labor union was destroyed in one of East St. Louis' largest industrial plants.

The Aluminum Ore Company employed about 1900 men in April, 1917.[1] The pay was higher than the scale in other East St. Louis plants, but the company refused to recognize the union. During the previous autumn in the wake of a brief strike which the workers won,[2] the company embarked upon a policy of increasing the Negro labor force in order to limit the future demands of white workers. According to Aluminum Ore's own statistics, in November, 1916, the number of Negro employees rose to 280, in December there were 410, and in February of 1917, 470 Negroes were working in the plant.[3] Whether these figures were understated or accurate, they indicated rapid proportional increases.

After the 1916 strike the whites accused management of locking them out, and in December the Aluminum Ore Employees Protective Association was incorporated.[4] During the months of December and January, when at least two hundred Negroes were hired, more than that number of whites were discharged, nearly all of them members of the Protective Association.[5] The whites were being punished for union activities, and race tensions mounted after Negro replacements arrived. Until that time there had not been much anti-Negro feeling at the plant. The working force had been all white before 1913 and during the three following years the number of Negro employees increased from ten or twelve porters to 280 industrial line workers in November, 1916.[6] The leadership of the Protective Association recognized the need to recruit members among Negroes.[7] A few joined shortly after December, 1916, and that was precisely the point at which management decided to hire colored men who had just migrated from the South.

By the spring of 1917 the Protective Association organizers considered a strike and planned to strengthen their deteriorating position by affiliating with the American Federation of Labor.[8] The AFofL advised against a walkout at that time, suggesting instead that the union increase its membership rolls in preparation for a later showdown.[9] This counsel was based on the belief that the Aluminum Ore management, when faced with the demands of a larger and more cohesive union, would accede without the necessity of a strike. However, in April the leaders of the Protective Association feared that the company was going to flood the labor market with more Negro migrants.[10] Furthermore, since the Association's treasurer had just been fired, there was apprehension that management was preparing to discharge other union officials.[11] The strike was called on April 18, 1917.

The company announced that as the plant manufactured war equipment for the army and navy, the "pro-German" labor leaders were actually in the pay of the Kaiser. One organizer was even accused of offering to fix the strike for ten thousand dollars.[12] The *East St. Louis Journal* commented, "When strikes are called now there is good reason for suspecting that something else than the interests of the workmen is at the bottom of them." [13]

During the first several days of the walkout, production was sharply curtailed, since at least one-half the workers did not report for work, and the union seemed to be winning. However, after the company drew upon its resources the strike caved in; although for a few weeks pride prevented the dying Protective Association from calling it off. A professional strikebreaker was imported from New York City who recruited a large corps of associates at a Chicago detective agency; all these men were armed with shovels and possibly guns.[14] The Protective Association complained that pickets were fired on by persons inside the plant.[15]

The Aluminum Ore Corporation also borrowed U.S. Government-owned rifles and ammunition. C. B. Fox, the company superintendent, had secretly obtained these weapons from E. M. Sorrels, a secretary of the Chamber of Commerce and an officer in the East Side Rifle Club.[16] Sorrels, who later received a job at Aluminum Ore, denied that his rifle club had been established for procuring the weapons from the Federal Government to meet the company's anticipated needs during the strike. However, he admitted that most of the rifles remained in crates until he made a secret midnight journey to the Aluminum Ore Corporation.[17]

Fox also obtained help from other government sources; two companies of Illinois militiamen were sent to patrol bridges and plants, "guard[ing] against property damage by persons who are sympathizers with the German cause." [18] The soldiers' presence was humiliating and seemed a gesture of intimidation not only to the Aluminum Ore pickets but also to employees in other corporations who threatened to strike. For example, East St. Louis streetcar motormen said they were told by company officials that the guardsmen—some of whom were housed in carbarns— would operate streetcars in the event of a work stoppage.[19] On the day after the arrival of the militiamen Fox's lawyers appeared in federal court,[20] alleging that the Aluminum Ore strikers were led by "alien enemies" of the United States, and they had interfered with the production of necessary war goods. The judge issued a restraining order limiting the activities of pickets, despite the fact that until then the strikers had conducted themselves in a generally orderly manner.[21]

By April 25, Fox's superior strength was so apparent that he not only refused to confer with the strikers' executive committee but also barred the members permanently from working in his plant.[22] He purchased a full page employment advertisement in the newspaper, and many former Protective Association members were among the hundreds applying for jobs. Fox told all of them that henceforth no employees could hold membership in the AFofL or the Aluminum Ore Employees Protective Association.[23]

His victory destroyed the Protective Association.[24] Although most strikebreakers at Aluminum Ore were white, the union members remembered only that Negroes had taken their jobs. In their frustration they seized upon this single point: if Negroes had not come to East St. Louis the union could not have been crushed. The Aluminum Ore Company's conquest brought to the surface memories of other lost strikes, particularly one which occurred the previous summer in the meat-packing industry. The recollections of the union leaders were distorted to serve propa-

ganda purposes, since in 1917 wide community support
was desired to stop the Negro influx. East St. Louis labor
organizers, in retrospect, dated the beginning of the Negro
migration with the meat-packing industry strike in July,
1916.[25] The unionists asserted that from eight hundred to
fifteen hundred Negroes had been shipped into the city to
break the strike, and that the whites, whom the Negroes
had allegedly replaced, did not regain their jobs after the
union was beaten.[26]

Since the unionists' recollections of the meat-packing
strike played an important role in the re-enforcement of
racist attitudes which led to the race riot, it is instructive
to examine the walkout and try to discover what actually
happened. There is no doubt but that the labor organizers
were correct in noting many similarities between the meat-
packing industry and Aluminum Ore defeats, but they
were inaccurate on two important points: the packers did
not discharge large numbers of union members as had occurred at Aluminum Ore, and the Negro influx into East
St. Louis did not begin in preparation for the packing
strike. Nor did the meat-packing industry seem to have
increased the proportion of Negro workers during the
months before the walkout, as had been the case at the
Aluminum Ore Company.

In the summer of 1916 the packing workers had attempted to gain union recognition; after thirty-six or
thirty-seven organizers at the plants were fired the employees struck in protest.[27] Besides recognition they demanded the reinstatement of their leaders and an agreement not to penalize those who participated in the strike.
Over four thousand workers stayed away from their jobs
and production at the plants was nearly halted.[28] The
strike was brief but bitter, and the public posture of several
industrialists was adamant. John W. Paton, the general
manager of the Morris Company stated, "There will be no
conference on the part of this company with the strikers.
When they get ready to come back to work they can come

as individuals. There will be no union in this plant. That is all we have to say to them now or any other time." [29]

At least one corporation (Armour) transferred Negro and white employees to East St. Louis from plants in other cities; these men worked during the strike but returned to their home communities after a few days when the walkout ended. [30] The superintendent of the Armour Company also admitted importing fifty or sixty Southern Negroes, but it is doubtful that many of them actually worked during the strike because: the plants suspended production almost completely; union men surrounded the factories, intimidating those who might have wanted to work; the local press contained almost no mention of the strikers' reactions to the colored migrants, although newspapers published the strikers' other views; and there were no reports of violence against colored men, while there were press accounts of white strikebreakers having been pulled from streetcars and beaten. The *East St. Louis Journal* observed that the violence of the pickets frightened several migrants who had arrived at a meat-packing plant: "sho don't want to work in that thar place."

Although the strikers had demanded union recognition, the corporation managers refused to settle for more than a promise not to discriminate against union members. The companies agreed to rehire all the strikers immediately—with the exception of union organizers. Members of the latter group were promised reinstatement as soon as they were needed. Since the initial firing of these men had triggered the strike, the acceptance of management's terms showed clearly who possessed the power. Two months later meat packers denied they had ever promised to re-employ the union leaders. Because the strike agreement had been violated, the workers threatened another walkout and among their grievances were interference with the union, low wages, and irregular work hours. [31] While several union men said they were fired and replaced by Negroes, there were no general complaints at that time against Negro packing plant workers.

The press reported only one incident of race tension in a packing plant—at Armour's sausage room about fifty white girls went on strike because Negro girls were employed to do scrub work. The company replaced the strikers with whites and Negroes.[32] Between 1916 and 1917, the plants increased their military contracts and expanded production. The labor force of both whites and Negroes was augmented, but the relative proportions, roughly sixty to forty, probably had not varied much during the year.[33] The manager at Swift admitted that forty or fifty Negroes were directly imported,[34] while other plant executives stated that they hired their Negro workers at the factory gates. Management had two reasons for maintaining the consistently large Negro proportions: race differences among the employees decreased the possibility of unionization, and Negroes did not object to performing low-paying, dirty, unpleasant tasks involved in fertilizer manufacturing and hog-killing.[35]

By 1917 the meat-packing corporations had created such a repressive atmosphere in the plants that the union organization drive was smashed without even the necessity of firing many whites. The employees' organization, which had one thousand to fifteen hundred members before July, 1916, dwindled to about thirty by the following year.[36] The employers used as a club the threat of hiring more Negroes and the labor leaders realized that another packing plant strike was absolutely out of the question. In 1917, both before and during the labor troubles at the Aluminum Ore Company, union officials charged in their newspaper that the meat packers had put their threat into operation. The *East St. Louis Mail* carried the following bannerlines: "Packinghouse Laborers 70% Colored," "Thousands Flocking Here To East St. Louis In Answer To Ads—Situation Will Be Serious If Industrial Depression Comes." [37]

According to the labor leaders' estimates, five thousand Negroes had already been imported; thousands had arrived in late April and early May (coinciding almost exactly with the beginning of the Aluminum Ore strike). The unionists contended that the manufacturers planned to bring in another ten or even fifteen thousand Negroes and their families as part of a far-reaching scheme to make East St. Louis a Negro town.[38] In a *St. Louis Republic* interview with labor leaders, one organizer said that five thousand were scheduled to be brought to the city during May and early June.[39] Union organizers charged that the "capitalistic organizations" were building "negro huts" in "colonies" situated close to various factories in the community. These were exaggerations and distortions, but the Negro migration had increased in 1917 and probably the labor leaders believed what they were saying. They also decided that their only hope of ever staging a successful strike was to bar migrants from the city.

On May 10, a committee from the Central Trades and Labor Union, primarily a federation of AFofL craft unions, conferred with Mayor Fred Mollman, pleading with him to inform Negroes in the South that there were no jobs in East St. Louis.[40] The Mayor was warned that unless conditions were corrected, there would be a holocaust that would make the 1908 Springfield race riot "a tame affair." [41] Mollman promised that in the near future he would call a meeting of city officials to deal with the problem. However, the union delegation left his office convinced he was ignoring them and "just letting things go to smash." [42]

The labor leaders waited two weeks but in their view the only development was an increase in the Negro population. On May 23, the Central Trades and Labor Union sent a letter to all delegates announcing that a public meeting with Mayor Mollman and the City Council was scheduled for the following week. The letter, which received wide circulation, demanded "drastic action . . . to get rid of"

the migrants.[43] That same evening, a flareup occurred
which was reported in the press as a race riot. Despite the
overstatement, "race riot" had become a topic of conversation in the community, and "race feeling is at fever beat
. . . the hatred is increasing daily." According to a union
organizer, "It was a terrible feeling in the air. Everyone
felt that something terrible was going to happen. On the
street corners, wherever you went, you heard expressions
against the negro. You heard that the negro was driving
the white man out of the locality." [44]

In the May 23 incident at Seventh and Piggott a score
of Negro teenagers and about the same number of white
youths threw stones at each other until stopped by the
police. The patrolmen blamed the Negroes and after firing
shots in the air they arrested several colored boys. Later
that evening "a mob of blacks" gathered to protest the
arrest of a Negro for allegedly spitting on the sidewalk.
In the melee one man was shot.[45]

During their campaign against "wholesale importation," labor leaders had the support of realtors who believed
that Negroes were causing a decline in property values.[46]
In May, 1917, newspaper stories appeared about Negro
residential invasion, and middle-class homeowners were concerned that colored people might distribute themselves all
through the city. Two or three improvement associations
held indignation meetings. The Fifteenth Street Association, for example, tried to stop a Negro doctor from moving into a desirable piece of property at Fifteenth and
Exchange Avenue. Another neighborhood group in Washington Park served notice that their area "is a white man's
part of town . . . forever restricted" against Negroes. Influential whites suggested the enactment of a residential
segregation ordinance. These activities indicated that racial hostility was by no means confined only to blue collar
workers.[47]

In the days before the union protest meeting, the local
newspaper continued to re-enforce and reflect the edginess

of the population: "Negro Immigration Here Continues." [48] During the last weekend in May more flareups occurred between Negroes and whites. On Saturday night, May 26, a clash of about fifty Negroes and whites erupted at Tenth and Piggott. In the *Journal*'s description, "threatening negroes are reported to have congregated and made insulting remarks concerning the whites." [49] The *St. Louis Republic* noted that although Negroes fired more than a dozen shots, they had been beaten decisively.[50]

Press accounts omitted mention of weapons which whites carried, although considerable attention was given to the automatic pistols and loaded revolvers which Negroes possessed. The *Journal* reported that henceforth local policemen would deal with armed Negroes by carrying two guns instead of one, and the *Republic* warned that a serious race riot might erupt. According to the newspapers, the Saturday clash climaxed a night of Negro criminality. Early in the evening, a Negro robber allegedly shot a white man "because he did not raise his hands quick enough." Shortly afterwards, an unidentified Negro allegedly fired at a white policeman, and several other Negroes were arrested for carrying concealed weapons. In the whites' stereotype, "gun-toting" was a peculiarly Negro trait, and the common belief was that about the first thing they did after arriving in East St. Louis was to purchase a weapon.[51] The typical white attitude was expressed in a letter to the editor of the local newspaper: [52]

It is a noticeable fact that whenever revolvers form part of a show window display they at once attract attention from passing negroes. The glitter of a polished metal or silver mounted revolver possesses a fascination for the colored sport that is hard to resist, and he has been known to make a series of small deposits with the dealer to obtain the coveted weapon. Our pawnbrokers can tell you that more pistols are pawned by colored men than by any other class. Their idea is that the gun serves the double purpose of defending them against their dreaded foe, "de wite man" and as a meal ticket when they get hungry. Negro gun-toters are fanatical on the subject of self-protection and are constantly confiding to each other what they intend to do to the first "bad man" who disturbs their peace. The way to stop about half of this mortal and terrifying practice is to penalize the sale of guns, especially to "cullud folks."

Actually, in the East St. Louis frontierland of 1917, whites also beat a well-worn path to the pawnshops where window displays urged, "Buy a Gun for Protection!" [53] Even before the racial tensions many white males felt undressed without their revolvers, which "were popping around here all the time." [54] Since white East St. Louisans were not routinely searched by the police, Negroes constituted the majority of persons arrested for carrying concealed weapons. On the few occasions when whites were apprehended, the local newspaper usually did not give the stories much attention. Thus differential treatment by the police and the press confirmed the whites' mental picture of Negroes as gun-toters.

At the height of the importation crisis, Mayor Mollman and the police charged migrants with responsibility for another alleged crime wave. [55] The same accusation had been made during the colonization controversy the previous autumn. Many East St. Louisans also attributed their own anti-race feeling to the "reign of lawlessness," and a rumor circulated that the "gun-toters" were plotting a race war. At the end of May that rumor was used by some whites to justify counter-measures, and they told each other that perhaps violence was the only effective method to frighten Negroes away from East St. Louis.

4
The First Race Riot and Aftermath: A Testing Action

ON May 28, sixty delegates of the East St. Louis Central Trades and Labor Union appeared before the Mayor and City Council. They lodged a formal protest against Negro migration. One hour prior to this meeting the street outside the building was packed with people, and the Council moved to the auditorium. Female members of a waitress and laundry workers union arrived early. Their presence was calculated to dramatize that white womanhood required protection from Negro criminals.[1] The remnants of the Aluminum Ore strikers were among the males in the audience. Hundreds of persons who could not be accommodated in the larger room returned to the street. The labor leaders demanded a showdown session at which to confront the City Council with a bloc of voters.

A newspaper advertisement announced the program: "Negro and cheap foreign labor [is being imported by the Aluminum Ore Company] to tear down the standard of living of our citizens. Imported gunmen, detectives, and federal injunctions are being used to crush our people. Come and hear the truth that the press will not publish." [3] But when violence erupted after the session, the labor organizers denied placing the advertisement and blamed unwanted newspaper publicity for attracting a large, unruly crowd. [3]

In the auditorium, Aluminum Ore strikers protested that company officials had refused to confer with them. Michael Whalen, the City Clerk (and a union leader) introduced Mayor Mollman who warned against "hotheadedness." He told his listeners that because manufacturers had recently imported thousands of Negroes, the City Council was preparing a plan to stop the migration. Mollman also announced that Southern governors had been requested to persuade Negroes to keep out of East St. Louis. One or two speakers tried to counteract the mob spirit of the audience by pleading with the group to remain quiet and not to attack the Negroes. [4] However, Alexander Flannigan, a lawyer and minor politician, arose and condemned Negroes for moving into white neighborhoods. From several parts of the auditorium workers shouted, "East St. Louis must remain a white man's town." In a voice filled with emotion, Flannigan cried, "there is no law against mob violence." According to the labor leaders, no one took Flannigan seriously because he was regarded as a local joke. [5] Actually, the lawyer's incendiary remarks were received with clapping and cheering, and no union representative challenged him. [6]

As the men were leaving the City Hall they heard that a Negro robber had just accidentally shot a white man during a holdup. The story was embellished as it passed among the crowd; within minutes people asserted that the shooting was intentional and the victim had died. [7] According to other rumors, a white woman was insulted, two white girls were shot, and a white woman was shot. Crowds shouted, "Lynch him!" "Get a rope!" "Close the pawnshops and take the guns away from the negroes!" Mayor Mollman rushed outside in a fruitless effort to persuade the people to go home. By that time there may have been as many as three thousand persons on the street.

Mobs rushed to the downtown intersection of Broadway and Collinsville Avenue beating every Negro in sight. At Collinsville Avenue the wheel trolleys of streetcars were pulled from overhead wires and men were dragged out of the darkened vehicles. A colored woman was threatened with lynching, but the mob fled after a white female passenger became hysterical. On Fourth Street near Broadway a gang broke into a restaurant, a barbershop, and a few saloons which Negroes had patronized. Some of these establishments were demolished. Large mobs of white men continued down Fourth Street (along Railroad, Walnut, to Trendley) in search of colored people. The Negroes offered very little resistance; except for a skirmish at Collinsville and St. Clair Avenues, solitary Negroes were attacked at will. Apparently there was very little gunplay —the victims were beaten, kicked, and left bloodied in gutters.

The police force was described as powerless, and for the most part confined their activities to taking the injured to hospitals or headquarters. They also arrested several Negroes for carrying concealed weapons. However, two detectives, Samuel Coppedge and Frank Wadley, prevented rioters from burning down several houses at Third and Missouri Avenue. Ironically these two lawmen were to be killed a month later in the most serious race riot of the century.

In desperation Mayor Mollman appealed to Major R. W. Cavanaugh, commanding officer of the Illinois National Guardsmen stationed in the city since the beginning of the Aluminum Ore strike. Cavanaugh replied that he lacked authority to order the men from their posts. The harassed Mayor called Illinois National Guard headquarters in Springfield,[8] and, while the mobs roamed his city, he was still on the telephone trying (and failing) to find someone with power to divert the two hundred soldiers for duty in quelling the race riot.

By the early hours of May 29 the mobs were tired out, and an unidentified riot leader was heard to say, "Come on, fellows, let's go home. Tomorrow night we'll be ready for them. We are not armed now, but tomorrow we'll all have guns. We'll burn the negroes out and run them out of town." [9] However, some of the whites proceeded to the rail-road depot to meet an Illinois Central train supposedly arriving with five hundred migrants. When the rioters realized the report was false they finally went home. [10] Shortly after two o'clock in the morning, hundreds of Negroes carrying battered suitcases were seen heading for the bridges that led to St. Louis, and, although many whites were still on the streets at that hour, the refugees were not molested. During the long night, damage to life and property had actually been comparatively light. Two or three Negroes were shot, some were severely beaten, but no one was killed.

By noon Governor Lowden had promised to dispatch six companies of national guardsmen, and there was every indication that they would be needed. The Mayor and police chief instructed every member of the force to report that evening and be ready to work through the entire night. Mollman announced that groups larger than five persons would be arrested for congregating and discussing the race riot question. Saloons and theaters were closed and school children as well as their parents were warned to keep off the streets. The sale of firearms and ammunition was stopped, and the police department across the river in St. Louis was asked to prevent Negroes from purchasing weapons. [11] The afternoon edition of the *St. Louis Post-Dispatch* did not have a calming effect when the paper reported that according to St. Louis police, "an unusually large sale of firearms to negroes were [sic] carried on in the pawnshops of Market Street." [12]

Although the whites had started the riot on the previous evening and proclaimed intentions of finishing the job, East St. Louis police officers continued to devote most of their attention to disarming Negroes. Detectives were stationed at the bridge approaches to search and arrest Negroes attempting to transport guns, while whites were allowed to pass without being stopped.[13] One automobile containing six colored men was halted and several revolvers as well as a large supply of ammunition were found under the hood.[14]

Hundreds of whites stood in front of the police station as scores of Negro "gun-toters" were brought in, and the street was finally cleared after the crowd became threatening. A handful of whites was also arrested; among them was Charles Lehman, official of the Aluminum Ore Employees Protective Association. When Lehman was apprehended he carried a riot gun and several shells.[15]

Despite the arms embargo against Negroes, some managed to smuggle weapons into East St. Louis. According to the *St. Louis Argus* (a Negro newspaper), light-skinned men shuttled back and forth carrying guns across the river. Since these people were light enough to pass for white, they were not searched. In their neighborhoods the Negroes reassured each other: "As long as the state or United States troops do not disarm us, we are able to take care of ourselves." [16]

In the afternoon edition of the *Journal,* there was a report of Negroes mobilizing at Sixth and Trendley and Tenth and Piggott.[17] Before sundown a group of whites congregated near the meat-packing plants in the Whiskey Chute area at Second and St. Clair Avenue, waiting for Negroes to finish work. One by one, the laborers were beaten. A block away, at First and St. Clair, a Swift packing plant employee was shot. As darkness was falling over the city, white youths fired shots into the air, marching unchallenged through the streets singing popular tunes. While the police made several rescues, they were unable, and often unwilling, to deal with the disorders. Many clearly permitted their racial sentiments to interfere with duty, and until the arrival of the militia, rioters realized that they possessed the power to make the city government absolutely impotent.

/Just before dark as the first group of guardsmen arrived from Vandalia, some whites on the streets commented that the town of Vandalia had no race problem because Negroes were not allowed even to live there./ The militiamen were dispatched to Whiskey Chute, where mobs ridiculed them: "Look at those tin soldiers. See their legs shaking. They've only got blanks in their guns, anyhow. It's just a bluff."/After the commanding officer ordered his men to load weapons, the rioters retreated./However, there were not enough soldiers to preserve order in other parts of the city/As late as eight-thirty in the evening only two companies of guardsmen were on patrol, and the whites moved against the Negroes before other companies arrived.

A mob invaded the district near First and Pennsylvania Avenue, hurling stones and bricks at the Negroes. Windows in homes were shattered and shots were exchanged on both sides. A few blocks away on Illinois and Summit Avenues, hundreds of shots were fired by Negroes and whites. At Third and Summit Avenue, several Negro shacks were literally torn to pieces, a few dwellings were set on fire, and oil-soaked rags were found outside of several others. The main rioting areas were from Second to Fourth Streets and Broadway to St. Clair Avenue.

/Time and again the rioters retreated in the face of firmness shown by the soldiers, and control was slowly regained as additional troops entered the city/For example, a group of whites established a fort behind a boxcar on the Louisville and Nashville railroad tracks at Third and Summit. When guardsmen approached with drawn weapons, resistance crumbled. Other mobs disintegrated at Fourth and Broadway and at Division and Collinsville Avenue after guardsmen issued an ultimatum to disperse./The pattern was repeated several times—dispersal, regroupment, dispersal—until it became clear to the whites that further violence would not be tolerated. Shortly after eleven in the evening the soldiers headed off a mob demonstration at the Aluminum Ore plant, and by midnight order was completely restored throughout the city.[19]

Although many Negroes were beaten earlier in the evening, only six persons were shot (three Negroes and three whites), and no lives were lost. Perhaps this record indicated something more than poor aim on the part of the rioters—their intentions were not to kill but rather to frighten the Negroes into leaving the city. However, whatever the initial motives, a blood bath might have resulted if the militia had not arrived. While the militia's attention to duty was lauded by the press, there were a few instances of guardsmen cooperating with the mobs. Some soldiers were heard to say, "We don't have to see everything," and several were arrested by Police Chief Ransom Payne for leading groups of men and boys in attacks on Negroes.[20]

In the next two days (May 30 and 31) false reports and rumors circulated throughout the community. Several Negroes were beaten, one was shot, and at least one white man was attacked. The soldiers patrolled the streets in borrowed automobiles, sealing off small Negro neighborhoods. These guardsmen also seemed to have spent a great deal of time searching Negro homes for weapons. The *St. Louis Argus* angrily noted that the militiamen's searches and arrests of Negroes were intimidations designed to drive colored people from the city. The St. Louis branch of the N.A.A.C.P. informed Governor Lowden that the militia was "discriminating in favor of whites."[21]

Probably because of the one-sidedness during the rioting, whites feared massive retaliation by the Negroes. The *St. Louis Republic* announced that St. Louis police worried about the arrival of East St. Louis Negroes who might attempt to storm gun warehouses. As expected, some Negroes came across the river, but most were in search of refuge, not guns. Newspapers observed that the majority of assaulted Negroes were not the migrants who arrived in 1917. The *Globe-Democrat* cited the case of John Lee who with his wife and four children had lived in East St. Louis for several years. An employee of the Swift Corporation, he was known as a hard-working, conscientious person who had been with the company ever since he came to the city. Lee was attacked on May 29 while returning from the packing plant; when police appeared on the scene, the terrified man begged to be escorted home and told rescuers that he would leave the city to find a peaceful place in which to raise his family.[22]

The *Journal* estimated that in excess of 6,000 Negroes left East St. Louis,[23] but the newspaper exaggerated greatly. Undoubtedly, to avoid trouble some Negroes went to St. Louis between May 28 and May 30; when the immediate crisis passed by June 1 or 2, most returned. If a large, permanent exodus had occurred, school enrollment statistics would have reflected it. However, between May and June there was no drop in enrollment.[24] Since the May riots caused no large and permanent departure of Negro families with school-age children, there is no reason to assume that other colored residents were frightened away.

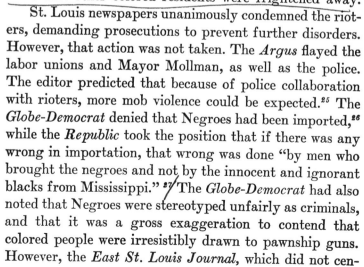

St. Louis newspapers unanimously condemned the rioters, demanding prosecutions to prevent further disorders. However, that action was not taken. The *Argus* flayed the labor unions and Mayor Mollman, as well as the police. The editor predicted that because of police collaboration with rioters, more mob violence could be expected.[25] The *Globe-Democrat* denied that Negroes had been imported,[26] while the *Republic* took the position that if there was any wrong in importation, that wrong was done "by men who brought the negroes and not by the innocent and ignorant blacks from Mississippi."[27] The *Globe-Democrat* had also noted that Negroes were stereotyped unfairly as criminals, and that it was a gross exaggeration to contend that colored people were irresistibly drawn to pawnship guns. However, the *East St. Louis Journal*, which did not cen-

sure the mobs, took another view, concluding that the
whites had rioted against the lazy, shiftless, and criminal
Negro migrants.[28]

In the aftermath of the riots not a single effective precaution was taken by anyone to prevent future disorders.
Employers did nothing to assure white workers of job
security or union recognition and thus hostility toward
Negroes increased. In early June, Mayor Mollman and the
leaders of the Central Trades and Labor Union asked the
Illinois State Council of Defense to investigate the background of the riots. A labor subcommittee of the Council
was sent to conduct the hearings and one of its three members was John H. Walker, Acting President of the Illinois
Federation of Labor. He had also participated in the May
28 meeting which sparked the violence. The Walker Committee, with the support of East St. Louis labor organizers,
blamed the riots on a deliberate conspiracy of employers to
import "an excessive and abnormal number" of Negroes to
East St. Louis. The Walker group condemned employers
but made no attempt to discover the identity of the rioters
or recommend the prosecution of mob members. These actions, in seeming to condone the riot, hardly discouraged
those who took the law into their own hands.[29]

Nor did Mayor Mollman make any effort to improve
the police department, despite its obvious inadequacy during the disorders. Furthermore, although Governor Lowden was aware of the East St. Louis police situation and
received warnings that more trouble was expected, he allowed most of the national guardsmen to be withdrawn by
June 10. A few days later hardly more than a hundred
soldiers remained in the city.[30] By June 20, most of these
also departed even though many people in town predicted
that the withdrawal would be a signal for renewed rioting.
Of course, there were still two militia companies on plant
security patrol, but their commanding officer, Major Cavanaugh, had learned no lesson from the May 28 disorders
when he refused to use his men against the rioters. In June,

1917, East St. Louis' only hope to avert disaster was the establishment of a clear procedure providing for Cavanaugh's immediate assistance when racial violence resumed. Evidently no such riot plan was conceived and certainly none was executed.

The city with a population of approximately seventy thousand was left unprotected despite the reappearance of all the obvious danger signs. In early June Negro employees at the Aluminum Ore Company were attacked by pickets. Once again, the police arrested Negroes—three workers were taken into custody for carrying concealed weapons to defend themselves. Almost daily Negro laborers were waylaid and beaten; [32] the *East St. Louis Journal* even stopped printing the incidents as news.[33] Since the police failed to provide protection, Major Cavanaugh's soldiers were finally used to escort Negroes to and from their homes.

The conversations of the whites turned again to the "gun-toters." Several pawnshops on Collinsville Avenue restored window displays of revolvers and the *Journal* reported that they "attracted a crowd of admiring blacks." [34] Negro crime stories were reappearing in the local newspaper and on June 15 the *Journal* carried a front page story about two Negro robbers. On page two of the same issue were other news notes—"Shot by Negro," "Negroes Blamed for Early Morn Robbery," and "Charge that Negroes Took All His Money." During the next several days there were similar accounts, and the *Journal* observed that these were the first Negro holdups since the May riots "attributed partly to the numerous shootings, stickups and other robberies committed by negroes." [35]

On June 17 an embryonic race riot mob of several hundred whites threatened a sixty-six-year-old Negro who was then beaten into insensibility. According to the *Journal,* he "had refused to give his seat on a Collinsville streetcar to an elderly [white] lady." [36] The following week other Negroes were attacked by white gangs, and the newspaper announced that "race rioting [had] resumed." [37] It was no coincidence that these last assaults occurred just after the dwindling corps of pickets at the Aluminum Ore plant decided for "patriotic" motives to call off their strike. They had experienced two months of bitter frustration and defeat; their union, having failed to obtain recognition, stood impotent before the U.S. marshals and Illinois militiamen. [38]

Despite the police having arrested none of the gangs of whites beating Negroes, Mayor Mollman later reported that colored people had "made no individual retaliations . . . to defend themselves." [39] Time and again, when they went across the East St. Louis-St. Louis Free Bridge, they were "abused, hooted, and chased," and in late June a Negro committee complained to Mollman. This delegation, headed by Dr. Le Roy Bundy and Dr. L. B. Bluitt, who was the assistant county physician, prophetically told the Mayor there was a real danger that a victim might kill one of the tormentors and plunge the city into a disastrous race riot. Mollman expressed surprise and dismay, indicating that he had judged race relations to be considerably improved since the first week of June. [40] His remark was somewhat strange, not only because of the repeated assaults, but also because during the entire month East St. Louis whites circulated the rumor that Negroes were arming to stage a July 4 massacre in revenge for the May riots. [41] The Negro variation of the same rumor was that the whites intended to slaughter them on July 4.

Mollman's professed ignorance was one more proof that as a city official he often postponed making unpleasant decisions. He and his political machine wanted to maintain the support of both the lower class whites and Negroes. To avoid offending white laborers he refused to protect Negroes, but since he also did not wish to alienate colored voters, Mollman told the delegation that their complaints would be investigated thoroughly. Because the Negro leaders were unconvinced, Mollman summoned Police

Chief Payne who adamantly announced that the patrolmen were doing their full duty.[42]

The forebearance of East St. Louis Negroes ended four days after that interview. Early on Sunday evening, July 1, several more white assaults on Negroes were reported. About seven o'clock that night one man was beaten and may have shot his white assailant.[43] The incident, like the others, occurred near Tenth and Bond Avenue. Between nine and ten o'clock an hysterical colored woman in a torn dress told a crowd of Negro men that whites had just beaten her and several others at Eleventh and Trendley. Someone shouted, "Let's go to 10th Street." However, several in the group advised them to return to their homes.[44]

Between ten-thirty and midnight, a Ford car (possibly two) driven by whites fired shots into Negro homes along Market Street, near Seventeenth. On a second foray, the residents were prepared and returned the fire, striking the automobile which disappeared in the night. Although the police did nothing about the whites, they received a report that armed Negroes were on a rampage. A Ford squad car was dispatched immediately to make an investigation. In the front seat of the police automobile were the driver and two detectives in civilian clothes. Uniformed officers sat in back and a reporter for the *St. Louis Republic*, Roy Albertson, stood on the running board. Early the following morning, the *Republic* published the newsman's account of the police encounter with the Negroes—without doubt this particular version helped to incite an East St. Louis population already on the verge of riot.

According to Albertson, the police car turned into Bond Avenue from Tenth, meeting "more than 200 rioting [armed] negroes . . . [who] without a word of warning opened fire." Samuel Coppedge, one of the detectives, was killed almost instantly and the other, Frank Wadley, died the following day. Albertson wrote that the Negroes had prearranged the murder. Other newspapers repeated this account of a premeditated, unprovoked, and senseless killing. The assailants were portrayed as so calloused that they opened fire upon lawmen who had extended an offer of protection.[45] Through this version, East St. Louisans were confirmed in their view that Negroes, stirred up by agitators and intoxicated by new Northern freedom, were the aggressors who had determined by any unlawful means to take control of the city.

In his article for the *Republic*, Albertson omitted certain facts which, although not excusing the crime, certainly explained it. Testifying during the autumn of 1917 before the Congressional Committee investigating the riot, Albertson admitted that the murder could have been a case of mistaken identity.

Tenth and Bond Avenue was almost totally dark, a street light was at least fifty feet around the corner from where the Negroes were, and the headlights on the police car were "very poor." In his original articles on July 2 and 3, he had written that Detective Coppedge flashed his badge, identifying himself to the Negroes; but at the Congressional hearings Albertson was asked, "How could a policeman show his star to a man in the dark, with the [automobile] stopping and off again in half a minute? What could [the Negroes] see about a star in the dark?" The reporter replied, "I don't know." Congressman John E. Raker suggested that the armed Negroes mistook the Ford police car for the Ford which white assailants had used to shoot into colored homes shortly before the lawmen had arrived: [46]

> Now, as a matter of fact, if marauders had gone through those negro quarters and had shot into the houses and terrorized those people, the way [the police car] drove in front of those negroes that night, irrespective of whether they were armed or not—and in the dark, without being able to see who was in the machine—isn't it reasonable to suppose they thought there was another gang of maraud-

ers coming there to kill them as well as destroy their property. Isn't it reasonable?

Albertson admitted that it was indeed reasonable.[47]

On the morning of July 2, Sergeant Coppedge's bullet-riddled car was parked before the police station in downtown East St. Louis. The Ford, with its blood-stained upholstery, "looked like a flour sieve, all punctured full of holes." [48] Laborers on their way to work gathered around it, talking about getting revenge.[49] A local attorney remarked that he would gladly act as counsel for "any man that would avenge the murders." [50] The attack upon the detectives gave East St. Louisans "proof" they needed that Negro "armies" were mobilizing for a massacre, and in the face of that threat the whites were ready to wage a race war.

5
The July Riot

WHILE some of the laborers stared at the car, others moved among the crowds announcing that within an hour there would be a protest meeting in the Labor Temple at Fourth and Collinsville Avenue. Tension mounted and by half-past nine in the morning the downtown intersections were filled with more people than usual. In a City Hall office Mayor Mollman was not feeling well,[1] as he was afraid of being attacked by laborers if he appeared on the street. Several prominent persons advised him to deputize a citizen army to prevent mobs from burning up the town,[2] but Mollman was unable to decide what to do. He knew quite well that the police wouldn't cooperate in trying to control the mobs, but during the previous night he had telephoned National Guard headquarters in Springfield and mistakenly believed that six militia companies would arrive that morning.[3]

While Mollman hesitated in his office, speakers were telling the Labor Temple audience to return with guns in the early afternoon. After the meeting, participants

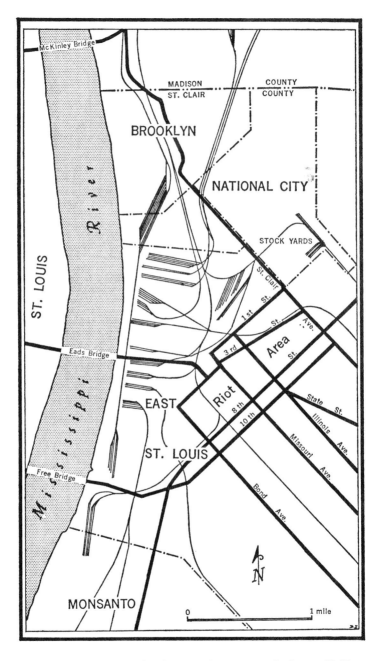

1. East St. Louis Area as it appeared about 1917

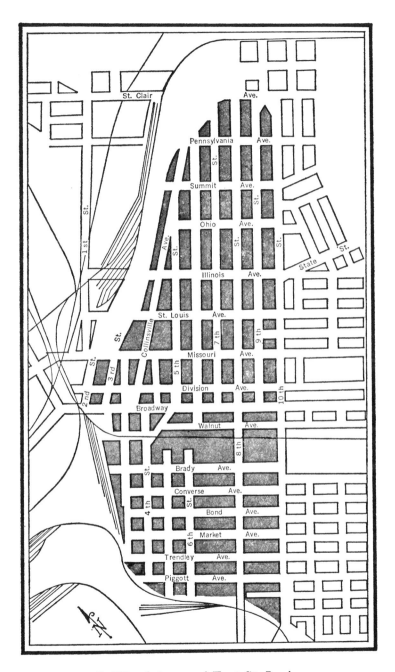

2. The riot area of East St. Louis

marched in military formation along Collinsville Avenue
(a principal business street) toward Broadway, which was
the most important streetcar transfer point in the city.
Within view of the large crowds on that street corner, the
first Negro was shot.[4] Observers described the whites as
being "in good humor . . . like waiting for a circus parade." [5] After the shooting, soldiers from the only militia
company that had arrived were assigned to patrol the main
business intersections as well as a Negro district near the
center of the city.[6]

Between ten o'clock and eleven o'clock, other colored
people were attacked along Collinsville Avenue between
Broadway and Illinois Avenue. This area became a bloody
half-mile in the following three or four hours. Streetcars
were stopped: Negroes, without regard to age or sex, were
pulled off, stoned, clubbed, and kicked.[7] A large group
of whites marched through the streets shouting that colored
people should leave East St. Louis immediately and permanently; [8] this demonstration of community support emboldened the rioters who after the noon hour began killing
Negroes along Collinsville Avenue. Although some newspapers reported that the mobs were composed of "10,000
blood-crazed whites," in actuality the assaulting gangs
were small, usually containing not more than twenty-five
persons. However, there was no doubt that they had the
encouragement of thousands of spectators watching from
the sidewalks.[9]

A few whites who attempted to protest against the violence were threatened; some were "hissed" and "hushed"
by women carrying hatpins and pen knives as weapons. A
chilling fear gripped and completely immobilized well-
meaning citizens who later rationalized their noninterfer-
ence. For example, a corporation executive recalled his
conduct on July 2: ". . . if you had been there you would
have been just as big a coward as the rest of us. We didn't
want to [interfere], not only for our own lives, but most of
us I guess—I didn't own all the property, you know. I

have my duties to my stockholders to protect the property, and it wouldn't have done any good." [10]

By the early afternoon, when several Negroes were beaten and lay bloodied in the street, mob leaders calmly shot and killed them.[11] After victims were placed in an ambulance, "there was cheering and hand-clapping." Near Main and Broadway, white prostitutes grabbed the hair and clothing of fleeing Negro women. An excited girl was heard to admonish her little brother who carried a rock, "Why haven't you got a gun?" Carlos F. Hurd, a reporter for the *Post-Dispatch*, described the fury of these white women, "dressed in silk stockings and kimonos, with last night's paint still unwashed on their cheeks": [12]

> I saw negro women begging for mercy and pleading that they had harmed no one, set upon by white women of the baser sort, who laughed and answered the coarse sallies of men as they beat the negresses' faces and breasts with fists, stones and sticks. I saw one of these furies fling herself at a militiaman who was trying to protect a negress, and wrestle with him for his bayonetted gun, while other women attacked the refugee.

A few yards away two or three Negro men held their hands high in a gesture of surrender, but were clubbed with gun butts. When they fell, young girls got blood on their stockings while kicking the victims, and the sight amused the rioters.

During the late afternoon, mobs invaded Third and Fourth Streets, south of Broadway, the same area they attacked in May. They advanced with the battle-cry, "They got Sam [Coppedge] and Frank [Wadley]. We'll get them." Shacks at Main Street and Brady Avenue, Third and Brady, and Third and Railroad Avenue were surrounded and set afire. When the Negroes attempted to escape their burning homes, four or five of them were picked off "as one shoots running or cowering rabbits."

The *St. Louis Republic* described the waiting game played
by armed whites who lined up along the railroad tracks: [13]

> A crazed negro would dash from his burning home, some-
> times with a revolver in his hand. Immediately revolvers
> by the score would be fired. He would zig-zag through the
> spaces between buildings. Then a well-directed shot would
> strike him. He would leap into the air. There were deep
> shouts, intermingled with shrill feminine ones. The flames
> would creep to the body. The negro would writhe, attempt
> to get up, more shots would be fired. The flames would
> eat their way to him, past him, and further east along
> Railroad Avenue.

Violence fed upon itself and the riot reached a climax
at Fourth and Broadway shortly after six o'clock that evening. On that street corner, the "shirt-sleeve gathering" estimated at one thousand chanted, "Get a nigger . . . get
another." In the Black Valley, small gangs lighted torches,
joking while waiting for Negroes to flee from the furnaces
which had been their homes. Residents faced a terrible decision—to remain inside and await incineration or to risk
slaughter by gunfire outside. Only a few chose the flames
and most who ran from their back doors into the alley actually escaped.[14] Reporters describing the violence said
"there was a visible coolness and premeditation about it . . .
this was not the hectic and raving demonstration of men
suddenly gone mad." [15]

At Fourth and Broadway, Paul Anderson, a *Post-
Dispatch* correspondent, counted six Negro corpses on the
street. He recalled, "I think every one I saw killed had both
hands above his head begging for mercy." One had cried,
"My God, don't kill me, white man." [16] Victims were not
permitted "to die easily," and when "flies settled on their
terrible wounds the dying blacks [were forbidden] to brush
them off." The mobs laughed at the final writhings of a
Negro whose skull had been partly torn away; even corpses
were clubbed and stoned. One man's face was a bloodied

mess, but when an ambulance arrived to take him to a hospital, rioters warned, "If you pick up that skunk, we'll kill you, too." The driver departed and the Negro was hurled into the flames. Three armed men shined flashlights on a Negro lying in a gutter. "Look at that————, not dead yet;" each fired a shot and disappeared.

Since it was said that "Southern niggers" deserved a "genuine" lynching, seven or eight men with a clothesline tried to hang a victim on a telephone pole. When the rope broke under the weight of his limp, almost-dead body, a new piece was substituted. A journalist ran to several mili-tiamen a few hundred feet away, begging them to save the man's life, but "I was not able to interest them in it." [17] Other witnesses also noted that these soldiers stood around doing nothing.[18] Mr. Hurd reported the lynching in the *Post-Dispatch:* [19]

> I saw the most sickening incident of the evening when they got stronger rope. To put the rope around the ne-gro's neck, one of the lynchers stuck his fingers inside the gaping scalp and lifted the negro's head by it, literally bathing his hand in the man's blood. "Get hold, and pull for East St. Louis," called the man as he seized the other end of rope. The negro was lifted to a height of about seven feet and the body left hanging there for hours.

After another Negro was captured someone shouted, "We're going to lynch the dog. Shooting's too good for him!" He was dragged to the pole by a rope tied around his neck. His life was saved only by the arrival of seventy guardsmen, but a few days later the victim died of injuries caused during the attempted lynching.

With the coming of darkness and additional soldiers the rioting slowed down but was not yet over. The square block at Eighth and Broadway was "burned to an ash heap" while more Negroes were killed. According to the *East St. Louis Journal,* two were shot by "khaki-uniformed" men. Afterwards, rioters "slapped their thighs and said the Il-

linois National Guard was all right." [20] Nearby, a reporter
said he observed a mob strike a Negro woman and a small
Negro boy, hurling the latter into a blazing shack.[21] At
least three other children lost their lives in the riot—the
county coroner declared that a boy approximately a year
old and a girl about two years of age died after being shot
in the head.[22] The death of another child was recorded in
the following terse police memorandum: [23]

> In the ruins of a negro shack at 4th and Division, rumor
> had it, a body of a cremated negro child, as if laying
> [sic] under a bed when the fire had destroyed it [sic]
> home. Mahany and Wilson investigated, and reported the
> rumor as being true. . . .

On that night of July 2 citizens encouraged the mob
with the chant, "Burn 'em out! Burn 'em out!" Fires destroyed over two hundred houses, and much of the burned
sixteen block area was in a vice district called the Black
Valley. The neighborhood's history gave whites an added
reason for condoning the destruction. In the words of the
St. Louis Republic, the Black Valley "had been occupied by
negroes of the lowest form of two-legged existence [who
lived in] a settlement of cocaine dives, houses of pollution,
gambling dens, and thieves' resorts." [24] Extensive property
damage was done between Fourth and Tenth Streets, in the
block south of Broadway. Homes were also burned on
Fourth Street and Seventh Street in the two blocks from
Broadway to Missouri Avenue, and on Second and Third
Streets in the block between St. Louis and Missouri Avenues. In addition, ten or fifteen houses were set afire over
two miles away in the vicinity of Nectar Street between
Thirteenth and Fifteenth.

By midnight the South End was bright with flames
which could be seen miles away. An observer in Belleville
(the county seat) reported from Signal Hill, "the flames
shot high into the air and were reflected in Pittsburgh
Lake until that body of water at the foot of the bluffs

looked like a sheet of fire." [25] Witnesses generally agreed
that local firemen adequately performed their duty with
the help of the St. Louis department. Although the mobs
threatened firefighters and on at least one occasion cut
hoses, they usually withdrew after fire equipment arrived.
Since by that time it was often too late to save the frame
dwellings, the mobs turned their attention to houses still
intact. While hosemen were trying to extinguish one blaze,
mobs were starting others. [26]

Some fleeing Negroes asked white residents for temporary shelter, but not infrequently these pleas were rejected.
For example, a woman refused to allow a Negro to hide
under a house because she said that her chickens would be
disturbed. [27] However, many refugees owed their lives to the
aid of sympathetic whites who hid them from mobs. [28] Loss
of life was also reduced considerably because by evening
the Negro residents had already fled from the city or been
rescued by militiamen who made street-to-street canvasses
of the Negro district bordering on the downtown area. As
the colored people were being evacuated, rioters warned
that death would be the price of their return. Many de-
serted houses were looted, and vandals destroyed household
belongings and furniture before arsonists took over. [29]

With the flames illuminating the night sky, hundreds
of tired, terrified refugees were brought by military escort
to the City Hall auditorium. Some suffered from burns or
beatings; many were separated from their families. The
moaning and wailing of these people "raised a Bedlam that
at times drowned out the bark of pistols and the crackling
of fires." [30] The lights suddenly went out in the building
and "the negroes screamed in terror, believing this was a
new plan to murder them wholesale. In a moment, the lights
returned; there had been a slight accident to the electrical
machinery."

In the sociology of race riots, it is a truism that early
reports generally exaggerate the extent of casualties, [31] and
East St. Louis was no exception. Whites guessed that as

many as 250 or even 400 Negroes lost their lives,[32] while
Negro sources (such as the N.A.A.C.P. and the *Chicago
Defender*) estimated that from approximately one hundred to two hundred colored persons had been slaughtered.[33] A Congressional Investigating Committee recognized the impossibility of stating with complete accuracy
how many individuals actually died, but its reports indicated that at least eight whites and thirty-nine Negroes
were killed.[34] The county coroner recorded that nine whites
lost their lives and it would appear that his figure is the
correct one.[35] Some of these victims were accidentally slain
by other whites.[36]

Ascertaining the number of Negro casualties involved
insuperable difficulties. East St. Louis municipal records
were inadequate; Negro corpses "were just thrown in like
you would gather up so many dead hogs in the yard." [37]
In order to save county funds, post-mortem examinations
were performed on only a few bodies, a situation which the
Congressional Investigating Committee considered as-
tounding.[38] The coroner held a blanket inquest for most of
the others, and many were never identified.[39] Apparently
several victims were buried in potter's field without even
having been under the perfunctory jurisdiction of the coroner's office.

The Congressional Committee seemed to have based its
reckoning on reports of local undertakers.[40] However,
many citizens took issue, believing that some officials had
not spoken frankly and that the Negro mortality list was
considerably higher than thirty-nine. The East St. Louis
Police Department indicated that about one hundred persons died, and this number was accepted by the St. Clair
County Grand Jury.[41] East St. Louisans disputing the
Congressional figures claimed that the true number of Negro fatalities would never be known because many corpses
were not recovered.

On July 4 and 5, after several "horribly mutilated
floaters" were found in the Cahokia Creek, this discovery

was considered as the first confirmation of reports that in
many cases, members of the mob threw bodies of their victims into the creek. There were statements that twenty-five
bloated corpses could be recovered.[42] However, the water
did not surrender any more of its dead, and it was unlikely
that over twenty beaten bodies had sunk to the bottom to
remain there forever. Some East St. Louisans felt that
while whole bodies might come to the surface, charred remains would not and without presenting any proof, they
contended that white mobs dumped into the creek the ashes
and burned bones of victims consumed by the fires.[43] Nor
was there substantiation for the claim that adult corpses
were entirely devoured in the flames, leaving absolutely no
traces.[44] Rumors of the wholesale incineration of Negroes
lacked foundation.[45] For example, it was reported that
many perished in a fire at the Broadway Opera House
where victims had allegedly sought refuge; however nothing was found in the rubble.[46]

In testimony before the Congressional Committee, Coroner C. P. Renner discussed his examination of Negroes
who had died in the flames: [47]

> *Congressman Johnson:* Doctor, to what extent were they
>   burned . . . ?
> *Dr. Renner:* They were just burned to a crisp; as much
>   as a human body can burn without being in ashes;
>   enough to be agglutinated together, showing the form
>   of the human body.
> *Congressman Johnson:* The bones were of course left.
> *Dr. Renner:* The bones were left and the skulls were left.
> *Congressman Johnson:* And the cooked flesh?
> *Dr. Renner:* The cooked flesh was in a crisp.

Of course, it might also be argued that other charred
remains of corpses had indeed been discovered but that the
arsonists secreted them in the aftermath of the riot. However, in the days following July 2, the mobs showed no
remorse or guilt; on the contrary they seemed proud of

what they had done and threatened further harm. Why should they have been frightened in view of the fact that many East St. Louisans were saying there would be no real post-riot investigation? But even if there had been a desire for concealment, it is difficult to understand how scores of corpses could have been hidden from the eyes of newsmen and soldiers arriving in the city. Those who claimed that the death toll was one hundred also used the argument that an undetermined number of Negroes was missing and not accounted for. However, there was simply no way of knowing how many colored people had been residents of the city before the riot, nor how many had fled to St. Louis and other communities during and after the riot. During the days following July 2, many Negroes remaining in East St. Louis heard from "a lot of people" living across the Mississippi River who were rumored to have died in the riot.[48]

In the East St. Louis of 1917, almost every statistic pertaining to Negroes had been exaggerated—the number residing there, the number of strikebreakers, the number who fled in the aftermath of July 2—and it seems reasonable to conclude that the Negro mortality estimates were also exaggerated.

A similar problem existed in connection with obtaining statistics on injured persons. Hospital records were incomplete and patients were not always identified by race. Of the nearly one hundred persons whom records showed as having been treated on July 2, the majority were Negroes. It must also be pointed out that some injured Negroes were afraid to be hospitalized and were believed to be concealed in homes. Several newspapers probably overestimated the number of wounded; for example the *St. Louis Times* suggested that the figure was as high as 750.

The earliest figures on property damage were also overestimated and were set at $1,400,000 to $3,000,000. Later a deputy state fire marshal placed the fire loss at $373,605. He stated that 244 structures were totally or partially destroyed in addition to 44 railroad freight cars which were burned. The Congressional Investigating Committee concluded that 312 buildings were destroyed.[49]

The July 2 killing of Negroes was indiscriminate. There was no evidence indicating that victims had participated in the murder of the police officers at Tenth and Bond Avenue. Some of those who lost their lives were among the oldest and most respected colored people in the city.[50] Most Negroes in the riot zone made no attempts to defend themselves, and the small number of casualties among the whites clearly showed the one-sidedness of the riot.

Observers decribed the colored people as being "scared to death," maintaining an "absolute[ly] passive attitude," hoping only for an opportunity to flee across the Mississippi River to St. Louis.[51] Nevertheless, some did defend their homes, by shooting at mobs who were trying to burn them out. For example, at about seven-thirty in the evening of July 2, over a hundred Negroes barricaded themselves in two houses near Sixth and Broadway, engaging in a gun battle with the white men outside. The whites, who had not expected such resistance, angrily complained that their lives were in danger and asked militiamen for help in flushing the colored people from their shelters. A guard officer lectured the attackers: "Now this is a two-handed game. You have got hold of some [Negroes] that [are] playing the game the way you are and you don't want to take hold of it." [52] After he arranged a cease fire the Negroes were escorted to St. Louis.

Beyond the riot zone, colored men in only a few instances organized small mobs which counterattacked sporadically. Two Negro gangs were active in the predominantly Negro neighborhoods between Thirteenth and Fifteenth Streets at Bond Avenue. They shot at passing automobiles and ambulances, and apparently killed one white man while wounding several others. A third Negro mob moved along Broadway between Eleventh and Thirteenth Streets, causing several casualties, including the death of one white man.[53] On other occasions, gangs attempted to burn down public schools at Twenty-sixth and Bond Avenue and Eleventh and Piggott where white families had taken refuge. The latter were hurriedly rescued by militiamen. Since these skirmishes hardly amounted to anything like a real Negro counterattack, the *St. Louis Republic* fabricated one for local readers: "Thousands of negroes, far from being cowed by the method of the white man's revenge, continued fighting back all day and far into the night." [54]

Whites in the city also passed along reports of massive Negro revenge, but police and militia investigations found no traces of such activity. Following one such report on the afternoon of July 2, the home of Dr. Le Roy Bundy (suspected of leading a Negro army) was searched for a large cache of arms. Nothing was found. Militiamen later learned that Bundy had stored two cartons in a nearby saloon, but these contained only automobile supplies and stationery. Large bands of armed Negroes were supposedly seen at Sixth and Bond and Nineteenth and Market; however investigations disclosed only the presence of three armed Negroes who were arrested by the militia.[55] There were also rumors of a pitched battle between Negroes and whites at Twenty-eighth and Tudor Avenue in the southern part of the city. When guardsmen arrived, they found twelve or fifteen armed whites were in the midst of attacking Negroes cowering behind a fence. The whites, who were not searched, complained that the Negroes had fired first. An examination uncovered no Negro with weapons or ammunition. In a house nearby were unarmed, frightened Negro men, women, and children.[56]

These investigations did not reassure whites, and the mounting Negro death toll served only to stimulate the invention of more rumors of Negro revenge. By evening it was reported that an invasion was plotted by colored people in the surrounding cities of Belleville, Alton, and

Brooklyn. However, the besieged victims in the downtown riot zone received no help from neighboring communities just as they had obtained none from the rest of the colored population in East St. Louis.

Several Negro accounts of the race riot bore no resemblance to the one just described. For example, W. E. B. Du Bois, a founder of the N.A.A.C.P., wrote that members of his race valorously and furiously repelled whites, forcing them to suffer heavy casualties: [57]

> The Negroes fought. They grappled with the mobs like beasts at bay. They drove them back from the thickest cluster of their homes and piled the white dead on the street, but the cunning mob caught the black men between the factories and their homes, where they knew they were armed only with their dinner pails.

The *Cleveland* (Ohio) *Gazette* stated that as many whites as Negroes were killed, but that the metropolitan newspapers had purposely under-reported white casualties. East St. Louis whites had suffered such a "high [death] toll" that they were afraid to allow another race riot. To illustrate the black fury, the *Gazette* reported that in one hospital alone there were at least "THIRTY-EIGHT DEAD WHITE[S]," and that the enraged Negroes had thrown other Caucasians into the Cahokia Creek.[58]

The militant *Chicago Defender* also reported a black army which had come from some unidentified city outside of East St. Louis and had desperately but unsuccessfully staged a military campaign of retaliation. According to the *Defender*, East St. Louis Negroes, forced to rely upon their own inadequate resources, counterattacked bravely: "The younger members of the Race were not afraid to die . . . the firing of the whites was promptly returned by hot lead from the Race quarters . . ."[59] Such accounts reflected the need to reassert race pride and were designed to defend colored people against the charge of cowardice, an accusation heard in 1917 and historically employed against Negro soldiers in wartime.

Why didn't Negroes organize a massive retaliation or at least take vigorous, sustained measures to repulse the mobs which burned their homes and shot them down? Some residents possessed no weapons because they were disarmed in June by militiamen or police officers during systematic searches of colored neighborhoods. But many armed Negroes actually fled from their homes leaving guns and ammunition behind—when the fires started, there was a constant rattle of small explosions. Ecological factors explained much of the Negro passivity of July 2. The riot occurred in the business center of the city where Negro pedestrians were heavily outnumbered by whites; violence also erupted in the adjacent area which contained relatively few Negro homes and/or was on the edge of a small colored district. Most of the East St. Louis colored population lived one to two miles from the riot zone, and on July 2 few white rioters dared to enter that neighborhood.

Perhaps, if Negroes had mobilized to rescue friends and relatives under attack in downtown East St. Louis, the white gangs would have scattered or withdrawn. On the other hand, although mobs of white attackers were relatively small, they possessed the support of many citizens, and a Negro rescue force might have marched into a large-scale race war. In such a battle the odds were against the Negroes who, of course, constituted a small minority in the city. Furthermore, at the time the riot was raging along Broadway, colored people living in the southwestern part of town believed their own neighborhood would soon be attacked. They were concerned with the protection of lives and property in their own immediate area, instead of risking a rescue operation elsewhere.

In the Black Valley downtown, residents were taken by surprise. They had not expected that their homes would be burned, and these tinderbox shanties were hopeless fortifications from which to wage an armed defense. They believed that the Illinois militia would offer protection, as had been the case when the same district was attacked during the May disorders. The very cyclonic fury of the mobs frightened Negroes into terrified inactivity, and this reaction was probably intensified by most of them having lived in the South where repression conditioned a fearful, passive acceptance of periodic race violence.

6
The Reaction of America
and East St. Louis

ALTHOUGH the editor of the *Springfield* (Mass.) *Republican* observed "a certain reluctance on the part of the press to discuss the depressing . . . abominable race riots in East St. Louis," [1] magazines and especially newspapers did devote considerable copy to the "startling and horrifying" details. The *Survey Magazine* published an account of a white social worker's tour in East St. Louis shortly after the riot and among the unforgettable vignettes was the following: [2] "I saw the ruins of their homes, into which had gone the labor and savings of years. The little thrift gardens had escaped the flames and the orderly rows where seeds had been planted gave the plots the appearance of miniature graveyards."

Political cartoonists from several metropolitan dailies created bitter sketches reprinted by many papers. Morris, the *New York Evening Mail* artist, drew a blazing East St. Louis background against which he showed a Negro woman begging for mercy on bended knees with her hands outstretched. A pair of terrified children held her tightly. Standing above her was President Wilson bearing a document labeled, "The World Must be Made Safe for Democracy." The caption of the sketch read: "Mr. President, Why Not Make America Safe For Democracy." [3] In a similar vein, Cesare, of the *New York Evening Post* staff, portrayed two Negro bodies crumbled in a gutter before a smoking shack labeled, "East St. Louis." The timely caption was, "Speaking of Atrocities"—obviously suggesting that white East St. Louisans were at least as barbarous as German soldiers were reputed to be. [4]

Editorial writers in Boston, Chicago, and St. Louis cited many reasons for the violence and among them, national or local politics was frequently included. The *Boston Journal* noted that particularly since 1912, when the Southern Democrats assumed control in Washington, the status of Negroes had sharply declined throughout the nation. The Chicago dailies especially stressed that the state of Lincoln had been disgraced before the nation. The *Tribune* declared that "the blood of victims spatters the state," [5] and the *Chicago Daily News* suggested that all Northern cities should establish measures to prevent future racial violence. [6] The *St. Louis Globe-Democrat* and the *St. Louis Post-Dispatch*, among other dailies, concluded that "Illinois cannot rest until the guilty are brought to justice." [7]

In the South editors used the riot to prove the hypocrisy of the North, which was accused of deluding the nation with "a roseate picture" of Negro living conditions above the Mason and Dixon line. The *Louisville Courier-Journal* reminded readers that East St. Louis was located in the home state of Abraham Lincoln "who guaranteed the black man freedom from bondage and equality before the law!" [8] Although the *Memphis Commercial Appeal* advised fellow Southerners not to condone their own system of race violence by pointing to the heinous crimes of July 2, the counsel was unheeded by editors tired of being con-

SPEAKING OF ATROCITIES
Cesare in N. Y. *Evening Post*

3. Cartoon which appeared in New York Evening Post

MR. PRESIDENT, WHY NOT MAKE AMERICA SAFE FOR
DEMOCRACY?
—Morris in N. Y. *Evening Mail*

4. Cartoon which appeared in New York Evening Mail
and reprinted here from Current Opinion

demned in Northern newspapers for barbarous treatment of Negroes.[9] Thus to the *Augusta* (Ga.) *Chronicle* the riot was a kind of poetic justice and a great equalizer: "Never again can one section of the country select and set apart any other section as barbarians to a greater extent than other places." [10]

Some Dixie leaders even suggested that only in the North was the Negro race living under terror. For example, the *Tampa Tribune* agreed that although its section of the country had occasional lynchings, in comparison with "the blood-thirsty, ravenous negro-hunters and negro-killers of Illinois, the average Southern mob is a Sunday school picnic party." [11] On the floor of the Georgia House of Representatives, Rep. Wright of Floyd employed irony in introducing a resolution which, while conceding to Illinoisans "superior judgment" in dealing with colored people, "earnestly recommended that they do select their victims one at a time and be sure of their guilt before they act." [12]

The *Atlanta Constitution* observed that nowhere in the South could a Negro be slaughtered for wanting to earn a living. Of course, racists such as Senators Tillman and Vardaman emphasized that the riot had roots in biology instead of region, and thus East St. Louis was an illustration of the "dauntless spirit of the white man" who would never yield to a "congenitally inferior race." [13] For many white Southerners, the disorders vindicated an idealized way of life which they alone offered Negroes. The *Atlanta Constitution* and the *Tampa Tribune* boasted that "our way is the best way, after all," and the *Nashville Tennesseean* declared that only Southerners recognized the sacred obligation "to protect and care for a race which we alone seem to understand." [14] According to the whites of Dixie, the Negro's life in comfortable Southern homes bestowed absolute security and contentment: ". . . the cotton is blooming in the old patch, roasting ears are hanging green from the stalks, red-hearted watermelons are ripe under the shady vines; blackberries are winking through the leaves. . . ." [15]

In a period when "contented" Negroes, "lured by smooth-tongued labor agents," were migrating from the South, the *Jacksonville Times-Union*, as well as countless other papers, used the July 2 riot as a cautionary tale for Negroes remaining in Dixie: "The negroes of the South may see in this East St. Louis affair just what will happen all over the North when there is no longer enough work for all and white men want their jobs." [16] Survivors of the riot were asked to disown Northerners, and the migrants were assured that "the gates back down in Dixie are open." [17]

However, some papers, such as the *Galveston Daily News*, *Houston Post*, and *Dallas Morning News* also used the riot as an occasion for temporarily dropping the veil of Southern idealization, and the editors inquired why Negroes had migrated to East St. Louis and other Northern cities. Observing that unfair treatment caused the exodus, they emphasized that Negroes desired not political-social equality but only economic and educational opportunities as well as the right to legal protection. Therefore, if the South reformed, it could stem the tide of migration, and by lessening job competition between Negroes and whites in the North, race riots could be prevented. [18]

The East St. Louis violence had a profound effect on Negroes all over the nation. Some found the news accounts so shocking as to be unbelievable, and the first reaction was to consider that they were invented by the Southern press in order to frighten migrants from going North. The *Cleveland Gazette* suggested that the attacks were painted blacker than the facts warranted. [20] On the other hand, the N.A.A.C.P. took the opposite position, accusing white newspapers of suppressing much of the horror committed upon Negroes in East St. Louis. [21]

Wherever Negroes congregated the riot was the chief topic of conversation as they searched for reasons which had provoked the violence. The race press reflected this concern. A few Negro writers considered that it was a German conspiracy to weaken Allied war efforts, while other editorialists viewed the outbreak as the work of a vindictive South determined at any cost to stop Negro migration.[22] There were expressions of fear that East St. Louis was only the forerunner of similar attacks scheduled for other cities. For example, the *New York Age* reported that at Saratoga, where Southern Negro women had only recently supplemented some white help in the Grand Union Hotel, the colored community was apprehensive that the "East St. Louis spirit could break loose here with a little spark to the powder." [23]

However, most articulate Negroes found the enemy neither in Germany nor the South, but rather among organized labor in the North. The Boston Equal Rights League wired AFofL President Samuel Gompers that the "bloodiest, most murderous massacre of colored Americans in the country's history at East St. Louis was committed by labor unionists." [24] Others declared that "it was the absolute conviction on the part of labor leaders that no Negro has a right to any position or privilege which the white man wants." [25] The *Cleveland Gazette* noted that since immigrant factory workers had been "treated like dogs" in their native lands, they planned to give the same treatment to American Negroes.[26] W. E. B. Du Bois wrote that in the conflict over bread and meat, Negroes were killed because they were black and strikebreakers.[27] The editor of the *Atlanta Independent*, a Negro newspaper, asked the tortured question, "What shall we do to be saved? If we don't work South we are jailed; if we do work North we are mobbed." [28]

Negro solutions to the conflict with labor unions ranged over the spectrum. At one pole was the *Washington Bee* calling upon colored people to remove themselves from competition with white workers and establish an autonomous, segregated economy involving the ownership and control of factories, stores, and jobs.[29] At the other pole were the *Messenger* editors, A. Philip Randolph and

Chandler Owen, demanding the death of the capitalist system and integration of Negroes in labor unions. The *Messenger* argued that since the problem was basically not racial, East St. Louis white workers would have shot down migrants of their own race: "Negro laborers would do the same thing if they were in the white laborers' places." [30]

Most colored writers naturally related the riot to the ethos of Christianity and Democracy, reminding white America that whenever economic interests were involved, Christian morality had been forgotten. Race journalists dissected the souls of white men, whose churches, newspapers, and other social institutions had allowed the mob violence.[31] Whites were told that the Negro is the most American of all races and "loyalty to the flag is a part of his religion." The riot was viewed as "The White Man's Burden . . . a shame that awaits atonement;" [32] and white America was doomed if it failed to recognize the mistreatment of Negroes across the nation were symptoms of an approaching moral disintegration. Jessie Fauset wrote in sadness and with resignation: "We are perfectly well aware that the outlook for us is not encouraging. . . . We, the American Negroes, are the acid test for occidental civilization. If we perish, we perish. But when we fall, we shall fall like Samson, dragging inevitably with us the pillars of a nation's democracy." [33]

A Negro minister about to become a military chaplain asked how his nation, "with so much filth in her own backyard," could participate in a "world-cleaning expedition" in Europe; the editor of the *Norfolk Journal and Guide* suggested that if the American government refused to restore peace between the races, not only in East St. Louis, but in the rest of the country, it should renounce its purposes for entering the world war and stand convicted among the nations of the earth as the greatest hypocrite of all times.[34]

While these writers acknowledged that the hour was late, they held tenaciously to the hope that it was not too late. In the *Crisis*, the N.A.A.C.P. magazine, Du Bois sounded the chord for articulate, educated Negroes of the North, when he wrote that whites could atone for East St. Louis and prevent other riots only by adopting a program of race equality: [35]

> To stop lynching and mob violence.
>
> To stop disfranchisement for race and sex.
>
> To abolish Jim Crow cars.
>
> To resist the attempt to establish an American ghetto.
>
> To stop race discrimination in Trade Unions, in Civil Service, in places of public accommodation, and in the Public School.
>
> To secure Justice for all men in the courts.
>
> To insist that individual desert and ability shall be the test of real American manhood and not adventitious differences of race or color or descent . . .

Race journalists called upon Negroes not to surrender to despair, and the editor of the *California Eagle* recalled what Sojourner Truth had told a despondent Frederick Douglass—that God was not dead.[36] But East St. Louis also provoked another kind of reaction—an insistent, angry demand for revenge. Sometimes the same voices which told Negroes that justice would inevitably triumph also cried for retaliatory violence. For example, the *Eagle*'s editor wrote, "It's up to the Negro to strike the first blow . . . be not afraid to die . . ." A Boston group threatened an uprising of Negro millions.[37] A writer for the *Cleveland Gazette* told Negroes to obtain U.S. Army riot guns and ammunition,[38] while a Chicago leader instructed an audience to "arm yourselves now . . . you in Chicago may be next." [39] That speech and others like it alarmed the Chicago Police Department.[40]

After further reflection, most Negroes adopted moderate views realizing that counter-violence was literally a dead end: "Those Negroes who advise the resort to firearms and throwing of bombs as a means of reprisal for

East St. Louis are playing with fire," said the *New York Age*. "We want law and order among whites and Negroes." [41]

In East St. Louis at least three-fourths of the white citizens were repelled by the riot and emphatically condemned it—according to the *Journal*.[42] There was ample evidence to demonstrate the inaccuracy of that statement. Most white residents appeared to show no remorse, and on the morning following July 2 a "mardi-gras" atmosphere characterized the city. Thousands spent the day downtown, since factories were closed, and the tone of the street crowds was lighthearted, with many persons displaying souvenirs, i.e., pieces of hats, jackets, and shirts taken from corpses. Sightseers toured morgues viewing distorted remains of victims. A soldier exhibited a two foot "cinder," telling the throngs, "There's one nigger who will never do any more harm." The cinder was part of a torso, and, after an ambulance arrived to remove it, a squad of militiamen "saluted . . . with shouts of merriment." When bodies were pulled from Cahokia Creek and other corpses recovered from smoking ruins which had been homes only the day before, hundreds of men and women stood by and cheered.[43]

After arriving from Springfield, Adjutant General Frank S. Dickson of the Illinois National Guard announced that there would be no more violence; newsmen were told that persons refusing to obey military orders would be summarily arrested. Several fires were started in abandoned houses at Fourth and Bond Avenue and Fourth and Trendley, but unlike the previous night most guardsmen assumed complete control and the blazes were extinguished. Negroes who ventured out of doors were attacked, but soldiers scattered the whites by firing rifles in the air.[44]

Two companies of soldiers supervised an officially conducted exodus of refugees, as truckloads of "quivering, bandaged blacks" crossed the Mississippi River to St. Louis. Unlike cities on the Illinois side of the river,[45] St.

Louis extended a welcome, boarding a large number of Negroes in the Municipal Lodging House. The press gave a considerable amount of coverage to this exodus of weary, weeping people.[46] The thousands of Negroes created problems for Missouri welfare officials who accused the Mollman administration of dumping their colored population on St. Louis.[47] Factory superintendents, still the only East St. Louisans wanting the refugees to return, told them that they would be perfectly safe under military protection.[48] Mayor Mollman was not so reassuring, saying that he was unable to guarantee their safety.[49]

The East St. Louis Chamber of Commerce feared that the refugees might accept jobs in the South, as bids were pouring in from Atlanta, Birmingham, Louisville, as well as a dozen other places, and several Mississippi plantation owners even offered to charter a steamboat. The *East St. Louis Journal* advised migrants to accept the offers. Although some refugees vowed they never wanted to see the North again, Red Cross surveys showed that few were anxious to go South. Many decided that for the time being they would find jobs in St. Louis, although a substantial group evidently went to Chicago.[50] The *St. Louis Argus* advised refugees to return immediately to East St. Louis, thereby refusing to allow any labor union to force the surrender of "our rights as American citizens." [51] Some accepted the counsel, while others reclaimed jobs in East St. Louis but continued to live on the Missouri side of the river.[52]

Of course, more Negroes would have returned if East St. Louisans had shown repentance, but the lack of sympathy was at least partly calculated to discourage colored people from ever coming back. After the riot the most common comment of the whites was, "The niggers started it and the whites did the finishing." [53] Perhaps the frequency and defensiveness with which the words were expressed indicated latent guilt feelings, but for most citizens there was no other evidence such feelings existed. According to a local postman, "The only trouble with the mob was that it didn't get niggers enough. You wait and see what we do to the rest when the soldiers go. We'll get every last one of them." A journalist from New York interviewed some of the city's leading citizens and editors—their composite statement revealed how much they condoned the riot: [54]

> Well, you see too many niggers have been coming in here. When niggers come up North they get insolent. You see they vote here and one doesn't like that. And one doesn't like their riding in the street cars next to white women—and, well what are you going to do when a buck nigger pushes you off the sidewalk?

At a July 4 picnic on the Belleville fairgrounds, a Negro porter was attacked,[55] while on the following day two more homes in East St. Louis were set afire.[56] Feelings ran so high that when one newspaper printed a story about Negroes having hidden in a grocer's cellar during the riot, the merchant requested a retraction.[57] In this social climate where a man feared to acknowledge having aided riot victims, it was not surprising that over a hundred Negro construction men at a government aviation field near East St. Louis were discharged on demand of white laborers.[58] During the weeks after the riot, East St. Louis whites resumed beating Negroes and made several new attempts to burn houses which colored people formerly occupied. Fire insurance policies on colored homes were cancelled, landlords asked tenants to vacate, and even furniture dealers demanded the return of merchandise being purchased on the installment plan. Negroes who owned homes in mixed neighborhoods discovered that as warnings "black hands" were painted on their property. Several white neighbors of a Negro sent the following note to the police department: "We the undersigned prefer for Mr. John Robinson to be away from his present location which he is buying on installments." Some Negro families who had not joined the exodus of July 2 and 3 departed after deciding that the pressure was unendurable.[59]

The East St. Louis Real Estate Exchange revived earlier plans for the localization of Negroes and appointed a committee "to determine what territory should be set off to the colored man and to have attorneys draft a bill to be presented to City Council." Prominent citizens again suggested that if large employers built segregated model towns outside city limits, Negroes would not be involved in East St. Louis politics and therefore the race problem would be solved. Other members of the Exchange contended that assiduous efforts should be made to encourage the migration of whites to the city.[60] In a full-page *Journal* advertisement, the Exchange asked readers to inform their friends about "the wonderful opportunities in East St. Louis for white people." [61]

The press encouraged as well as reflected racial tensions. For example, on July 5 the *Republic* and the *Journal* informed East St. Louis that a white woman was "slashed across both cheeks by a negro . . . [who] apparently was anxious to get revenge upon some white." Another "woman sufferer . . . is said to have been so seriously abused that she may not recover . . . her name is kept secret for fear the negroes may attempt some new outrage." Local police officials stated they had no knowledge of these attacks.[62] The newspapers also informed readers that Negroes had struck back because of vindictiveness, an attribute characteristic of most migrants—the *Journal* exempted the old residents, who were supposedly regarded as race traitors by the rest of the colored population.

According to these editors, the race riot resulted because white politicians had encouraged Negroes to demand equal treatment and rights with the whites, and colored people even began to think they were as good in every way as white people. Negro ministers, although well-meaning, became interested in this "erroneous" doctrine of equal rights and preached that colored people were entitled to the same privileges as whites.[63] Negroes who were committed to this ideology boasted that they would seduce every white woman in town as soon as white men were conscripted into the army. Thus the majority of East St. Louis Negroes were identified as criminals, rapists, and dupes of corrupt politicians. The *Journal* even suggested that the "foreign" Negro migrants would never have come to East St. Louis if they had been denied the right to vote, as in the South.[64] The *Republic* warned that if they did not permanently depart or at least rigidly segregate themselves "the whites will strike again, maybe more cruelly." [65]

Such remarks seemed to justify the riot, rather than explain it, despite these newspapers also condemning the white rioters. Tenseness in the community increased even more after the *Journal*, the *Republic*, and two Belleville newspapers published a flood of incendiary stories concerning testimony allegedly presented at the coroner's inquest.[66] Unproven and unsupported rumors were reported as indisputable facts. The *St. Louis Republic* bannerlined, "25,000 Whites Were 'Doomed' in Negro Murder Plot," and in this account the July 2 riot had actually headed off a Negro plan to slaughter women and children on July 4 at Jones Park. During the black invasion, prominent white citizens were to have been assassinated. Afterwards, according to these reports, Negroes were to resume the march through the city, killing and pillaging as they saw fit. Other newspapers embellished the story. The *Journal*, noting that the invasion force was to contain 1500 armed men in three divisions, stated that the mass assault would have succeeded if one division had not been discovered by Sergeant Coppedge at Tenth and Bond Avenue. By implication, the whites who burned or shot Negroes on July 2 and sent the black armies fleeing across the Mississippi River actually performed a community service.

After these accounts were published, the *Post-Dispatch* interviewed members of the coroner's jury and discovered that nothing was said at the inquest to afford any founda-

tion for the alleged Jones Park massacre.[67] The *Journal*
and the *Republic* may very well have been searching for
circulation-builders, taking advantage of the hearings being held behind closed doors. Newsmen were excluded,
placing a premium upon their imagination and enter-
prise.[68]

Since an already excited population had been stirred
up, many persons hysterically circulated a new batch of
rumors about another impending Negro invasion. In the
week after the riot, fearful families were unable to sleep.
A white businessman justifiably held newspapers responsible for creating an atmosphere in which half the women
in town were scared to death.[69] A mighty black army was
seen everywhere—sometimes turning out to be Negro refugees sleeping in fields and sometimes railroad work crews
composed of sunburned whites. Frightened whites evacuated their homes in the middle class sections of Lands-
downe, Rosemont, and Washington Park. Vigilance committees were even hurriedly organized in nearby towns such
as Wood River.[70]

Through the summer, East St. Louisans told each
other that Negroes were drilling in St. Louis and that the
Industrial Workers of the World (I.W.W.) was master-
minding plots against East St. Louis. Unfounded reports
of ammunition purchases by Negroes were frequent, and
AFofL officials said that on reliable authority many colored homes were actually arsenals. Stern denials were issued by Brig. General Henry R. Hill, commanding officer
of the national guardsmen in the city. His men had already
made additional searches of Negro districts, confiscating
any weapons they found. The *St. Louis Argus* reported
that as a result of militia searches, Negroes again were
defenseless against renewed mob action by whites. The
Chamber of Commerce also urged all citizens to deny
rumors that rioting would be resumed when the troops
were withdrawn, and even the *Journal* was enlisted in the

drive to calm down an uneasy population that it had helped to arouse in the first place.[71]

Although the militia was preserving order during this potentially explosive period, prominent East St. Louis citizens and particularly those of the Chamber of Commerce, contended that if the soldiers and the police had performed their duty on July 2, there would have been little violence.[72] Since the conduct of the Illinois National Guard had been so vehemently condemned by these businessmen as well as by Mayor Mollman and the press, Governor Lowden was pressured into appointing a Military Board of Inquiry. Business and civic leaders hoped the investigation would prevent a repetition of militia misconduct in the event there was a resumption of rioting. Unfortunately the Military Board of Inquiry was biased, but, despite that, the transcript of testimony provided a great deal of information about the breakdown in the agencies of law enforcement on July 2.

7
The Riot and Agencies of Law Enforcement

THE agencies of law enforcement in East St. Louis during the July riot were the East St. Louis Police Department and the Illinois National Guard. Both organizations were ineffective at best and there were many indications that both were guilty of ignoring or even aiding the mobs. Their performance in general was in a manner opposite to their intended function and each came under investigation.

From July 16 through July 18, 1917, the Military Board of Inquiry heard scores of witnesses describe the conduct of the Illinois National Guard during the riot, and subsequently a report was transmitted to the Adjutant General of the Illinois National Guard. The document was not released to the public, despite the impatience and consuming curiosity of newspapers.[1] State officials decided that publication of the report would be far more politically damaging than its suppression, probably because the findings deviated so sharply from the testimony of most nonmilitary witnesses.

At the hearings, prominent East St. Louisans stated that the militiamen not only allowed the killing of Negroes, but in several instances may have been the slayers. Charles F. Short, owner of the Short Moving Company, testified that on the afternoon of July 2, a soldier shot at a Negro in an alley at Fourth and Broadway: [2]

> My wife called me to the back door and said a soldier was shooting at a negro. I ran to the back door and saw three militiamen on bended knees with their guns pointed east at a yard—they hollered, "Get back, you black sons of bitches." I looked down and saw a negro with his hands in the air one block from us and where these soldiers were and as I looked out at the soldiers one man, I think in the middle, fired; I don't know whether any more fired but I heard a crack and saw the stuff come out of the barrel of the gun.

Charles Rogers, general manager of the Grant Chemical Company, told the Board that early in the evening of July 2, at Sixth and Walnut he observed a group of "unoffending negroes . . . huddled together in fright" before their burning homes. Nearby a militiaman stood guard and several whites jeered, "What are you doing with a gun? You couldn't shoot it." The young soldier retorted, "the hell I can't," and fired on the Negroes.[3] Mr. L. C. Haynes, vice-president of the East St. Louis and Suburban Railway, testified that he walked past Eighth and Broadway where whites were hurling bricks at the Negro shacks: [4]

> A soldier was . . . sitting on his heels . . . with his gun drawn . . . prepared apparently to aim at these [Negro] flats, apparently from all appearances ready to shoot if a darky would show himself.

It will never be known how many Negroes were wounded or killed by the militiamen. The Military Board of Inquiry said that an examination of hospital and undertakers' records was made to determine the number of

Negroes with wounds from Springfield rifle projectiles. Only two were found and the Board concluded that the pair had fired first on the guardsmen.[5] This last statistic, offered without evidence, illustrated the Board's disinterest in a real investigation. As indicated previously, hospital records were incomplete since some wounded Negroes through fear refused to be hospitalized for treatment. Morgue records were particularly useless. If the Board members had called Coroner C. P. Renner as a witness, they would have learned that, while most victims died of gunshot wounds, only two Negro bodies received post-mortem examinations, making it impossible to state how many soldiers' bullets resulted in killings.[6] Finally, even if post-mortems had been done on all Negro corpses, such examinations could not have determined how many of the bullets were actually fired by soldiers. Some civilians owned Springfield rifles or borrowed them from militiamen.

The testimony presented at the Military Board of Inquiry showed clearly that, although some militiamen fired upon Negroes, most of the violence was done by civilians. The major accusation against the guardsmen was that they were present during the killings, and made little or no effort to interfere. As noted earlier, at least six or seven guardsmen stood around like "passive spectators" during the hanging at Fourth and Broadway, and ignored pleas to save the victim's life.[7] A few blocks away at Collinsville and Broadway a bloodied Negro sought the protection of eight guardsmen. Their mute answer was to turn bayonets on him, forcing the victim back into the arms of five assailants.[8]

Charles Quackenbush, an executive of the St. Clair County Gas and Electric Company, testified that later in the evening of July 2, five or six rioters threw an injured Negro into the flames near Seventh and Broadway, while two soldiers on patrol took no action.[9] About the same time on Missouri Avenue between Seventh and Eighth Streets, Negro residents were shot fleeing from blazing homes, but during the fires a squad of twenty-five guardsmen marched down the street, making no effort either to help Negroes or arrest rioters.[10]

Even when soldiers saved victims, they usually did not arrest the whites. For example, at the railroad depot a soldier caught three women stripping the clothes off a colored girl; although a rescue was made, the assailants were permitted to go their way.[11] Shortly after two o'clock in the afternoon at Broadway and Collinsville, fifteen or twenty militiamen, forming a ring around three Negroes, held off a group of rioters. Although the soldiers drew guns, they made no attempt to use them or take prisoners. Since no firmness was demonstrated, the mob surged forward, kicking the Negroes who were eventually rescued by soldiers.[12]

Scores of East St. Louisans noted that the militiamen were laughing and joking, as if it was a picnic rather than a riot.[13] G. E. Popkess, a local reporter, complained that the first group of guardsmen arriving for riot duty looked like members of a ragtail army, and their dress reflected their attitudes. Some appeared in overalls without any semblance of uniform, while others lacked army hats, shoes, or leggings.[14] Popkess heard them tell the crowds, "the black skunks . . . are no friends of ours." One soldier asked him, "You got your negro picked out for tonight?" [15]

The members of the Military Board of Inquiry attempted to convey the impression of wanting to punish soldiers guilty of collaborating with the rioters on July 2, and witnesses were requested to give the names of offenders. Since no one was able to provide that information, the Board inquired about other identifying data such as company number, rank, and insignia of the soldiers. Witnesses said they were unable to recall such details and some citizens added that they would not recognize the militiamen if they encountered them again.[16] The officers conducting the inquiry considered it most curious that no one named a single soldier.[17] Despite such protestations members of the Board ignored witnesses who indicated that they might be able to pick out the soldiers if they saw them again.[18] For example, Miss Martha Gruening, a New York reporter, testified about an encounter with two militiamen who told her with great amusement that during the riot they had thrown several Negroes into a creek. Miss Gruening remembered the company to which the soldiers belonged, indicating also that she could identify both men if given an opportunity. While these soldiers' crimes may have been fabrications intended to shock a gullible lady, the Military Board made no arrangements to permit the possibility of identification.[19]

At the time of this hearing, many militiamen who had been in East St. Louis on July 2 were still on duty, and the Board could have paraded them before the witnesses. In only one case was this done.[20] The task would not have been insuperable, particularly because many complaints concerned acts committed between noon and half-past six on the day of the riot, when there were only a few militia companies in the city. Since witnesses were able to pinpoint street locations and time of occurrence, military records would have revealed which squads were in the areas. Although the Board members said they had exhausted every endeavor to find the guilty guardsmen, several citizens considered that they had been discouraged from giving evidence.[21] The hearing was dubbed "a trifling inquiry" by Congressman Ben Johnson of Kentucky, who chaired the Congressional Committee which later conducted its own investigation of the riot.[22]

    The Military Board of Inquiry based its report essentially on testimony of militia company officers.[23] This testimony differed so markedly from statements of most non-military witnesses that it is difficult to believe both accounts concerned the same riot. The Board asserted that "on the whole the troops employed at East St. Louis discharged their duty according to the best of their knowledge and ability . . . they displayed courage and energy. Many of them have been recommended by the reports of their commanding officers for individual gallantry and devotion to duty." [24]

Actually only a small minority of the militiamen showed "devotion to duty." [25] Among these were a captain who attempted to take a rioter into custody only to have a factory worker interfere by inciting a gathering crowd. The officer drew his gun, forced the mob back, and completed the arrest.[26] Several guardsmen stopped another mob headed toward the Relay Railroad Depot. The rioters retreated after one of the guardsmen fired into the air.[27]

Invariably when firmness was shown the mobs fell back just as they had done during the May riots. In the early afternoon of July 2, the rioters were still testing guardsmen to see how far it was possible to go, and until five o'clock the city might have been saved if the soldiers had behaved differently. Instead the mobs became emboldened by their indifference. Even at the particularly violent intersection of Fourth and Broadway, forceful action by seventy militiamen frightened the street crowds into submission. At least three hundred men meekly surrendered and were arrested.[28] However, the soldiers' efforts were not sustained and during the rest of the evening more Negro deaths resulted.

Faced with overwhelming evidence that Negroes were killed in the presence of guardsmen, the Board concluded that the soldiers were so greatly outnumbered by mobs that the victims' lives could not have been saved.[29] Undoubtedly the guardsmen who were sent to prevent the riot arrived too late—the Illinois National Guard had acted slowly in transporting the men. Mayor Mollman transmitted an urgent request for help at two o'clock on the morning of July 2,[30] and as Table 1 below indicates, during the next fourteen hours (until 4 P.M.) only about one hundred men arrived. In the next three hours (until 7 P.M.) while the Negro death toll mounted, only sixty-three reenforcements entered the city.

TABLE 1

Illinois National Guard Units in East St. Louis During July Riot *

CO.	REG	TIME OF ARRIVAL	DATE	OFFI-CERS	MEN
G	4th	8:40 A.M.	July 2	3	27
H	4th	10:20 A.M.	July 2	2	32
I	4th	12:50 P.M.	July 2	3	44
E	4th	4:00 P.M.	July 2	3	60
B	4th	7:00 P.M.	July 2	3	66
F	4th	8:00 P.M.	July 2	3	41
D	4th	1:45 A.M.	July 3	2	68
A	4th	2:00 A.M.	July 3	1	62
C	4th	2:30 A.M.	July 3	3	50
F	3rd	3:00 A.M.	July 3	2	54
L	3rd	4:15 A.M.	July 3	3	110
L	4th	7:30 A.M.	July 3	—	27
Prov. Co.	5th	8:00 P.M.	July 3	3	100
C	1st Cav.	8:30 P.M.	July 3	3	77
M	4th	3:30 A.M.	July 4	3	63
6 Co.	2nd	8:30 A.M.	July 4	not given	600†

* Adapted from "Report upon the Conduct of Officers and Men, Illinois National Guard on Duty at East St. Louis, July 2, 1917," dated August 2, 1917, p. 10.
† Approximate.

The influence of an inadequate number of soldiers was further dissipated by the necessity of dividing them into small units for street patrol. These detachments were usually unsupervised and isolated from each other. On some streets there were only one or two guardsmen, hardly enough to disperse the crowds. However, during the afternoon there were downtown intersections (such as Illinois and Collinsville and State and Collinsville) which contained squads of fifteen or twenty guardsmen,[31] and although the street crowds were large, the actual assaulting mobs were small.

The Military Board of Inquiry, unwilling to suggest cowardice or fraternization, emphasized not only insufficient numbers but also the inexperience of militiamen.[32] The Board pointed out that, since over sixty per cent had joined the militia less than two months before the riot, there had been no opportunity to provide training in the use of bayonets and rifle-butts to scatter crowds. Furthermore, the Board noted that on July 3, when the shorthandedness had been relieved by over eight hundred guardsmen, "all witnesses agreed that the . . . conduct of all troops on duty was excellent." [33]

Actually, several East St. Louis citizens complained publicly about the conduct of some guardsmen on the day after the riot. Among these were E. J. Steger and Joseph N. Keys. Steger, a real estate broker, saw a Negro house being looted at Eleventh and Bond Avenue and a rioter preparing to burn it down. Steger found a militiaman, who disclaimed authority to arrest the arsonist.[34] Keys, an executive of the Sanders Motor Company, testified that on July 3 eight or ten militiamen patrolled Seventh and Broadway, while looters invaded a Negro home at Eighth Street, breaking windows, banging on a piano, and stealing household goods and furniture. On the following day the dwelling was burned down.[35]

Unquestionably, the most important witness was Colonel S. O. Tripp, the commanding officer of the guardsmen. Since the Military Board of Inquiry gave no credence to evidence reflecting unfavorably on the Illinois National Guard, the colonel left the hearing room without even a reprimand.[36] Tripp, an assistant quartermaster general, lacked any knowledge of riot control and was described by one reporter as "a very excellent man as an office clerk." [37] Clad in civilian dress, he arrived in East St. Louis at eight o'clock on the morning of the riot, and from that time until noon (while mobs rioted a block away) he remained in a

City Hall office mapping out a plan of campaign for the day. At nine o'clock only thirty guardsmen were on duty out of five hundred whom he had expected to arrive during the morning.[38] Though other military resources were available in the city, Tripp waited until two o'clock in the afternoon before requesting the assistance of these two militia companies guarding East St. Louis war plants.[39]

Tripp was confident that when the five hundred guardsmen arrived from other Illinois cities they could handle any disorders. However they failed to report according to his campaign plans, and some companies did not entrain for East St. Louis until several hours after receiving travel orders.[40] Since many militiamen were farmhands, valuable time was lost locating and transporting them to local railroad depots for the journey to East St. Louis. For example, Captain S. H. Cohen of Company M, Fourth Illinois Infantry (Champaign) landed in East St. Louis at three o'clock on the morning of July 4—when his orders were received he was in Springfield and twenty men (including two lieutenants) were also away.[41] Many other companies arriving in the riot city were not at full combat strength.

Because Tripp remained in his East St. Louis office throughout the morning he underestimated the seriousness of the riot.[42] He also ignored the advice of his second-in-command, Lt. Colonel E. P. Clayton, who as early as eight-thirty in the morning suggested that even if the five hundred guardsmen came to East St. Louis on schedule, more than that number would be required to put down the expected disorders.[43] Whether or not Clayton exaggerated, he had some experience with race riots, having commanded the militia companies which restored order in East St. Louis several weeks earlier. However, Tripp replied that no determination of the need for re-enforcements would be made until he personally toured the city after lunch. (It was not until three o'clock that afternoon, following the deaths of several persons, that Clayton—acting on his own initiative and responsibility—telephoned the Adjutant General's office in Springfield and requested six additional companies).[44] Colonel Tripp finally left the desk at noon but went to a restaurant for a meal lasting over an hour. A short distance away, two Negroes and a white man were killed. With luncheon completed he made his first inspection of the troops, but by that time the mobs had multiplied.

When he testified before the Military Board of Inquiry, Tripp said that he had instructed subordinates to use force in preserving order on July 2.[45] However, four months later in an appearance before the Congressional Investigating Committee he admitted that militiamen had been told that unless fired upon, they were not to shoot rioters.[46] Congressman Johnson replied, "But as long as [mobs] weren't killing anybody but negroes, you didn't want to fire."[47] Despite censure from the legislators, Tripp was supported by the Military Board of Inquiry which contended that in the large street crowds of July 2, it would have been impossible to fire upon the lawless elements without risking the lives of spectators "innocent of evil intent."[48] (However, lives of white spectators were risked when soldiers shot Negroes though the Negroes were usually innocent of anything except the desire to avoid injury or death.)

Perhaps because guardsmen did not fire on the whites, some citizens thought that they had no ammunition—an opinion which hardly contributed to a restoration of order. After the riot Tripp allegedly told the county coroner that the militiamen had no bullets,[49] but as far as the *Post-Dispatch* was concerned, even if the soldiers lacked ammunition they had bayonets: "One looks in vain in the police and hospital reports for instances of rioters treated for bayonet wounds."[50] In his brief testimony at the Military Board of Inquiry Tripp was not even questioned about the matter.[51] Board members had already found plenty of evidence to indicate that guardsmen had access to an adequate supply of bullets.[52] However, in some individual cases it was quite true that soldiers patrolled without ammunition because they removed the cartridges.[53] Others confessed to the mob that their weapons were not loaded.[54]

Several witnesses told the Military Board of Inquiry that if Tripp had supported a declaration of martial law, the number of Negro deaths would have been cut substantially. At three o'clock on the afternoon of the riot, Mayor Mollman urgently requested Colonel Tripp to declare martial law.[55] Although the Mayor and the Chamber of Commerce had criticized the militia for inactivity, they believed that only such a declaration could frighten the mobs.[56] Tripp was warned that without drastic action the town would be burned down by nightfall. Since he was still out of touch with the riot, he insisted that "the situation [was] in hand" [57] and told Governor Lowden that martial law was undesirable "because we would lose the help of city officials." At the time of Tripp's telephone conversation with the Governor, the entire East St. Louis city government had almost completely collapsed.[58]

In this debate over martial law, both Tripp and Mollman favored a procedure which would have given to the other the primary responsibility for restoring order and the primary blame for failing to quell the violence. During the race riot Mollman was so terrified that he refused to appear on the streets.[59] For practical purposes the Mayor had already relinquished authority to Tripp, but he wanted desperately to legalize the transfer of power.[60] However, Tripp preferred to consider himself in strict subordination to civil officials.[61] The Military Board of Inquiry upheld Tripp in this controversy and held that according to an Illinois Supreme Court decision, martial law could not have been declared unless the courts were unable to function.[62] On July 2 the courts were evidently in session, although no riot cases were heard.[63]

The Board's summary report may be contrasted with conclusions of the Congressional Committee which later investigated the riot. The legislators charged Colonel Tripp with blundering ineffectiveness and cowardice. In their judgment, responsibility for much that was done and left undone must rest on him. The Congressional Committee based its portrait of the hapless colonel primarily on a lengthy interview with him: [4]

When the adjutant general's office summoned Col. Tripp in the early hours of the morning he answered the call to duty arrayed in a seersucker suit and a dainty straw hat, after having, as he informed your committee, hastily packed his hand bag with a lot of toilet articles. Thus ready for any emergency he took the first train for East St. Louis. He brought no uniform with him, and, although it was his duty to face and quell a riotous mob, at no time was he garbed as a soldier. Evidently it was his intention to secure some bullet-proof coign of vantage from which he could view the turbulent scenes in perfect safety. . . . It is the unanimous opinion of every witness who saw Col. Tripp on that fateful day that he was a hindrance instead of a help to the troops; that he was ignorant of his duties, blind to his responsibility, and deaf to every intelligent appeal that was made to him. His presence in East St. Louis was a reproach to the assistant adjutant general who sent him there and a reflection on the judgment of the governor for burdening his staff with so hopeless an incompetent. . . . When Col. Tripp was asked why he spent four hours in the city hall, with East St. Louis in the hands of a murderous mob, and failed to go to the scenes of conflict and take charge of his troops who were sorely in need of a commander, he absolved himself of all responsibility by answering, "The President never goes out of his office;" and so, by comparing himself to the Commander in Chief of the Army and Navy of the United States, he was perfectly satisfied with his conduct. "Me and the President" was, in his opinion, a complete defense.

In a last-ditch attempt to extricate himself Tripp contradictorily told the legislators that during the riot he was not the commanding officer of the militia in East St. Louis. The colonel agreed that he had been sent as Governor Lowden's representative and ranking officer, but denied being superior in command. In Tripp's view Lt. Col. Clayton had actually been the troop commander.[65] Unfortunately, Clayton lacked any knowledge of this arrangement as did everyone else.[66]

The Congressmen, believing that the riot should have been quelled promptly by militia guns and bayonets, included a description of the guardsmen which differed considerably from the one written by the Military Board of Inquiry:[67] "The conduct of the soldiers who were sent to East St. Louis to protect life and property puts a blot on that part of the Illinois militia that served under Col. Tripp." The Congressional Committee asked Governor Lowden to authorize another investigation of the militiamen's conduct. Although the legislators said that Lowden had a responsibility in this matter that could not be evaded, the Governor decided that the best thing for the Illinois National Guard, if not for the people of Illinois, was to bury the evidence and hope that the riot would be forgotten.

The guardsmen, with their own personal race prejudices, upon arriving at East St. Louis had no trouble following the cues of the police department. Every unbiased observer noted that on July 2 the hearts of the East St. Louis policemen were not in their work.[68] They "shared the lust of the mob for negro blood," but more by inactivity than anything else were guilty of allowing the shooting of Detectives Coppedge and Wadley to be used to arouse the mob.[69] When a merchant rushed to police headquarters to report a lynching, the night chief of police laconically replied, "Well they are getting what they gave Coppedge and Wadley." Some of the policemen did not bother to report for duty, preferring to stroll about town observing rioters in action. Others spent the day loafing at the police station, while a few apparently joined mobs clubbing Negroes. Lawmen were "laughingly held captive" when rioters beat or shot their victims, and desperate pleas for help were ignored:[70]

Two negroes came out of a house in the middle of the block, on Broadway, between Fourth and Fifth Sts., about half-past seven in the evening and falling on their knees before the policemen, begged for mercy. "Keep walking, you black ———," shouted a police sergeant. Both were shot half a block away. An ambulance came but drove on again when a policeman shouted, "They're not dead yet, boys."

Although policemen failed to respond to emergency calls, they relayed false reports of Negro reprisal attacks on the outskirts of the city. Militiamen were thus diverted from downtown riot areas, and the *Post-Dispatch* noted, "The purpose seems to have been to scatter the soldiers so that they would not interfere with the massacre. But they were not interfering. They were not interfering any more than the East St. Louis police." Chief Payne obviously considered that the soldiers were kindred spirits of the police—at the Military Board of Inquiry he testified that militiamen staunchly performed their duty.[71]

Police officials also protected the mobs by ordering patrolmen to confiscate cameras of newsmen, thereby destroying invaluable evidence. A *Globe-Democrat* photographer was arrested and several cameras were smashed.[72] Besides refusing to arrest mob members, the police interfered with the few guardsmen who attempted to take rioters into custody. Lt. Colonel Clayton apprehended one man during the afternoon, personally transporting him to the police station for booking. The desk sergeant made no entry in the arrest blotter and permitted release after Clayton left the building.[73] This incident preceded the departure from the police lockup of scores of persons whom guardsmen had arrested at the Fourth and Broadway hanging.[74] Police generosity did not extend to Negroes placed in protective custody after eluding the mobs; in at least three cases an officer charged a fee to open cell doors.[75]

A week later the secret coroner's inquest was held at the police station, ostensibly as a precautionary measure to prevent rioters from fleeing.[76] However, newsmen charged that the secrecy ban was actually imposed to suppress evidence against police and city officials, as well as the rioters.[77] According to the *Post-Dispatch*, no lawmen at the inquest made any identifications of the rioters, and the typical police attitude was, "I don't know anything and I don't want to know anything." Chief Payne and his department were accused of being disinterested in gathering evidence leading to indictments and prosecutions. Critics also said that terrorism was employed to intimidate citizens who witnessed the riot and wanted to give testimony. One member of the coroner's jury declared that the lawmen wished only to incriminate Negroes.[78]

Police records on the riot have been lost or destroyed, although one small file still exists. It does suggest that much police activity involved checking rumors that Negroes organized a massacre of East St. Louis whites and planned the killings of Detectives Coppedge and Wadley. Prominent colored men were arrested on the assumption that as political leaders they must have promoted dissatisfaction and participated in the alleged plot. Among those taken into custody were Fayette Parker, a member of the St. Clair County Board of Supervisors, N. W. Pardon, a former assistant state's attorney, James Vardaman, a city detective, and Dr. L. B. Bluitt, the assistant county physician.[79]

Little attention was given to apprehending whites who killed Negroes on July 2. According to one memorandum addressed to Chief Payne and dated three days following the riot, a police sergeant stopped John Tisch, a white man, who was carrying a suitcase containing expensive-looking women's wearing apparel. Although Tisch was suspected of looting, the officer casually asked how many Negroes he had killed on July 2. The man had no fear of replying, "I got my share." [80] Tisch was eventually tried after Attorney General Brundage sent assistants to prosecute rioting cases, but the police sergeant did not appear as a witness. Nor has any evidence been uncovered to show that the police department informed Brundage of what the defendant had said.

Aside from racial prejudices—which, as already mentioned, were apparent even before the rioting—the East St. Louis Police Department was not known for its effectiveness. In 1917 the city, with a population of approximately seventy thousand, maintained an understaffed law enforcement agency composed of only thirty-six patrolmen and sixteen plainclothesmen to provide protection around the clock.[81] (Six plainclothesmen were Negroes—nearly all received orders to go home on July 2).[82] According to an earlier revision of the city code,[83] there should have been fifty uniformed policemen and fourteen plainclothesmen, and, although that number was insufficient, it became regarded as a standard. In the years before World War I, despite substantial population gains, the size of the law enforcement agency remained essentially stationary.[84] Moreover, as officers retired or resigned, not all were replaced.[85] Mayor Mollman indicated that shortly after taking office in 1915 there were only about thirty-six patrolmen, and during the following two years the numerical strength of the department remained unchanged. He complained that the city government was financially bankrupt and could not afford to increase its payroll. The small number of law enforcement officers was particularly inade-

quate, considering the proximity to St. Louis, the mobile
population, and the fact that as a railroad terminus East
St. Louis was gridironed with tracks serving twenty-seven
railroads, facilitating the concealment and flight of lawbreakers. Above all else, the community was one which accepted a considerable amount of home-grown lawlessness.

Since the municipal treasury was empty, police recruits
were hired at a starting wage of seventy dollars a month,[86]
and the pay for a twelve hour workday was actually lower
than the hourly wages an unskilled laborer earned in the
meat-packing plants. Under these conditions, capable men
were rare and one newsman observed that "it is purely ac-
cidental if you get competent policemen to work for that
money." [87] Qualified applicants were even harder to find
during the 1917 industrial upswing which accompanied
America's entry in World War I. The Congressional Committee investigating the riot was incredulous after hearing
about police wages, and Rep. Henry A. Cooper of Wisconsin commented, "There is plenty of money in this
city . . . I cannot understand it . . . is there no such thing
here as civic pride?" [88]

The law enforcement agency was also weakened by its
policy of making police jobs political appointments, and
a crucial qualification was an ability "to deliver" precincts
on election days.[89] Officers supporting defeated candidates
often lost their jobs. A few years before the riot, law enforcement officers proved loyalty to the party in power by
arresting rival precinct workers on the street outside of
political meetings.[90] Another requirement for steady employment was a "non-compulsory" contribution to the
Mayor's campaign fund—sergeants, twenty-five dollars;
detectives, twenty dollars; and patrolmen, fifteen dollars.[91]
When these details were complied with, it was difficult to
discharge an officer. Only gross incompetence subjected
him to suspension (but not discharge) by the Board of
Police and Fire Commissioners, who were also political
appointees of the Mayor and City Council. Even then,

cases could be appealed to a police trial board, composed of politically prominent judges from the county, circuit, and probate courts.[92] These judges sometimes ignored recommendations of the Board of Police and Fire Commissioners.[93] For example, one officer pleaded guilty to intoxication on duty. After suspension by the commissioners, he appealed to the police trial board, selecting as his lawyer, Joseph B. Messick, Jr., whose father was chairman of the board. The case was dismissed.[94]

It was worth fighting to keep a job that paid so little, since there were many opportunities for gratuities. The East St. Louis force possessed an earned reputation for corruption, and it was said, "The reason that a policeman is called a 'cop' may be because of his skill in copping the graft." [95] The Congressional Committee noted that enterprising police officers rented houses to prostitutes.[96] According to the Committee, a year before the race riots, Frank Florence, assistant chief of detectives, became infuriated after his property was raided by H. F. Trafton, a member of the police morality squad. Using his service revolver, Florence ordered Trafton to raise his hands in the air. In that position—with his hands held up to the height of his head—Trafton was killed. Although several witnesses had seen the slaying Florence was acquitted.[97] Florence was the same officer who two years earlier made an "apparently unauthorized" raid on a house of prostitution. According to rumor he was drunk when he arrested thirty-two persons there, but the madam of the house told city officials that he held a grudge against her for recently vacating the establishment she had rented from him.[98]

East St. Louis's tolerance of its police department appeared unlimited until after the riot when scores of indignant businessmen held a mass meeting at City Hall, charging that police corruption and laxity had insured a long reign of lawlessness which brought on the racial violence.[99] The Chamber of Commerce formed a Committee of One Hundred, demanding that Mayor Mollman re-

organize the department from top to bottom, replacing the
three police commissioners, as well as the chief of police,
the night chief, and the chief of detectives. Illinois Attorney General Brundage concurred and announced that
in preparing riot cases for prosecution, the local law enforcement agency would be by-passed.[100]

Mollman replied that the Committee of One Hundred
could not dictate to him; however two weeks after the riot
the police commissioners were responsive to pressures of
the business community and suspended the chief of police
as well as the night chief. The grounds for suspension were
inactivity during the riot and failure to cooperate with the
coroner's jury investigation. The commissioners thought
that this action would save their own jobs, and one member, Nelson Schein, even publicly confessed that political
interference had made it impossible to administer the police
department.[101] Despite these gestures, the businessmen insisted upon a clean sweep. Mollman decided to oblige, since
by then he was annoyed that the police commissioners
seemed to be implicating him as a member of the political
net dominating the department. Within a week all three
members of the Board of Police and Fire Commissioners
were fired.[102] The Mayor's apparent concession to the Committee of One Hundred was also caused by an offer to raise
$105,000 among industrialists for the purpose of obtain-
ing additions to the force and higher salaries for patrolmen.[103]

The Committee of One Hundred, expecting that the
money would give them a major voice in selecting new
police commissioners, submitted a list of six names from
which Mayor Mollman and the City Council were to choose
three. However, Mollman and his friends had no intention
of going that far; they named only one man from the list
and two others not entirely acceptable to the Committee.[104]
The businessmen also seemed to have second thoughts
about giving away all that money. They not only distrusted
Mollman's ability to maintain law and order, but, being

economy-minded, they considered the possibility of persuading Governor Lowden to keep the national guardsmen in East St. Louis, thus making a larger police department unnecessary. Halfway measures were finally taken: in place of doubling the force, the law enforcement agency was augmented by only about fifteen men; instead of large pay increases, patrolmen received an additional ten dollars a month.

The new Board of Police Commissioners proved to be far more independent than Mollman anticipated. Their independence led them to recruit patrolmen without first checking political credentials with City Council—the City Council repeatedly complained of their non-recognition in making these selections.[105] Furthermore, the Board appointed as Police Chief, Frank Keating, Mollman's political enemy. In his first official act, Keating announced that commercialized gambling would be banished, and, of course, Mollman resented the implication that there were gamblers in the community to banish. The Mayor was also piqued when the commissioners suspended his confidant Maurice Ahern, (who doubled as secretary to both Mollman and the Board) after an indictment by a grand jury on charges growing out of the riot.[106]

Within a few weeks there were rumors that Mollman and the City Council intended to force the resignations of the new Board.[107] In early 1918 he accused them publicly of allowing wide-open gambling in East St. Louis. The commissioners, with the support of the press, retorted that the Mayor opposed them precisely because they were succeeding in cleaning up the town. If Mollman believed he could get his way without a fight he was mistaken. The Ministerial Alliance requested a petition for his recall, and the *Journal* told readers that he "must be circumvented in his mad attempt to re-establish through the personal control of a subservient police department a reign of municipal debauchery and corruption." [108] The *Post-Dispatch* demanded a grand jury investigation, strongly urging the

City Council not to fire the commissioners—"the plan the gangsters have in mind." [109] By a vote of twelve to four, the City Council confirmed Mollman's candidates for a new police board.[110] Police Chief Keating was replaced by a grocer and the East St. Louis Police Department was again dominated by the same politicians who had influenced it before the race riots.

8
Court Trials of the Whites

SINCE the East St. Louis Police Department gave little assistance in the investigation of whites who rioted on July 2, the Committee of One Hundred particularly tried to enlist the support and cooperation of Hubert Schaumleffel, the State's Attorney of St. Clair County. However, Schaumleffel, a member of the same political ring as Mayor Mollman, was quoted as saying that because the riot reflected public sentiment, grand jury indictments would be difficult to obtain.[1] He remarked wryly that his investigators were unable to find witnesses who saw any citizens committing violence during the race riot. On July 3 he had appeared at the preliminary hearing of persons apprehended in the Fourth and Broadway hanging. Some courtroom observers thought Schaumleffel handled the proceedings with levity as if the whole affair had been a joke. Because of a lack of evidence nearly all of the defendants were released.[2]

The business leaders and newspaper editors turned directly to Governor Lowden, who sent Assistant Attorney

General C. W. Middlekauf to East St. Louis.[3] Upon his arrival Middlekauf angrily condemned Mollman, the police department, and especially Schaumleffel. He told the Committee of One Hundred, "Think of it, gentlemen, the greatest crime in the history of the state and the State's Attorney told me that he had no witnesses a week after the riot." [4] The Assistant Attorney General took personal charge of a grand jury investigation and appealed to businessmen for help in obtaining evidence against the rioters.[5] He was supported by Circuit Judge G. A. Crow, who told the grand jurors to be "fair, fearless, and unbiased." [6]

For nearly one month the panel heard witnesses and to the surprise of almost everyone, on August 14, indictments were requested against eighty-two whites and twenty-three Negroes. A few weeks later, indictments were drawn against an additional thirty-nine persons, including Mayor Mollman.[7] The Mayor was accused of malfeasance, but the charges were later dropped.[8] Newspapers reported that the accomplishments of the grand jury "surpassed public expectation," but the "journey [has] just begun." The *Post-Dispatch* suggested that if prosecutions were pressed with equal zeal, potential rioters in East St. Louis and other Illinois cities would be deterred.[9] During the summer over one hundred persons were arrested; the county jail held nearly fifty accused rioters and about fifty others were out on bond. Some of those who were indicted had apparently anticipated that eventuality and disappeared or joined the army to escape the reach of the law. Strain and anxiety were evident and according to the reports of agents, "many persons lived almost in terror for the day when the hand of a policeman, detective, or deputy sheriff will fall on his [sic] shoulder and he will hear that he has been indicted for complicity in the riots." [10]

On August 18, S. L. Schulz became the first white rioter to plead guilty and be sentenced. Schulz confessed to clubbing a white meat-packing employee who came to the rescue of a Negro friend when the latter was mobbed near the stockyards. The *Globe-Democrat* reported that there was panic among other arrested whites after Judge Crow sentenced the defendant to a one-to-ten year term for assault to murder and a one-to-five year term for conspiracy to riot.[11]

As later events proved the white rioters need not have worried, since what was sufficient evidence to indict was often considered inadequate to prosecute. Despite the editorials calling for punishment, East St. Louis was satisfied with only a few vicarious convictions. Only a handful of rioters were placed behind bars in deference to public opinion in Illinois and the rest of the nation. In a gesture appearing to balance the scales of justice, almost the same number of Negroes and whites went to prison. However, of the nine whites sent to the penitentiary only four were charged with homicide—despite the fact that at least thirty-nine Negroes were murdered. On the other hand, of the twelve Negroes who went to prison, eleven were convicted of killing the two detectives.[12] The editor of the *Chicago Defender* was accurate in emphasizing that "the [Negro] Race has received decidedly the worst of it." [13]

After the few court trials were held, the ritual was considered fulfilled, and many rioters were assured by the Illinois Attorney General's office that only slight punishments would be imposed if they pleaded guilty. Pleas were made at bargain prices—assault with a deadly weapon went for a thirty day jail sentence or even a fifty dollar fine. Men who admitted that they had participated in the rioting received ten day jail terms or were ordered to pay a few dollars to the county.[14] Middlekauf probably had no other alternative, for in order to take cases to court he required more witnesses than the men and women who had already come forward to testify in a handful of circuit court trials. Representative John E. Raker commented on this fact during the Congressional investigation, by observing that East St. Louisans lacked the courage to stand up, point their finger and say, "I saw this man participating in that mob." Raker wanted to know how it was possible that on the night of July 2 when "the town was lit like a blazing sun so everybody could see it, everybody was as blind as a bat . . . how did these people's eyesight all fail?" [15]

A total of forty-one persons were found guilty of misdemeanors—twenty-seven paid small fines and fourteen received short terms in the county jail.[16] Among these allegedly petty criminals were men who shot Negroes. For example, the grand jury had originally indicted seven police officers—three for murder and four for rioting and conspiracy. In an arrangement with representatives of the Assistant Attorney General, charges against the entire group were dismissed on condition that three lawmen agree to plead guilty to the crime of rioting. The policemen drew slips out of a hat and those choosing numbers one, two and three were charged; their fines amounting to $150 were paid by the rest of the group.[17] The *St. Louis Argus* criticized the "audacity to so distort the law as to make it a lottery, when the murder of Negroes is the issue." The Negro newspaper noted that the license to kill and maim had been set at only fifty dollars.[18] It is difficult to understand the basis of this unorthodox judicial procedure; perhaps the Assistant Attorney General did not bring this case to trial because he believed that regardless of the evidence no jury in St. Clair County would convict policemen.

The defendants' lawyer was Dan McGlynn, a leader in the Committee of One Hundred which was supposed to help Middlekauf in prosecuting rioting cases. The Congressional Investigating Committee sharply attacked McGlynn's loyalties and conduct: [19]

On one side was his membership on the executive committee of the "Committee of One Hundred" and his possession of important secrets of the prosecution disclosed to him by officials of the attorney general's office, and on the other was his desire to save [the police officers] from the punishment which they so justly deserved. All his talents and influences were placed at the service of these assassins, forgetting his duty as a citizen and regard for the ethics of his profession.

In the case for which McGlynn acted as counsel two Negroes were killed and another lost an arm. According to the original murder charge, on July 3 a group of policemen and guardsmen received instructions to close a saloon. Some witnesses said that the police officers entered with drawn guns and killed the Negroes on sight. Others recalled that the colored men met death attempting to flee. The soldiers later stated that although the Negroes did not display any weapons the police gave the order to fire and did most of the shooting. The police version was that the Negroes fired first and only the soldiers used their guns. A coroner's jury concluded that the evidence substantiated the militiamen's account.[20]

Despite the way this case was dealt with, there were six major court trials stemming from the race riot. Four of these trials involved white defendants. The scale to weigh guilt was calibrated differently for whites and Negroes. The whites were sentenced after culpability was overwhelmingly established; however the Negroes were imprisoned on inadequate evidence.

During October of 1917 in order to test whether a St. Clair County jury would find whites guilty, the prosecution presented what was considered its strongest case.[21] Herbert F. Wood, a forty-year-old railroad switchman, and Leo A. Keane, a seventeen-year-old railroad messenger, were charged with the murder of Scott Clark, who had been beaten and dragged by a rope at Fourth and Broadway. There was much sympathy for the defendants, and according to the *St. Louis Times*, "feeling in East St. Louis is bitter as a result of the opening of the trial . . . [a] new race riot looms." [22] East St. Louisans contributed to a small legal defense fund for the indicted whites, and these two men were represented by several lawyers, among whom was a former mayor.

Assistant Attorney General Middlekauf contended that Clark's death resulted from a conspiracy among whites to drive Negroes from the city. Since this implied that labor unions had been involved in the violence, defense attorneys attempted to ask potential jurors whether they were prejudiced against labor organizations. After the prosecution objected, Judge Crow barred the question. Middlekauf tried to eliminate talesmen with race prejudice and several candidly admitted that they would not vote to convict whites for crimes committed in a race riot. The jury which was finally selected contained neither blue collar workers nor, indeed, any East St. Louis residents at all.

During the trial Colonel E. P. Clayton testified that shortly after seven P.M. on July 2, he and a detachment of militiamen arrived at Fourth and Broadway; upon reaching the street corner he observed defendants Wood and Keane among the men dragging a Negro. Clayton grabbed Wood, ordering a guardsman to take Keane into custody. On the witness stand two infantrymen confirmed Clayton's account.

Mrs. Scott Clark, the widow of the man whom the rioters attempted to hang, told the jury that when the racial disorders began she and her husband sought refuge in the cellar of their house at Fourth and Railroad Avenue. After whites set fire to that dwelling the walls began to cave in and the Clarks fled next door. Within a short time this second house was ablaze so the couple decided to take their chances outside. They headed for the railroad tracks nearby, where a guardsman seemed to offer protection, and the three proceeded to Fourth Street. Approaching Broadway through an alley, they saw a Negro hanging from a pole. When a mob attacked the Clarks, the soldier made no attempt to save them. One rioter, identified as defendant Wood by another witness, struck Clark on the forehead with an iron bar, knocking him to the ground. Someone suggested, "drag him around a little while," but the rest of the mob shouted, "Hang the nigger." A rope was knotted around his neck, while Mrs. Clark turned away because "I couldn't stand to see no more." Paul Y. Anderson, the *Post-Dispatch* reporter, testified that Clark pleaded, "My God, don't kill me!" The men started to lynch him on the same pole that already held the other dangling body, but since the rope was too short to pass over the pole, Clark was pulled along Broadway. Although guardsmen rescued him, death came four days later from a fractured windpipe resulting in strangulation.

Both defendants admitted being on Broadway, but only as spectators attracted by large columns of smoke. A defense witness testified that at Fourth Street he saw Wood staring at the corpse hanging from the telephone pole, and the defendant had commented, "That's pretty tough." Nevertheless, under oath Wood acknowledged buying a gun on the day of the riot; when arrested he carried an automatic pistol and thirty-two steel-jacket cartridges. The former chief of detectives took the witness stand, naming Keane—easy to identify at the riot because he wore a green cap—as being one of the moving spirits of the mob prior to the attempted hanging of the deceased.

Silas Cook, a defense lawyer, tried to rebut the testimony of the guardsmen. He told the jury that the Illinois National Guard wanted Wood and Keane convicted to justify arrests of scores of innocent sightseers at Fourth and Broadway:[23]

> Why was it that only soldiers testified they saw Wood and Keane have hold of the rope? There were plenty of East St. Louis people there, but not one of them said they saw these defendants holding the rope. Isn't that strange? Have you stopped to think of that?

The prosecutors were portrayed as overzealous men determined to find scapegoats; Cook and his legal associates declared the defendants "are as innocent as was Jesus Christ before Pilate."

Demanding the death penalty for Wood, Middlekauf told the jury that if the defendants were permitted to beat and kill Negroes, Illinois would have other race riots. Obviously he feared that the jury might be reluctant to convict whites for the murder of a Negro during a race riot: [24]

> If negro hunts are considered permissible, we will have to keep soldiers in every city in this state, and we can't send them to Europe. If it had been a dog whom these men dragged through the streets with a rope about its neck, you would all agree that they ought to be punished for malicious mischief. If it had been a beautiful girl, hardly anyone would say that the offense was not deserving of the death penalty. No one would be satisfied with anything less. But remember that this old negro section hand had the same right to his life that the girl would have. The law makes no distinction of sex or color.

In less than two hours' deliberation Wood and Keane were found guilty and sentenced to fourteen year terms. Afterwards, the *Post-Dispatch* noted that a "stronger case against [them] could not have been made." The *Chicago Defender* was disappointed and told Negro readers that the punishment should have been more severe.[25] However, the *East St. Louis Journal* and the *Belleville Daily Advocate*, among other newspapers, were elated that "the law still reigns. . . . This vindicates the people and officials of St. Clair County from the country-heralded charges against them of race prejudice." The *Chicago Herald* declared, "The start thus made is wholly hopeful. Let the good work go on . . . the horror cannot be wiped out by a few vicarious convictions."[26]

Because the transcripts of both the Wood-Keane trial and the one which followed it have not been found, the discussion here has been based upon newspaper accounts. The major dailies in St. Louis and East St. Louis reported these court trials against white defendants in a very objective manner, with almost no attempt to reach a verdict before that of the juries'. However, one exception was the *East St. Louis Journal*'s account of the Wood-Keane proceedings, in which several defense witnesses were described as having given "no strong testimony." According to the newspaper, "the circumstances against the accused men appear to be unusually strong. . . ." [27]

The second court trial of the whites was also held in October 1917. Assistant Attorney General James Farmer presented the prosecution's case, charging three men with killing William Keyser, a white hardware merchant, shortly after one o'clock on the afternoon of July 2. The defendants were Harry Robinson, a middle-aged shoemaker; John Dow, a teen-aged ice wagon driver; and Charles Hanna, a young teamster. The prosecution did not attempt to show that they actually fired the fatal shot; rather the case rested on the contention that the men were members of a mob who in conspiring against Negroes accidentally caused Keyser's death. One of the lawyers representing the defendants was Alexander Flannigan, who had told a union audience on May 28 that there was no law to curb mob violence. In accordance with Judge Crow's earlier ruling, neither side asked prospective jurors if they were union members, although inquiries about occupations were permitted. Flannigan used most peremptory challenges against farmers and businessmen, but when the jury was finally impaneled, at least half of its members were farmers. There were no East St. Louis laborers, a fact which caused comment.

The key witness for the prosecution was Mrs. Edward Cook, a Negro whose husband and son were killed in the same incident which brought death to Keyser. Mrs. Cook told the jury that on July 2 her family was returning by streetcar to their home in St. Louis after having spent the morning fishing in Alton. At Collinsville Avenue, between Illinois and Missouri Avenues, the wheel trolley of the car was pulled from its overhead wire by a mob led by defendants Hanna and Dow: [28]

> We heard men holler, "Stop the car!" Then that man (Hanna) reached through the window and grabbed my dress, and tore it partly off. . . . He said, "Come on out you black bitch, because we want to kill you. . . ." Then he and that other man (Dow) came into the car and said, "All you white people get out. We're going to kill these niggers." The white people got off. I told them that we all didn't live in East St. Louis and hadn't hurt anybody there. . . . That man (Hanna) took my husband by the collar and pulled him to the back platform and threw him off and shot him. I saw that. . . . That man (Dow) took my boy and started to drag him out. I took hold of him. "You've killed my husband," I said. "Don't kill my boy." He jerked him away, beating him over the head with his revolver, and that was the last time I saw my son alive. . . . Then that man (Hanna) came back and dragged me out of the car, and men beat me, and kicked me, and pulled my hair out. A white man got in front of me and called out, "Don't kill the women folks." The men started beating him, and I crawled on my hands and knees into a store. . . . Well, I fell over in this doorway, and at that time some tall white fellow came running there and said "don't beat her any more," he begged and said, "please don't beat her any more." "I am not going to let them kill you," he said, "stay back there." And so he threw his arm across the door like that and I was behind him and he says, "in the name of the Lord don't kill the woman;" and then some way or other they got me into the ambulance, and there was another fellow lying there, a colored fellow on the side of the ambulance, and I saw he had a big handkerchief and I took it and wiped the blood out of my eyes, and when I looked down I saw my husband lying there and my boy right under me; they had their eyes open and they were dead.

Taking the witness stand, Abram Keyser described how his father was accidentally killed by the same bullet which took the life of Mrs. Cook's teen-aged son. Keyser recalled that his father was standing in front of their store observing the mob that had invaded several street cars and beaten Negro passengers. "As I got to the door of the store I saw an Alton car had been stopped, and saw a negro boy, a tall boy, running toward us. When he got almost to us, there was a shot—only one shot—and the boy fell and my father fell, too. My father died about ten minutes later." The witness stated that defendants Robinson and Dow were in the group from which the shot was fired. Others presented corroborative testimony. Lewis P. Ward, a white passenger on the streetcar, identified Dow as a mob member; Mrs. Ada Walters said she saw Dow and Hanna take a Negro from the vehicle. She recalled that a day later, Dow bragged about killing many Negroes and disposing of their bodies in the Cahokia Creek. Additional witnesses testified that Hanna pursued fleeing Negroes, kicked an unconscious man, and threatened to kill an ambulance driver for attempting to transport a Negro victim to the hospital. Max Sozinsky and his daughter Fannie asserted that on the morning of the riot, their Collinsville Avenue pawnshop was burglarized by a mob containing defendants Robinson and Dow. Thirty-six revolvers and twelve boxes of ammunition were stolen. Sozinsky also said that over an hour later he saw Dow, with a pair of ice tongs hanging from his shoulders, pulling a Negro boy from the street car window.

Defense lawyer Flannigan, although denying that his clients participated in the mobs, suggested that unidentified white gangs had been provoked by Negroes. Excluding that line of testimony, Judge Crow ruled that a conspiracy of one group could furnish no legal defense for the conspiracy of another. The defense then attempted to show that the bullet which killed Keyser might have come not from the whites in front of his store, but from a Negro

mob which was allegedly in the alley. However, according
to the *Post-Dispatch*, the defense attorney "failed to get
any witness to say that there was any way in which a bullet
from the alley in the rear could have struck Keyser, without first having turned a corner." [29]

Since there was overwhelming evidence connecting defendants with the white mob on Collinsville Avenue, they
portrayed themselves as sightseers who, for only a brief
time, were near the crime scene. Hanna said he was at
work during most of the day, but his employer was unable
to account for his movements in the early afternoon when
the murders occurred. Nor did Dow's alibi cover the crucial time between noon and one-thirty in the afternoon.
Robinson's employer testified that the defendant worked
in the shoeshop until noon which seemed to account for the
time when the pawnshop was burglarized. However, the
prosecution sought to discredit that alibi by reminding
Robinson that he had told the coroner's inquest about
standing in front of the pawnshop during the burglary.
He denied ever making such a statement and, since the
testimony had not been recorded verbatim by the coroner's
stenographer, it lent little support to the prosecution's
case.

In his closing argument, Assistant Attorney General
James Farmer told the jury that the Collinsville Avenue
mob was more savage and wanton than the Indian tribes
which used to roam St. Clair County. Dow and Hanna
were found guilty and sentenced to fifteen years in the
penitentiary. The jury was unable to reach agreement
about Robinson and his case was scheduled for retrial;
however, after pleading guilty to conspiracy to riot, he
received five year's imprisonment. [30]

In the third trial, Richard Brockway, a middle-aged
railway claims agent, was charged with conspiracy to incite rioting. James Farmer portrayed the defendant as "the
leader who started that awful holocaust of murder, arson,
and rapine." As usual, the selection of a jury involved end-

less wrangling—with the examination of nearly 350 tales-men. Foreman Edward Sims caused considerable comment because he was a Negro teamster who looked "almost white." Sims would have been rejected, as were several other Negro talesmen, if defense attorneys had been aware earlier of his racial background.

Several witnesses testified that on July 2 in front of the police station they heard Brockway tell a group "that niggers [are] going to take the town." He persuaded listen-ers to march to the Labor Temple for a protest meeting, where he demanded revenge for the shooting of the detec-tives. Favoring the organization of a Home Protective League, Brockway allegedly instructed the men to return with weapons later that afternoon in order to drive the Negroes out of town.[31] Immediately following adjournment of the morning meeting, Negroes were beaten and shot.

Many prosecution witnesses reported other incendiary statements Brockway was supposed to have made. A Negro minister testified that on the morning of the riot Brockway saw him talking to a colored man. The defendant turned to a policeman, allegedly saying, "Officer you'd better get those damned niggers off the street; we're going to kill every nigger in East St. Louis in a minute." Another wit-ness declared that Brockway stated, "We ought to go down there and get those niggers and burn their shacks." [32]

Defense attorneys presented the defendant as a peace-maker who expended superhuman efforts in a fruitless at-tempt to stop the riot. Witnesses asserted that Brockway had favored a declaration of martial law to save Negro lives and had been deeply concerned about the carnage.[33] Brockway claimed that only for the sake of preserving peace did he advise a policeman not to permit Negroes on the street. He said that his sole reason for attending the Labor Temple meeting was to recommend a policy of restraint. He further contended that out of contempt for the rioters he helped many Negroes to safety. Brockway concluded with the amazing statement to the jurors that because his peace mission had been so successful, he heard only a few shots fired and saw no Negroes assaulted.[34]

The defendant's statements differed considerably from remarks attributed to him a few months earlier at the coroner's inquest. For example, Brockway told the coroner that he had indeed seen white mobs assaulting Negroes on the day of the riot. Brockway also admitted to the coroner that it was he who instructed the men to return to the Labor Temple on the afternoon of July 2. At the trial he denied ever having made such statements. The prosecution was unable to show that Brockway personally committed acts of violence, and several witnesses testified that they had not seen the defendant among the rioting mobs.[35] However, the jurors were reminded that he was accused only of organizing a group of whites at the Labor Temple, and under Illinois law he was held responsible for actions flowing from the conspiracy.

The state called reporters from the *Post-Dispatch* and *Globe-Democrat* who described scenes of mob fury; the Negroes, rather than having a gun in each pocket, were shown as passive victims pleading for their lives.[36] The prosecution repeatedly emphasized that on July 2 the purpose of the Home Protective League organizers was not *defensive* action to protect their families from Negro aggression: [37]

> Q. There was nobody assaulting the whites' homes at that time, was there?
> A. I do not know.
> Q. You did not hear anything of that kind, did you?
> A. No, sir.
> Q. There was nobody saying that anybody was attacking the whites' homes or trying to hurt the white people at that time, was there?
> A. I did not hear any.
> Q. Nobody said anything of that kind there.
> A. No, I do not think so.

Q. What they were talking about was killing negroes, wasn't it. . . .

The jury found Brockway guilty and he was sentenced to five years in the penitentiary.[38] At this trial, two co-defendants were also convicted. Nineteen-year-old John Tisch, a meat-packing plant employee, received five years in prison after witnesses testified to seeing him fire several shots at fleeing Negroes.[39] Another witness stated that Tisch had boasted of "getting his share of niggers." John Johnson, a twenty-nine-year-old railroad switchman, received a one year sentence after testimony convinced the jury that he prevented two soldiers from arresting a rioter.[40] Johnson denied the accusation, but according to earlier statements presented at the coroner's inquest he had admitted ordering soldiers to release the rioter.

In the final court trial of the whites, three men—Mike Evanhoff, a coal and ice dealer; Edward Otto, a steamfitter; and Daniel Walsh, a railway yard clerk—were fined five hundred dollars each for conspiracy to riot. Many persons testified that the defendants were in a mob which burned Negro homes in the vicinity of Thirteenth and Gross on the evening of July 2.[41] Witnesses George Reeves and Ada White stated that they saw Evanhoff and several others enter their house about one o'clock on the morning of July 3.[42] The intruders went from room to room breaking windows, furniture, and dishes. Reeves said he hid in a closet while the men were there. When soldiers drove up in an Armour meat truck to rescue the Negroes, Evanhoff reportedly remarked, "We ain't done them half bad enough—ought to kill all the damned niggers." [43] After the refugees were taken into protective custody their homes were burned.

Rachel Cary testified that she saw Edward Otto at the front door; he pointed a gun, demanding to know where Negro males were hiding. Mrs. Rosa Augustus told the jurors that Otto broke down her front door with an ax and shot into the house. She said he shouted, "If any of you niggers are in there you better get out." Carrying a baby in her arms, she fled through the back door into an alley and a short time afterwards the house was ablaze. Other witnesses reported that Walsh also fired into Negro residences.[44]

In all these trials of white persons, witnesses placed the defendants at the riot scenes. In all except one case, specific violent acts of the rioters were observed. The one exception was Brockway, but there was no question that his actions, while not violent in themselves, gave encouragement to the mobs. Attorneys Middlekauf and Farmer effectively presented the prosecution's case in these trials, and the fairminded juries rendered the only possible verdict under the circumstances.

9
Court Trials of the Negroes

STEMMING from the race riot were two trials of Negroes. In both proceedings defendants were charged with participation in a conspiracy resulting in the murder of the two detectives. People v. Parker *et al.* was the very first of all the riot cases and was tried in early October, 1917. People v. Bundy was the last riot case, taking place in March, 1919. The complete transcripts of both trials have been located, offering an opportunity to examine at first hand the evidence upon which jury verdicts were based, to determine if witnesses changed their testimony during the period between the two trials, and to compare the press versions of witnesses' testimony with what was actually said in the courtroom.

Although twenty-one Negroes were originally indicted for the murder of the detectives, when the first case went to trial there were thirteen defendants (among them Fayette Parker, a member of the St. Clair County Board of Supervisors). The Negro community feared that, since this was the opening riot trial, the prosecution was actually seeking to blame the colored race for the July 2 violence and thus have a pretext to release all whites from indictments.[1]

At most of the sessions the courtroom was filled—about half of the spectators were Negroes. Also, almost all the defense witnesses were Negroes. The jury contained only three East St. Louis residents, all of whom were businessmen.[2] Negro newspapers took notice of the fact that the jury included no colored members.[3] In his opening statement for the prosecution, Assistant Attorney General James A. Farmer said that under the leadership of Dr. Le Roy Bundy, Negroes had planned an uprising, provoking the race riot to avenge real and fancied grievances. Farmer, employing a precedent used in the Haymarket Riot trials, sought to prove a conspiracy and thereby hold the defendants responsible for crimes resulting from it. He told the jurors that instead of trying to show that these Negroes actually fired the shots killing Coppedge and Wadley, the prosecution wished only to prove that Parker as well as the other twelve men participated in conspiratorial meetings and were in the mob at the murder scene. Judge George A. Crow admitted all testimony tending to show the congregating of armed Negroes, whether or not such gatherings related directly to the slaying.

The prosecution called William Walker, a Negro saloonkeeper, who testified that between eight and nine o'clock on the evening of July 1—less than four hours before the murder—he saw defendant William Palmer and a companion walking past Sixteenth and Colas St. Both men had shotguns.[4] Another witness, Calvin Glasby, reported that at Fifteenth and Piggott between nine and ten o'clock he observed defendants O'Fanniel Peoples, Charles Foster, Marshall Alexander, and two others who were not on trial, and, in his opinion, Peoples possessed a gun. One of the non-defendants had allegedly told Glasby[5] that he planned to go to Tenth and Bond—the place where the two detectives were shot a few hours later—because whites had previously beaten Negroes there. Other white and Negro witnesses testified that during the three hours before midnight unidentified gangs of Negroes roamed the streets in the area which was to be the murder scene.[6]

Taking the stand, Fred Peleate stated that around midnight he heard noises outside his house at Twelfth and Market; among the armed Negroes he allegedly saw was defendant George Roberts carrying a shotgun or a rifle. The witness added that a few minutes later Roberts was marching at the head of a gang of seventy-five or one hundred armed men within one block of Tenth and Bond.[7] Peleate's identification might be disputed, since he also testified that less than an hour earlier Dr. Le Roy Bundy was seen driving a black car near Tenth and Bond.[8] At his trial Bundy was able to present incontrovertible evidence proving that he was not in East St. Louis on the evening of July 1, 1917.

Witnesses for the prosecution reported that a few minutes past midnight they heard a churchbell pealing, after which about a dozen automobiles left a gas station owned by Bundy.[9] They testified that a short time later there was a volley of shots, "like someone attacking in war." Jurors were told the Negro gangs had not formed spontaneously, but that the bells had been the signal for the uprising.

In view of there being no surviving officer in the detectives' car who could identify even one of the slayers,[10] the most important witness for the state was Edward Wilson, a Negro ice and coal dealer. He testified that when the gunshots followed the bell ringing, he looked outside and observed Negroes on the corner of Fifteenth and Piggott, three blocks away.[11] Out of curiosity he walked over and said he saw twelve armed defendants, several of whom were intensely discussing a car they had just shot at.[12] There is evidence that Wilson may not have been an unbiased witness. On the day following the shooting police suspected him of involvement; he was arrested and jailed for more than a week.[13] Whether guilty or not, Wilson had a motive for being influenced by overzealous investigators, and he obtained release from custody shortly after appearing at the coroner's inquest where he identified several Negroes as having fired into the car. At the time of his incarceration, three defendants (Peoples, Smotherman, and Palmer) were also being held, and their attorneys declared that Wilson confided to the three men that he would do anything to be freed.[14] At least one defense lawyer believed that Wilson had actually been leading a mob near Tenth and Bond.[15] The state's star witness denied all of these accusations.

Samuel W. Baxter, a defense attorney, tried to show an inconsistency between Wilson's testimony at the coroner's inquest and the statements which the witness had just made in the courtroom.[16] In early July when Coroner Renner had asked Wilson which men were seen at Fifteenth and Piggott, the record showed that he gave the names of just four persons, and only one of these (Peoples) was a defendant in the murder trial. Later in his appearance at the coroner's inquest, Wilson decided to change the statement and told Coroner Renner that he knew five or six Negroes at Fifteenth and Piggott. When Renner asked which man had talked about the car being fired upon, the witness identified Dr. Bundy. However, at the murder trial Wilson denied that the coroner's transcript was complete and he stuck to the story about recognizing twelve defendants on the street corner, five of whom were discussing the shooting.

Since the accuracy of Dr. Renner's transcript had become an important issue in the courtroom, the coroner's stenographer was called as a witness. She was unable to recall whether she had written down Wilson's statements verbatim or whether a summarized account of the testimony had been dictated to her by Renner.[17] Because of the uncertainty, Judge Crow ruled that the transcript was improper evidence. This discrepancy between Wilson's testimony at the inquest and the trial was crucial, and the coroner might have clarified it had he been summoned to the witness stand.[18] If the Negro had originally identified twelve men, it is inconceivable that Renner would have omitted from the transcript any names of alleged slayers and accessories, particularly since Wilson was the only witness supplying this information.

In view of Judge Crow's ruling, the defense attorneys were powerless to present an effective challenge. Unfortunately for the witness, however, he named Dr. Le Roy Bundy as having been among those on the street corner. After the 1919 murder trial of the Negro dentist, Wilson's testimony was discredited by the Illinois Supreme Court. But if he had not told the truth regarding Bundy, what about some (or even all) of the defendants in the 1917 trial? Had they actually been at Fifteenth and Piggott shortly after the slaying? Had Wilson really overheard them talking about the crime? According to Wilson, the street corner gathering discussed a car they had just shot into, but nowhere in his testimony was there any mention that the car carrying the detectives was the subject of the discussion. The men (who may or may not have been the defendants) could have talked about another Ford automobile which only a short time earlier was driven through a Negro neighborhood by white "joyriders" who shot into colored homes. Some Negro residents rushed outside and fired back.[19]

Defense attorneys stated that their thirteen clients were not in the armed Negro gangs which moved about the streets of East St. Louis on the night of July 1, and that the defendants had no knowledge of a plot against whites. They contended that, while no Negro conspiracy was proven, there had been a white conspiracy. They wished to introduce witnesses to show that even before the May 28 riots, whites had harassed Negroes in a campaign to run them out of the city. Judge Crow undercut this approach, holding that a conspiracy by whites was a separate, illegal action which could be no legal defense.[20]

Following Crow's decision, the defense was confined to presenting alibi witnesses to account for the whereabouts of the accused on the evening of the shootings. They also disputed the prosecution's contention that the churchbell had been a signal for the shooting.[21] The Negroes claimed that the bell rang *after* the firing.[22] The Assistant Attorney General noted that the defendants' friends and relatives might easily have been confused, and the *Journal* made the point that none of these witnesses was white.[23] Ten of the thirteen defendants were found guilty and sentenced to fourteen years in the penitentiary.[24] On appeal, the Illinois Supreme Court upheld the convictions.[25]

Several newspapers convicted the Negroes days ahead of the jury. Early in the trial, the *Post-Dispatch* ran a column head, "Testimony Tends to Show Negroes had Planned Riot." [26] The *Journal* observed, "An abundance of strong evidence to show that Bundy . . . was the master hand in planning the outbreak of blacks . . . was introduced by the state. . . ." [27] A similar statement was made by the *St. Louis Republic*.[28] According to the *Globe-Democrat*, a considerable amount of outside money was spent for the Negroes' defense; the paper noted that the lawyers admitted they were retained at big fees by a national Negro organization.[29] This was a reference to the N.A.A.C.P., which sent W. E. B. Du Bois to East St. Louis shortly after the riot to collect evidence.[30] The Association helped to establish a modest legal defense fund and among the contributors were such Negro organizations as the Masons and the Odd Fellows.[31]

There were many instances of inaccurate, biased newspaper reporting of witness testimony. For example, according to the *Journal*, "Mrs. George W. Wodley of 1714 Bond Avenue, which is just a few doors from the former home of Bundy, testified that she saw large numbers of negroes enter Bundy's home at various times between May 28, the day of the first race riot and July 1. Many of the negroes were armed, she said, and all seemed to be drilling for the proposed reprisal of the blacks. Many meetings were held at the negro leader's home, she stated, and at these gatherings they are supposed to have mapped out their proposed massacre." [32] In reporting Mrs. Wodley's testimony, the St. Louis newspapers also mentioned the "secret meetings" and "assemblies of negroes at Bundy's place." [33] An examination of the actual trial transcript indicates that the witness on one occasion had seen about twenty Negroes in Bundy's house. She admitted having no idea of "what they were doing outside of being there." She said that she could not recall any other time when Negroes congregated at Bundy's home. The witness thought that four guns were brought into the house but she made no comment about Negroes drilling in preparation for a "massacre." [34]

According to the *Post-Dispatch*, Henry Krudwig, a white saloonkeeper, testified that he saw Negroes bringing arms into a Negro tavern which Bundy visited "every few days." [35] On the witness stand, Krudwig had mentioned nothing about Bundy. [36] The most biased newspaper was the *St. Louis Republic*, which quoted Andrew Gaa as testifying that near midnight he saw Bundy driving a red automobile to a Negro tavern. [37] The trial transcript actually indicates that under cross-examination, the witness made the following statement: [38] "The machine stopped in front of Bayles, that was Bayles place and a gentleman got out, whoever he was, he looked like Bundy to me; I won't swear to it, I could not swear to it." In reply to the question about whether Bundy's car was seen, he said, "Why it looked like Bundy's car. I am not sure, there are lots of cars like it in town, I only can state it was a red car." [39]

The *Republic* noted that William Walker "told how he had heard the ringing of church bells calling negroes to arms." [40] The *Post-Dispatch* claimed that the witness "testified he saw negroes assembling earlier in the night." [41] As mentioned previously, Walker had simply said that two armed Negroes were walking along the street between eight and nine o'clock in the evening of July 1, and that over three hours later he heard the ringing of church bells. In the testimony [42] he had made no connection between the two occurrences.

The *Republic* considered that "the most startling development yesterday . . . was the testimony of Edward Keshner" (a vice-president of the Union Trust and Savings Bank in East St. Louis). "He told of how he had seen scores of automobiles occupied by negroes crossing the free bridge between 8 and 9 o'clock, July 1. These negroes drove to the district where the negroes later mobilized on the night of the murders, it was said . . . negro residents of St. Louis had secretly pledged their support to negroes of East St. Louis and were members of the mob which murdered Coppedge." [43] According to the *East St. Louis Journal* and the *St. Louis Post-Dispatch*, Keshner added that the Negroes in this "unusual procession" of automobiles "appeared very much excited" and "he remarked to his wife that 'something must be going on.' " [44] The trial transcript actually indicated that Keshner had testified only to observing eight or ten cars filled with Negroes crossing the bridge from St. Louis early in the evening of July 1. He was asked, "Could you tell from anything you saw whether they were armed?" He replied, "No, I could not." [45] That was all there was to his testimony.

It is not possible to determine to what extent trial-by-newspaper influenced the jury, but journalistic distortion of testimony should not be ignored. An examination of the trial transcript indicates that the state's evidence against the defendants was weak—even the prejudiced *St. Louis Republic* quoted the prosecutor's admission that his case was "not the strongest in the world." [46] On the night of July 1-2, Negroes had indeed shot the detectives, but aside from Wilson's questionable testimony, there was nothing to link most (if any) of these particular defendants with the crime.

The verdict which was arrived at was feared, but not

really expected, by the Negro community. Race newspapers commented that the jurors allowed themselves to accept the word of witness Wilson ("a disreputable policy writing Negro") and to reject the statements of the defendants (nearly all were identified as "citizens of good repute" who belonged to Negro churches and fraternal orders).[47] The *Chicago Defender* summed up the sentiment in declaring that the convicted men received a "bum deal" and were "victims of race prejudice pure and simple." [48]

As soon as the ten Negroes went to prison, East St. Louis focused attention upon the Le Roy Bundy trial which was considered of even greater importance. The press had noted during the preceding trial that the prosecution made a stronger case against Bundy than against the defendants found guilty of murder.[49] If the dentist did not have enough of a burden, there were hints that German money had supported his activities.[50] Shortly after the race riot, newspapers had reported that the "black king" received a "thick bundle of bills" to arm Negroes for their advancement, that he "marked for execution . . . prominent [white] men," and that he was an "aggressive political agitator . . . [who] is alleged to have boasted that the negroes would 'get even' with the white people." The *Journal* and *Republic* had even falsely reported that at the coroner's inquest many Negroes named Bundy as the man who plotted the murder of the two detectives.[51] Condemning the press for having inflamed public opinion against their client, Bundy's attorneys obtained a change of venue for his trial.[52]

Although Dr. Bundy was certainly no black king, before the race riot he had occupied a leading position among Negroes in East St. Louis and had been a member of the St. Clair County Board of Supervisors. A man in his mid-thirties, he came originally from a prominent Cleveland family. His brother served at the American legation in Liberia and his father, Rev. Charles Bundy, was a presiding elder in the African Methodist Episcopal Church as well as a trustee of Wilberforce (Ohio) University.

Le Roy Bundy was a fiercely independent, ambitious man who was dissatisfied with only a dental practice; he invested money in a gasoline and auto repair station, a car rental service, and an automobile dealership. To East St. Louis whites he represented the spirit of a new and undesirable kind of Negro—over-ambitious, argumentative, even bumptious, and anything but accommodating. He was known as a strong supporter of equal rights for Negroes in an era when the term was hated and feared by local whites, who accused him of preaching discontent among colored people.

Demanding equal political participation for Negroes, Bundy tried to obtain equal political rewards. He viewed himself as a super-ward leader, and in local elections forced both political parties to compete for his influence among Negroes. In exchange he persuaded constituents to follow his lead; sometimes money was paid for their votes, but often payment was in the coin of services (obtaining a few political jobs or getting them out of trouble with the police).[53] Negroes admired his self-confidence, although some thought his hot temper might get him into trouble with the whites. The *Chicago Defender* described Bundy as "a good mixer," a man of "natural leadership," and the sort of person that "the ordinary fellow looks to for guidance."[54]

In national politics he was a Republican, but as an opportunist in local political affairs he was close to the Mollman administration. The "outs" in attacking the "ins" often tried to accomplish their objective by assailing Bundy and his constituents. In East St. Louis politics, Bundy's white allies even moved against him when their purposes were served. For example, despite Bundy's having collaborated in local elections with Mayor Mollman's political boss, Locke Tarlton, Tarlton did not hesitate to make Bundy a dupe in the Democratic party's efforts to link Negroes with the alleged colonization conspiracy in 1916. Amid publicity the Negro leader was arrested and then quietly released.

Bundy's independence also brought him opponents among local labor leaders. He favored unionization but was not reluctant to criticize AFofL locals for not admitting Negroes.[55] Union officials accused him of double-crossing the labor movement when in June, 1917, as a witness before the Illinois Council of Defense investigation of the May 28 riots, he refused to charge factory owners with spearheading the migration of Negroes to East St. Louis.[56] The labor organizers concluded that Bundy's actions stemmed from ulterior motives, indicating his involvement in the "importation plot."

Possessing so many enemies, Bundy not only became the key suspect as the commander of a Negro army which killed Detectives Coppedge and Wadley, but he also found it impossible to obtain a fair trial in southern Illinois. In August, 1917, the dentist fought hard against extradition after his arrest in Cleveland, and his lawyers told Ohio's Governor James Cox that their client would be lynched upon return to East St. Louis.[57] Cox agreed to sign extradition papers only after receiving definite assurances that the Negro would be protected by Illinois authorities.[58] When Bundy was finally transported from Ohio to the county jail in Belleville, Illinois, the sheriff took the precaution of detouring to avoid East St. Louis.[59] Between the time of his arrest and trial about a year and a half elapsed. His attorneys, in delaying the proceedings, obviously hoped that with the passage of time community hostility would recede.

Bundy's arrest had transformed him into a celebrity among colored people across the country. Proclaiming him a "RACE leader," Negro newspapers declared that the case was not "the trial of an individual but . . . the trial of the Race." [60] The N.A.A.C.P. administered a modest legal defense fund, and, typically, local newspapers commented that powerful influences were working to set him free.[61] Despite N.A.A.C.P. support, the dentist's fierce independence created conflict with the Association, which had assumed that he would follow its guidance; his refusal resulted in an estrangement that probably hurt his case.

Bundy's troubles with the N.A.A.C.P. stemmed from an amalgam of arrogance and fear. He wanted financial and moral support, but refused to accept the demand for a rigorous accounting of legal defense funds. The Negro dentist also demanded a larger battery of attorneys than the Association considered desirable or necessary.[62] Bundy was under great strain from the ordeal of arrest and incarceration in the county jail, where he remained many weeks, until the state permitted release on bail. He was frightened at the possibility of trial by a kangaroo court. Since Bundy had been identified as the instigator of a Negro conspiracy, if convicted he could not receive less than fourteen years in the penitentiary, and there was every expectation that a life sentence, or worse, would be imposed.

If his risks were great, he evidently wanted to meet possible destruction in an atmosphere of glory and adulation. To this politician in trouble, there seemed tremendous satisfaction in taking his case to the people; he wished to tour the country seeking help from Negroes.[63] The N.A.A.C.P. insisted that to avoid financial scandals, funds collected from personal appearances should become part of a fiscal plan, but Bundy balked since the plan was more limited than he desired. Furthermore, after lawyers had obtained several trial postponements, the Association suggested that he earn a living again by resuming a professional career. Bundy, the dentist turned celebrity and race hero, was not much interested in filling teeth; for living expenses he preferred to use money collected at public meetings and he refused to report these funds to the Association.

This attitude created a feud with executive committee

members of the St. Louis N.A.A.C.P., who denounced the personal appearance tours as "junkets." By April, 1918, they were not on speaking terms with him and recommended that the national office withdraw from the case. In New York City, the N.A.A.C.P. was naturally reluctant to take that action and Bundy was invited to present his side to Association leaders.[64] W. E. B. Du Bois described the meeting as a painful fiasco—Bundy replied that an accounting of funds had been made to individual contributors but that since the Association gave so little support he was not obligated to submit financial reports to it. Reluctantly the N.A.A.C.P. publicly announced withdrawal from the case.[65] Continuing the speaking tours, Bundy discovered the quarrel had not hurt him with such prominent Negroes as A. Philip Randolph and Chandler Owen.[66] The *Chicago Defender* admonished the Association for its handling of the Bundy case,[67] while the *Cleveland Gazette* denounced the organization for making a vicious attack on a race leader and deserting him. The *Gazette* advised readers to resign from a "white-men controlled" Association which stood for the persecution rather than the advancement of colored people.[68]

Bundy's trial was finally held in March, 1919, at Waterloo, Illinois—an agricultural community located over twenty miles from East St. Louis. Assistant Attorney General James Farmer headed the prosecution and told jurors that the dentist had transported and stored weapons and been present when Detectives Coppedge and Wadley were shot.[69] Most prosecution witnesses had previously testified against Negro defendants in 1917, but in the 1919 trial the fragility of their evidence was skillfully exposed by defense attorneys Thomas Webb and Samuel W. Baxter.

Mrs. George Wodley was supposed to play a major role in linking Bundy with the conspiracy.[70] She testified that during the first week in June she passed his home and saw him "pointing and gesturing" to about twenty Ne-

groes. (The *Post-Dispatch* and *Globe-Democrat* told readers that Mrs. Wodley had said Bundy "harrangued" his
audience.) As previously mentioned Mrs. Wodley did testify that Negroes carried four shotguns into his house, but
defense attorneys suggested that, since the dentist also
operated an automobile service station adjoining his property, he usually kept expensive tools at home and the witness may have seen long wrenches instead of guns. Mrs.
Wodley also said that she observed Negroes in front of the
gas station apparently testing cars for some purpose and
slowly driving them up and down the street. She concluded
that the drivers looked at her and other whites in a "pecul-
iar" and "almost antagonistic" manner.[71] Since her remarks were to support the prosecution contention that
Bundy was "drilling" Negroes, defense attorneys called
Dr. Thomas G. Hunter who testified that when his car was
serviced at Bundy's, the mechanic routinely tested the
vehicle in front of the garage. Hunter also observed that
Bundy sold cars and provided buyers with driving lessons
across the street from the service station.[72]

To supplement Mrs. Wodley's testimony about the
storage of guns, prosecutor Farmer presented Henry L.
Krudwig, a white tavernkeeper, who reported that a few
weeks before July 1 he saw Negroes carrying shotguns into
James Bayles' saloon. (Bayles, in hiding, was described in
the *Post-Dispatch* as "a close personal and political friend
of Bundy.") The witness asserted that Bundy patronized
Bayles' tavern, but cross-examination by defense attorney
Thomas Webb revealed that the Negro dentist had also
been a customer of Krudwig's, who ran a saloon across the
street. Furthermore, no evidence was given to link Bundy
with the weapons brought into Bayles' place. No effort had
been made to conceal the delivery of guns, and Webb suggested that they were used by the Odd Fellows Lodge in
drill formations.[73]

Prosecutor Farmer employed a third attempt to con-
nect Bundy with the storage of weapons and presented

Charles J. Miller, who was outside the police station on May 29 when Negroes in a red car were arrested for smuggling seven revolvers and ammunition from St. Louis. (At the 1917 trial he estimated there had been thirty revolvers.) Despite the fact that under cross-examination by Mr. Webb, Miller admitted that the dentist was not among the passengers in the car,[74] the *Globe-Democrat* reported, "The most important testimony presented yesterday was offered by the state in an effort to prove that arms and ammunition were assembled at Bundy's home. . . ."[75]

Although the prosecutor did not assert that Bundy's red car was used, he emphasized (as in the earlier trial) that the defendant owned such a vehicle.[76] Many citizens believed that Bundy was involved in the May 29 smuggling expedition,[77] so the State's Attorney tried again to make an indirect connection by picturing the defendant as a close friend of the passengers arrested in the red automobile. Defense attorney, Samuel W. Baxter, introduced witnesses who testified that Bundy had not participated in the smuggling incident. The red Hupmobile which the police impounded had been sold by him months earlier to a businessman named John Owens.[78] On May 29, after Owens learned that his chauffeur and several others were arrested for hauling weapons, he asked the dentist to accompany him to the police station and help recover the car. Bundy's appearance at police headquarters led whites to conclude that he still owned the vehicle and had purchased the guns. Furthermore, since Owen's chauffeur frequented Bundy's garage, some citizens, including State's Attorney Hubert Schaumleffel, believed that the man was employed there.[79]

Defense counsel Baxter tried to turn the discussion of the smuggling incident to his client's advantage by placing on the stand several Negroes who had actually driven to St. Louis in the Hupmobile to buy weapons.[80] Baxter wanted these men to tell why they went, and through this testimony he hoped to demonstrate obliquely that Negroes had been beaten by whites in the weeks preceding the May 28 disorders. In this manner he sought to skirt Judge Gillham's ruling that a white conspiracy was no defense for a Negro conspiracy. However, the prosecutor's objection to this evidence was sustained by Gillham.

The rest of the testimony essentially concerned events occurring on the day of the Coppedge murder. The prosecution wanted to show that the "uprising" was planned in collaboration with St. Louis Negroes. As in the 1917 trial, witness E. P. Keshner testified that about seven o'clock in the evening he saw Negroes driving across the bridge into East St. Louis. However, only in the Bundy case was the witness given a thorough cross-examination, exposing how little factual information he possessed. Keshner admitted he did not know who were in the cars, what their destinations were, or why they crossed the bridge. He agreed that the automobiles were not bunched together or even necessarily in the same party. And he also acknowledged that on a warm beautiful Sunday, it was not too unusual for some Negroes to be out driving.[81]

Several other witnesses stated that after nine in the evening they saw colored occupants of a red car and a black car stop at various streets near the murder scene and talk with congregating Negroes. Mr. George Vatter said he noticed the cars at Twelfth and Trendley, with over one hundred Negroes walking behind them.[82] Mrs. Mary Fisher testified that shortly after the vehicles left Eleventh and Trendley, about fifteen or twenty armed Negroes walked past.[83] The *Post-Dispatch* quoted Mrs. Fisher as testifying that the cars came "from the direction of Bundy's house." [84] However, she had actually said that she did not know whether the cars were travelling north or south as they moved on Trendley from Tenth St. Furthermore, Bundy's house was about one mile south and west of the place where the automobiles were observed. Neither witness saw Bundy, although local newspapers noted that the prosecutor's "intended implication[s]" were that the red car was Bundy's, the black one Bayles', and that the vehicles were used "to carry armed negroes to the rendezvous." [85]

The state next called three other persons who asserted that about eleven in the evening, they actually observed Bundy in a black car within one block of the murder scene.[86] One of these witnesses had been arrested for "conspiracy and rioting" in August of 1917, but the charges were later dropped. According to some citizens, he drove a Ford car through a Negro neighborhood and shot into Negro homes—the act provoking angry Negroes to kill the detectives when the latter arrived shortly afterwards in their Ford police car.[87] Bundy's lawyers were not permitted to question the witness about his alleged role in precipitating the riot.[88]

Other white witnesses declared that between half-past eleven and a few minutes before midnight, they were shot at by Negroes as they walked along Bond to Twelfth. They swore that Bundy resembled one of the assailants.[89] Bundy's attorney compared their testimony with statements which the men made at the 1917 trial of the Negro defendants. There were obvious discrepancies. For example, in 1917 witness Thomas Barrett had acknowledged an inability to identify his assailants since "they had their caps pulled down over their eyes." Witness William Tojo had said in 1917, "I don't know the three that shot at us." [90] In a dramatic effort to emphasize the conflicting statements, Bundy's counsel introduced the man who had acted as court reporter at the 1917 proceedings.[91]

The prosecution presented Mr. and Mrs. John Stapp, who swore that shortly before and again shortly after the time of the murder, armed Negroes headed in the direction of Bundy's home at Seventeenth and Bond. However, under cross-examination by Mr. Webb, they admitted that they had not actually observed the Negroes stopping there, nor could either witness identify Bundy as being in the group.[92] Despite these qualifications, the *Journal* and

Globe-Democrat[93] reported that Mrs. Stapp "described having seen cars filled with men leaving Bundy's place immediately after the ringing of a church bell"—allegedly about ten minutes before the murder.[94]

Earl Bateman testified that a loud volley of shots awakened him around midnight at his home near Tenth and Market. Looking outside he allegedly noticed a light-skinned man at the head of an armed Negro group. A gang member supposedly shouted, "Bundy, we had better turn this next corner; if we don't they will head us off." Under questioning by defense attorney Webb, the witness agreed that the Negroes were on a dimly lit street about fifty feet from him, and he refused to swear that the defendant was definitely present.[95]

Undoubtedly the most damaging testimony against Bundy was given by Edward Wilson, who according to the *Globe-Democrat*, was a "sensation in court" because he presented "the first positive identification . . . of Bundy as a member of the mob." [96] As in the previous trial, he said that he walked over to Fifteenth and Piggott and met a group of armed Negroes, one of whom was Bundy. They were talking about having shot into a car driven by whites.[97] However, unlike the other Negro trial, the defense seemingly possessed sufficient evidence to discredit his testimony. Two witnesses testified that following the July riot, Wilson told them that he had implicated Bundy only after being beaten by the police in the county jail and threatened with a murder indictment. The State's Attorney accused these two witnesses of trying to help Bundy because of friendship and race loyalty: "You mean all you colored men wanted to get the colored dentist out of trouble? That is what you mean?" [98] Defense attorney Baxter presented Ben Colby, who recalled that about one o'clock in the morning of July 2, Wilson visited Bundy's garage to borrow equipment for repairing a tire. The witness maintained that Wilson told Bundy at that time about having come from Fifteenth and Piggott where he heard Negroes admit they fired into an automobile.[99] Obviously, if Wilson had brought this news to Bundy, then Bundy could not have been on the street corner as Wilson had sworn.

Bundy's defense was based on two premises: the Negroes had not planned violence on July 1, and he took no part in the detectives' murder. In far more detail than in the first trial, Baxter was prepared to present evidence of the whites' harassment of Negroes during the hours before the slaying. He called Mat Hayes to the stand, but Judge Gillham, after hearing the testimony, barred it from the jury. Hayes had stated that between nine P.M. and ten P.M. on July 1, a screaming Negro woman told an aroused crowd that whites had beaten her at Eleventh and Trendley. Assistant Attorney General Farmer argued that the witness's comments were not competent evidence. Baxter replied that the testimony was presented only to demonstrate that Bundy was not among the congregating Negroes, that the woman's complaint had helped to trigger the Negroes' unplanned retaliatory reaction, and that earlier there had been no organized movement. Other witnesses were called to supplement the stricken testimony but their remarks were also excluded.[100]

The defense attempted to explain why large numbers of Negroes congregated around Bundy's service station at Seventeenth and Bond during the weeks before July 1. Witnesses emphasized that Bundy's garage was the only one in the city owned by a Negro; Seventeenth Street was a main thoroughfare in a large Negro neighborhood; Seventeenth and Bond was also an important streetcar stop where many Negroes boarded vehicles; and a short distance from the dentist's garage was an open field which Negroes used for recreation.[101]

A crucial part of Bundy's defense was the assertion that neither he nor his red Hupmobile was in East St. Louis on July 1 between half past nine in the evening and midnight. He testified that, since a large amount of money was invested in the newly established service station, he

sometimes earned extra funds driving a car for hire. On
the night of the murder Bundy said that he drove three
men and a woman in a black car to an amusement park
near Belleville; returning with the party about midnight.
His statements were substantiated by some of the passengers and several people who had noticed him at the park.
After discharging the fares Bundy went to his office on
Collinsville Avenue where he was seen by witnesses shortly
after midnight.[102] Challenging that alibi, the prosecution
presented Martha Campbell who stated that her recently
deceased sister, who, according to Bundy, was the woman
passenger, could not have been in Bundy's car because she
was sick in bed on July 1, 1917.[103] The defense, suggesting
that Miss Campbell was mistaken about the date, appeared
confident that the dentist's whereabouts had been accounted for completely. Since the prosecution reiterated
many times that the defendant owned a red Hupmobile, the
defense produced a witness who disclosed that several local
Negroes owned similar cars. Finally, two colored school-
teachers were called to the stand, swearing that on the
evening of July 1, they borrowed the defendant's red automobile and drove with friends to Brooklyn, Illinois.[104]

With the alibi established, Baxter sought to explain his
client's flight from East St. Louis a few hours after the
shooting. Because Bundy had fled to St. Louis and then to
Cleveland, white people in southern Illinois considered his
action proof of guilt. At the trial, N. W. Pardon declared
that as Bundy's lawyer and friend, he visited the latter's
home at five o'clock on the morning of July 2 and advised
an immediate departure from East St. Louis.[105] Pardon
wished to tell the jurors that the advice was offered because of fear for the personal safety of the dentist, but
Judge Gillham ruled that the witness would not be allowed
to state why the flight had been urged. Defense attorney
Baxter objected strenuously, emphasizing that two significant points should have been admitted into the record:
Bundy feared reprisals and went to St. Louis because the

press linked him with the gun smuggling expedition following the May 28 outbreak; and after learning of the blood bath across the river on July 2, he decided to put greater distance between himself and the East St. Louis whites.

The prosecution asked for life imprisonment, and the Negro press was "stupefied with surprise" after the jury found Bundy guilty.[106] Under the leadership of Chicago politician Oscar De Priest, a Negro committee was organized to secure financial support for the preparation of an appeal to the Illinois Supreme Court. The jurists, after examining the evidence, reversed the conviction and remanded the case for a new trial. On the basis of that decision, the prosecution recognized the tenuousness of its case and made no attempt to try the defendant again.[107] The Illinois Supreme Court was satisfied that the state had demonstrated the existence of a Negro conspiracy on the night of July 1, but the judges concluded that Bundy's involvement had not been shown. The testimony of Edward Wilson, the principal witness, was completely discredited. The Supreme Court also repudiated discrepancies in the statements of other witnesses and considered Bundy's alibi to be unshaken. Lastly, the court, agreeing with defense attorneys, ruled that Judge Gillham "erred" in denying Bundy an opportunity to show if possible that innocence and not guilt had motivated the flight from possible mob violence on the day following the shooting.[108]

Although justice triumphed in this case, it did not for at least some of the defendants in the Parker case. Ironically their convictions were later used to show that justice was color-blind. After all, it was said, both Negroes and whites were sent to prison because Negroes murdered the detectives and white retaliation resulted in the riot of July 2. It did not seem to matter that the evidence in court against the white defendants was incontrovertible, while the evidence against Negro defendants was tenuous at best. Although innocent men were allowed to suffer, their im-

prisonment probably served one useful purpose: juries
might not have convicted white rioters if the Negroes had
not been found guilty.

After the verdicts against the white rioters, there
seemed to be a shift in public opinion and far less talk
about a resumption of violence against Negroes. The court
trials were of value not so much because they underscored
the strength of punitive deterrence,[109] but rather because
in providing a platform for recounting the acts of violence
against Negroes on July 2, the conscience of the community seemed to have been penetrated.

Of course, the change in local sentiment was due not
only to the court trials. It also occurred because the Congressional Committee arrived during the trials and held an
extended public inquiry into the background of the race
riot. These hearings were publicized across the country
as well as in East St. Louis, and although no fundamental
reforms were made in the economic or political system, the
inquiry strengthened the resolve of many East St. Louisans to avoid further racial violence.

10
The Call for Federal Intervention

IN the wake of the July riot, Washington received innumerable appeals for intervention. After the Executive branch of the national government responded with silence and equivocation, the United States Congress made the East St. Louis race riot its responsibility.

On July 3, 1917, Woodrow Wilson's secretary, Joseph Tumulty, told the press that the details of the riot were so sickening that he found it difficult to read about them.[1] Despite these sentiments of a national figure close to the President, no help came from Wilson. Several Northern white editors criticized the President's silence. The *Christian Register* considered it imperative that Wilson tell the country what he thought about race violence, and the *New York Evening Post* recognized that his failure to condemn the riot was part of a pattern indicating an unsympathetic attitude toward Negroes. The *Syracuse Post-Standard* saw little difference between the President's views toward Negroes and those expressed by such Southern racists as Senators Tillman and Vardaman.[2]

In contrast to Wilson, Theodore Roosevelt was incensed by the "appalling brutality" of East St. Louis. His remarks prefaced a Carnegie Hall speech honoring Russia. Samuel Gompers also shared the platform, and interpreting the former President's angry comments as hostile to organized labor, he declared that the racial violence, while deplorable, had occurred because employers imported Negroes to East St. Louis. When Gompers sat down, Roosevelt crossed the stage and shook his fist in the AFofL leader's face: "I am not willing that a meeting called to commemorate the birth of democracy in Russia shall even seem to have expressed or to have accepted apologies for the brutal infamies imposed on colored people . . . Let there be the fullest investigation into these murders." [3]

The Negro press was stirred and although some editors, such as Du Bois, had previously condemned Roosevelt for racism, the former President received unanimous praise.[4] The Negro reaction to Roosevelt's statement emphasized the growing bitterness that they felt toward Wilson, and the fear that his silence indicated federal consent of mob violence.[5] A Baltimore Negro delegation seeking to persuade Wilson to issue a proclamation was unable to obtain a White House appointment. Replying that he wished to conserve his time, the President sidestepped the interview because it was obvious what the group really wanted—recognition by the national government of a responsibility to intervene and protect Negroes from local lawlessness.[6] Articulate Negroes across the country observed that despite an avowed belief in the states rights doctrine, American Presidents had intervened in capital-labor struggles when Caucasian lives or property seemed seriously threatened (e.g., Cleveland interceded in the Haymarket Riot, Roosevelt in the anthracite coal fields, and Wilson sent federal troops during the Colorado coal strike of 1914).[7]

The N.A.A.C.P. and other Negro organizations tried to exert pressure on Wilson by sponsoring a "Silent Parade" in New York and other cities. The marchers sought to use the East St. Louis riot to arouse the public conscience and gain support for federal legislation or a Constitutional amendment outlawing lynching and other forms of mob violence. On New York's Fifth Avenue, thousands marched to the beat of muffled drums draped with black handkerchiefs, petitioning for action on their grievances. The placards and banners told their story: "We Are Maligned As Lazy And Murdered When We Work"; "We Have Fought For The Liberty Of White Americans In 6 Wars, Our Reward Is East St. Louis"; "Pray For The Lady Macbeths Of East St. Louis." [8] After the parade a committee led by N.A.A.C.P.'s James Weldon Johnson called at the White House. Mr. Tumulty assured them that although no Presidential interview could be arranged, their aspirations were understood by Wilson. The delegation left after listening to "general and platitudinous phrases." [9]

Other Negro groups participated in a concerted public campaign blanketing Wilson with "Protest and Petition" forms which announced that, after East St. Louis, Americans of Negro descent were "restless and were feeling unsafe." The Negro press published many "open letters" to the President. After an anti-Wilson letter was printed in the *Norfolk Journal and Guide*, a Richmond postmaster refused to allow it in the mails. The *Journal and Guide*'s editor engaged a Washington lawyer who had the ban lifted. The offending letter was written by a youth announcing his refusal to join the military service unless Wilson and the U.S. Department of Justice eschewed hypocrisy and insincerity and guaranteed to protect Negroes from mobs like those in East St. Louis.[10]

Washington also received requests for another kind of intervention—a federally sponsored investigation of the East St. Louis riot—and like previous proposals for an anti-lynching and anti-riot law, this one also represented a demand for federal responsibility to protect Negroes when state or local governments failed to do so. The earliest appeals for a federal inquiry came from the "outraged public sentiment" of East St. Louis business leaders, who considered it the only measure which would force the city to prevent another race riot after Illinois national guardsmen were recalled.[11] This position was echoed by the *Post-Dispatch*, which doubted the willingness of state investigative and judicial agencies to conduct a fair investigation.[12]

Within two weeks after the riot the appeals crystallized into a plan for calling a federal grand jury under the direction of Judge Kenesaw Mountain Landis. Landis, who later became famous as Commissioner for the American and National Leagues of Professional Baseball Clubs, had been United States District Judge for the Northern District of Illinois since 1905. In December 1916, he had gained prestige with the "church people" of East St. Louis when he forced Mayor Mollman and Chief of Police Payne to confess publicly that they had allowed saloons to remain open on Sundays in violation of state law. Among those favoring a Landis investigation were Illinois Senators Sherman and Lewis, Congressman Rodenberg, U.S. Attorney Karch, and the Committee of One Hundred.[13]

Since the assignment of Landis required the authorization of President Wilson and his Attorney General, Thomas W. Gregory, the latter asked U.S. Department of Justice lawyers to examine the legal basis for intervention by the federal judiciary. They advised Gregory that appropriate jurisdiction lay in Section Nineteen of the U.S. Penal Code and the 1866 Civil Rights Act. Section Nineteen made it possible to prosecute persons conspiring to violate rights and privileges guaranteed by the Constitution and federal law; under the Civil Rights Act, Negroes possessed the right to equal benefit of all laws protecting the security of persons and property. A Justice Department attorney informed Gregory "that, if evidence can be procured showing that either the State, the county, or the municipal authorities failed to perform the duties required of them by the Illinois law in relation to these people because they were Negroes, there is a basis for a [federal] grand jury investigation and such an investigation should be had." [14]

From East St. Louis, U.S. Attorney Charles Karch notified Gregory that "the violence against the negroes and the consequent denial of their constitutional prerogatives and immunities, were directly due to State action," i.e., East St. Louis, St. Clair County, and Illinois officials had acquiesced in the violence because of sympathies with racist mobs. In Karch's opinion, Section Nineteen also supplied the basis for taking action, and he favored the appointment of Judge Landis with whom he had recently conferred at the request of the Department of Justice. [15] A few days after Karch's letter was written, a local newspaper quoted him as saying that although the United States Government might not have explicit legal grounds for a grand jury investigation, "the fact that federal troops [the Illinois National Guard was federalized on July 25, 1917] are now being held on duty [in East St. Louis] and unable to go to Europe, if needed, probably would afford the basis for federal jurisdiction." [16] However, despite a *New York Times* announcement that the Department of Justice had decided to go ahead with an investigation, [17] neither Virginia-born Woodrow Wilson nor Texas-born Thomas W. Gregory were disposed to permit a federal inquiry. In their view jurisdiction to intervene did not exist since no evidence was uncovered indicating the violation of federal statutes during the race riot. [18] The Wilson Administration, strongly backed by Southerners who barred Negroes from ballot boxes, had no desire to use federal powers to investigate the denial by state officials of constitutional prerogatives.

Even if the national government had decided to send a judge to conduct the riot inquiry, there was never any real possibility of obtaining Landis's services. In a confidential letter to the Attorney General, Karch reported that the jurist had incurred the animosity of Illinois's Joe Cannon, former Speaker of the U.S. House of Representatives. Cannon was determined that Landis would never again handle cases in the judicial district of which East St. Louis was a part.[19] Although Landis had privately told Karch that Section Nineteen afforded ample basis for an inquiry at least, after Wilson and Gregory ruled against convening the grand jury, a story appeared in the *New York Times* showing that the jurist changed his mind or had it changed for him: "Landis . . . took the view that it was questionable whether as an infraction of state law, the riot was a proper subject of [federal] judicial inquiry." [20]

Even while Gregory's attorneys were involved in deliberations, L. C. Dyer, St. Louis's Representative in Congress, introduced a joint resolution requesting the Senate and House Committees on the Judiciary to sponsor the riot investigation.[21] Dyer maintained that a Congressional inquiry was justified because the riot had interfered with interstate commerce.[22] Illinois's Senator Sherman supported a similar resolution, and two weeks after the riot he told the United States Senate that East St. Louis contained all the ingredients for an even greater racial explosion.[23]

Negro groups, of course, supported the Dyer resolution, and among those who exerted pressures were the National Association of Colored Women and the N.A.A.C.P.[24] Race papers such as the *St. Louis Argus* wanted to avoid disappointment and seemed cautious in regard to the expected accomplishments of a Congressional inquiry.[25] The *New York Age* was somewhat pessimistic, fearing that the only result might be a recommendation for a federal law preventing Negroes from migrating to the North.[26]

In August there was a modification of the plan for a joint House-Senate subcommittee to investigate the riot, with the House passing a resolution establishing its own subcommittee composed of five members.[27] (Rep. John E.

Raker, California; Rep. Martin D. Foster, Illinois; Rep. Henry A. Cooper, Wisconsin; Rep. George E. Foss, Illinois; and Rep. Ben Johnson of Kentucky, who acted as chairman.) Hearings were conducted in East St. Louis from mid-October until mid-November of 1917 following the summer violence, and nearly five thousand pages of testimony were taken. During the opening days, committee members established a reason to legitimize their presence and meet the objections of those Americans who felt that a branch of the national government was capriciously interfering in a local problem. The Congressmen presented several witnesses who testified that the riot had obstructed the flow of interstate commerce between Illinois and Missouri.[28] For example, Phillip W. Coyle, traffic manager of the St. Louis Chamber of Commerce stated that from May 28 to July 10, there had been an interruption of over one hundred thousand tons of material which was normally sent between St. Louis and East St. Louis.[29] Furthermore, St. Louis shipping companies found it difficult to employ Negroes, who feared to unload goods in East St. Louis.[30] Packing plant superintendents reported that the riot delayed fulfillment of wartime government contracts.[31] The Armour Company noted that during the week after the riot, when Negroes refused to work, there had been a fifty percent drop in the number of cows killed and a seventy-five percent reduction in the number of hogs slaughtered.[32] As late as October and November, many companies allowed colored laborers to leave work one hour earlier because the men were afraid to be on the streets when darkness came.[33]

After the obstruction of interstate commerce was inserted into the record, the Committee turned its attention to the background of the riot. The legislators requested and received transcripts of testimony taken by the Illinois National Guard Military Board of Inquiry and the Labor Committee of the Illinois State Council of Defense. However, the U.S. Department of Justice refused to grant access to its records on the race riot, since in the opinion of

Attorney General Gregory, "it would not be in the public interest." [34]

During the four weeks of hearings scores of witnesses from all strata of the East St. Louis community were given an opportunity to testify—from bank presidents to labor organizers, from bailbondsmen to influential political leaders, from newly arrived Negro migrants to colored professional men who had lived in the city for a large part of their lives. A great deal of the testimony was based on verifiable facts, but a substantial portion was hearsay evidence requiring further investigation. Unfortunately, several factual errors appeared in the final report because some leads were not adequately explored by the Congressmen, e.g., the charge of importation, estimates of Negro crime, and the size of the Negro population in East St. Louis.

After a month of listening to accounts of graft, corruption, prostitution, murder, race prejudice, and community apathy, one legislator told the press, "I had never dreamed that such a condition existed in this country—or on the face of the earth." [35] On the eve of the Committee's departure local newspapers had only praise for the tireless, dedicated performance of the members. The editor of the *Globe-Democrat* recalled that when the possibility of the investigation was first discussed, he had opposed it, believing that Illinois was able to put its own house in order. However, after observing the diligence of the Committee, he concluded that the inquiry cleared the air, bringing an awareness that "there is no depth to which prostituted politics, in a long tolerant or indifferent community will not descend." [36] Other newspapers similarly commended the Committee.[37]

The Congressmen returned to Washington, spending several months sifting through all the data which had been collected. Despite the expectations of some East St. Louisans, no indictments or courts-martial resulted from the hearings. Nevertheless, the report presented to Congress was a stinging condemnation of the community's mores, clearly showing how the activities of employers, labor organizers, and politicians created a milieu which made the race riot possible. The remainder of the present volume examines the roles of these principals, drawing upon the legislative transcript of testimony and supplementing it with other data.

11
Employers and Employees of East St. Louis

NO evidence presented at the Congressional hearings proved that union leaders plotted to cause the July riot, but these men repeatedly inflamed the whites, using racist propaganda to rally the community against employers and frighten Negroes into leaving the city. When the union officials publicly warned of a race riot, their remarks were interpreted by followers as a threat to cause one. The labor organizers sponsored the May 28 protest meeting triggering the first riot and paving the way for the second, although in their official pronouncements, at least, they did not counsel violence as the means of getting rid of the Negroes. Nevertheless, union officials did not demand non-violence of the rank and file when other speakers promoted mob disorder on May 28.[1] Afterwards the rioting was condoned by the union leadership.

The Congressional Committee did not find any basis to conclude that union leaders participated in the violence of July 2. Despite the fact that rioters held a meeting at the Labor Temple that morning, there was no indication that labor organizers attended or even arranged it.[2] More-over, although most rioters were blue-collar workers, many were not union men.[3] On the other hand, whether or not union leaders could have stopped the violence they had helped to create on July 2, they made no efforts to quell it.

At the Congressional hearings, the legislators learned that the hysteria producing the race riots could not be understood apart from the history of conflict which char-acterized labor-capital relations in East St. Louis during the early years of the twentieth century. Until nearly a decade after the panic of 1907, an employers' market ex-isted with a surplus of Negro and white labor creating cut-throat competition for factory jobs. Before business improved in 1916, common laborers earned seventeen to twenty cents an hour. Every day, large numbers of men stood outside factory gates "waiting and begging" for work.[4] Some with jobs paid foremen twenty-five cents in tribute each day for the privilege of working. Earning such low wages, even those with steady employment found themselves only "two or three weeks out of the poorhouse," and most common laborers were "right at the back door of the poorhouse." [5]

Job security was virtually non-existent and workers were frequently laid off. Since there was "no permanency of labor," many men worked at one plant for a few weeks before being laid off and moving on to another.[6] During some weeks a common laborer might work forty or fifty hours; during others only twenty. It was not unusual for unskilled meat-packing employees to have no jobs for three or four months each year.[7] In the pre-World War I years many East St. Louis families shared dinners of molasses, bread, and coffee,[8] while survival often depended on the public soup kitchens.[9] Plant managers were as unconcerned about the living conditions of their employees as they were about working conditions in the factories. Several industrial plants did not install washrooms, lockers, or safety devices until compelled by state law.[10]

Leaders in the AFofL craft unions encouraged common laborers to obtain protection through the formation of strong industrial locals in the large plants. The bargaining position of unskilled workers was weakened as long as Southern and Eastern Europeans flocked to East St. Louis, but the natives were unable to take measures against the "foreign element" except to make ineffective demands for restrictive immigration legislation. Employers counted on the clannishness of immigrants and the prejudice of native-born workers to forestall unionization.[11] Only World War I cut the immigrant flow; by that time many resident aliens were also eager to improve their living standards by becoming strong unionizers.

However, as late as 1916, probably not more than four hundred unskilled persons in the entire city were members of recognized labor unions (among them were some track workers, teamsters, and hod carriers).[12] Common laborers staged unorganized strikes, but as already indicated, these often ended in defeat. Even occasional victories resulted in worsened relations between labor and management. For example, in the spring of 1916, track workers of the East St. Louis and Suburban [transportation] Company demanded a 2½ cent raise from 17½ to 20 cents an hour and struck after their spokesmen were fired. During the walkout which lasted several weeks, the men affiliated with the AFofL, winning the raise and the right of collective bargaining; however the company had the last word and deliberately embarrassed the union by hiring unorganized labor—some of whom were Negroes— at 22½ cents an hour.[13]

Actually, between 1916 and 1917 the wartime economy and organizational efforts by labor leaders had forced the wages of local unskilled labor from seventeen cents to about twenty-seven cents an hour,[14] but the cost of living had also skyrocketed and the wage scale was lower than in nearby cities.[15] The unskilled workers believed that without unions they possessed no job security and when the war ended they would be even more subjugated by employers than before. In the view of labor leaders, the wartime economic upturn provided a perfect opportunity for factory laborers to achieve their demands at last. However, the Negro migration provided management with a labor reservoir which hurt the union organizational drives.

Why didn't union organizers attempt to undercut the industrialists by embarking upon a sustained program to incorporate Negroes into the East St. Louis labor movement, just as some immigrants were integrated a few years earlier? Eugene Debs, in asking the question, termed the race riot "a foul blot upon the American labor movement. . . . Had the labor unions freely opened their door to the Negro instead of barring him . . . and, in alliance with the capitalist class, conspiring to make a pariah of him, and forcing him in spite of himself to become a scab . . . the atrocious crime at East St. Louis would never have blackened the pages of American history." [16]

It was quite true that despite AFofL pronouncements of friendliness toward Negroes, the national headquarters was not very interested in organizing them.[17] The AFofL claimed a policy of no race discrimination, but the leadership did not force its national and international unions to adopt the policy. In East St. Louis the craft unions excluded the small number of colored men who could have qualified for membership. Without union affiliation skilled colored workmen were compelled to accept lower paying and sometimes lower skilled jobs.[18] For example, a Negro manual trades teacher, employed by the Board of Education as an electrician during the summer months, lost his position because the Board was pressured into insisting that he join the union, which refused to accept him as a member.[19] Negro carpenters and painters, also facing a union bar, were allowed to work only on small repair jobs, and even then they were condemned by the whites who denied them affiliation.[20]

Union leaders invented rationalizations for their race prejudices. For example, Alois Towers, in testifying before the Congressional Committee, said that as far back as the turn of the century, only Negro employees at the Missouri Malleable Iron Company were allowed to shoot craps, while white foremen had customarily bought beer for the Negro women who visited colored workers at the plant.[21] According to Towers, such treatment made Negroes headstrong and they boasted that having been brought to East St. Louis by employers, they intended to seduce "lots of white women" after the white men were sent away to war.[22]

Despite such illustrations of prejudice, Debs was guilty of distortion and oversimplification in condemning union racism. He ignored the fact that the exclusionist policy of craft unions directly affected the opportunities of only a few East St. Louis Negroes, since most laborers in the city, both white and colored, were unskilled. Furthermore, because the industrialists refused to recognize and even crushed unions appealing to unskilled laborers, the race riot grew out of competition, not between organized white labor and unorganized Negro labor, but between unorganized and unskilled whites and Negroes.[23]

While it was true that racist craft unions did provide leadership and guidance to whites who were particularly seeking to organize factory laborers, before the riot several union locals actually made overtures to encourage unionization of unskilled Negroes.

The failure of this effort was due to Negro prejudice against unions as well as union prejudice against Negroes. Negro suspicion stemmed from a rural Southern background which branded labor organizations as alien, instilling a traditional faith that only employer paternalism gave protection against the hostility of lower class whites.[24] When the migrants arrived in East St. Louis those attitudes were reinforced by employer admonitions to eschew the union organizers. Nevertheless, before the riot there had been colored members in teamsters and hod carriers unions, as well as in the meat-packing employees' local.[25] (During the 1916 meat-packers strike, William Bagley, a Negro, was a leader of the workers at the Morris Company.)[26]

In April of 1917 an embryonic Negro labor organization existed at the East St. Louis Cotton Seed Oil Company; the members conducted a losing strike and the incident provided another reason why Negroes were not strong unionizers. At the plant the men labored twelve hours a day for 16⅔ cents an hour. The company's production involved grinding the cotton seed hulls into a fine powder, and the work was incredibly fatiguing, unpleasant, and unhealthy. Despite a handkerchief worn over the face, dust entered the mouth and nostrils. The men demanded a raise in pay and staged a walkout, but the company easily replaced them.[27] Negroes such as these were not likely to be much impressed by limited overtures on the part of white union organizers who themselves had failed to force recognition of unions particularly benefiting unskilled laborers. Consequently, between 1915 and 1917, organizers found indifference and disinterest when they tried to establish colored locals among saloon porters, barbershop porters, waiters, and freighthouse workers.[28]

After the May 28 riots, several labor leaders arranged a conference at the Labor Temple with prominent Negroes (among whom were Dr. Lyman Bluitt, the assistant county physician, and Dr. Le Roy Bundy). The conferees, recognizing that Negro suspicion of unions contributed to the racist attitudes of unskilled whites, formed an interracial committee to promote unionization among Negroes and thereby lessen tensions between the races.[29] The July riot erupted before the group could take action, but even if the violence had not occurred, an enormous amount of sustained effort would have been required to erase the

mutual suspicions between white and Negro unskilled
workers. While some union organizers declared that Negroes were welcome, many rank-and-file whites had an entirely different notion. These whites could not forgive
Negroes who had been used by employers in crushing
strikes, nor did Negroes wish to make common cause with
men who assaulted them almost nightly.

The Congressional Committee recognized that the
whites' fear of Negro migration was due, in large part, to
the economic insecurity imposed by industrialists. Nevertheless, although the corporation managers were most
heavily responsible for the social climate which culminated
in the race riot, they were also most directly responsible
for helping to create a public determination to avoid a
repetition of the event. More than any other single group,
the capitalists favored federal intervention and used their
considerable influence to bring the Congressional Committee to East St. Louis. Before and after the race riot the
behavior of the plant managers was consistent: in both
periods their primary goals were higher profits and the
protection of corporate property. They opposed mob violence largely because it threatened to frighten away the
Negro labor supply and might have resulted in burning
down factories as well as Negro shacks. If the two resident
companies of militiamen had protected Negro lives instead
of corporation property on the morning of July 2, there
probably would not have been a race riot that day.

The corporation managers regarded only their conduct as blameless. In early July, 1917, an executive of a
meat packing plant charged that labor agitators conspired
with the IWW and pro-German propaganda interests to
cause the riot.[30] Testifying before the Congressional Investigating Committee a few months later, the heads of the
East St. Louis factories declared that local labor leaders
were a direct cause of the violence.[31] These industrialists
seemed unaware that the destruction of unions, the crush-

ing of strikes, or East St. Louis's uniformly low wage scale had any bearing on the events of July 2.

The factory managers contributed almost no funds for modest social welfare programs designed to alleviate the grossest aspects of poverty, and preferred instead to blame the workers for being perpetual paupers. They condemned the barrel house which sold cheap liquor,[32] but they completely ignored the intolerable living conditions which made blue-collar laborers escape their frustrations at the saloons.

The typical view of an East St. Louis factory superintendent was expressed by a former President of the local Chamber of Commerce, C. B. Fox, general manager of the Aluminum Ore Company. Fox asserted, "My principal business was running the Aluminum Company. That is what I make my bread and butter at. That is the principal business I have got." [33] At the Congressional hearings, Representative Raker characterized Fox's approach to labor relations: "The main thing was to get the men in the plant to work and get the work, and then out again . . . you have never gone out in and about the town to see the conditions of the laboring people, where they live." Representative Cooper asked the witness: "Now do you, as a practical man, know of any more certain way to bring about civic degeneration such as has been seen in this city, than for influential men, men in easy financial circumstances, employers of thousands of laboring men to be absolutely indifferent to conditions under which labor lives?" However, in Fox's opinion, "You can do too much . . . welfare work." [34]

Like other corporation managers, Fox employed Negroes in lower-paying, unskilled work, but he admitted excluding them from clerical and skilled positions.[35] Although Negroes were the most economically deprived group in East St. Louis, the factories supported no Negro welfare projects. Only minuscule amounts were given to the whites, and some of the companies made annual dona-

tions to the Industrial YMCA which sponsored two playgrounds and several evening Americanization classes for
foreigners.[36]

The Rev. George Allison, a Baptist minister and a
tireless worker for social reform in East St. Louis, sadly
complained to the Congressional Committee: "Any man
who has a financial interest and knows no moral nor social
obligation with it is a criminal." [37] He received no cooperation from industrial leaders when he attempted to establish
a day nursery primarily for children of working widows.
The youngsters were often locked at home during the day
because their mothers could not afford to provide super-
vision and two or three children perished in fires. Allison
particularly appealed to the meat-packing companies
where most of these women worked, and one superintendent
frankly admitted that neither he nor the companies, which
were controlled from Chicago and New York, felt any
responsibility for East St. Louis social problems.[38] Fox's
reply was that only the national office of his corporation
had authority to make adequate contributions for welfare
projects, but that they were not interested.[39]

Irwin Raut, the executive secretary of the Industrial
YMCA, tried in vain to obtain corporate funds for a building and a real program. Weeks before the race riots he
observed: [40]

> East St. Louis is the only town of its size, so far as my
> knowledge goes, which has not provided a Y.M.C.A. for
> its young men. This is due perhaps to the fact that the
> wealth of the city is controlled by non-residents who
> do not come in contact with the conditions. I understand
> that although there are 20,000 industrial workers in East
> St. Louis the largest locally owned concern employs 85
> people.

In his appeal to employers he pointed out that the wounds
of industrial unrest would be healed only if corporations
took an interest in the social welfare of employees. Among

his repeated warnings of danger was the following: "There are many pressing [social] problems that need immediate attention. I feel that when the day of reckoning comes we will find that it has not paid to delay giving attention to them." [41]

In April, 1917, Raut and the Industrial YMCA sponsored a conference on Negro health and housing conditions, which were seriously aggravated by the migration. Many Negroes as well as whites lived in old, overcrowded, dilapidated shacks without running water or sanitary facilities. Youngsters played on vacant lots in pools of stagnant, slimy water and this environment probably contributed to the outbreak of smallpox in the early months of the year. It is instructive to quote an excerpt from a report written by an "expert from the Colored Department" of the national YMCA, who visited East St. Louis for nearly two weeks in early April, conducting a survey on conditions among colored people. [42]

> The housing condition is about as bad as can be found in any city the size of East St. Louis. The physical and sanitary conditions are positively dangerous. If such remains very long, it will breed disease and will menace the health of the entire community. . . . For the most part, the houses are in the very worst part of the city where there is no sewerage nor pavement. When it rains, water backs up in the [muddy] streets, and people who go to their work have to wade through water, and the children as well, [sic] to get to school. The children sit in the school room with wet feet, and consequently catch colds and are liable to get down with pneumonia or consumption.

The property owners were secure in the knowledge that Mayor Mollman's administration—controlled by realtors —was hardly likely to condemn unsanitary housing. [43] The landlords were among the "better class" of citizens, who

took advantage of the housing shortage by raising rents:
"They [Negroes] are offering to pay more rent than we
have been getting . . ." [44] According to the YMCA survey
of Negroes, "The rent paid for houses, as a general thing,
is high, and the amount paid for some of the vicious places
is criminal." When notices of rent increases were received
by white tenants they tended to blame the Negro migrants
for causing the housing shortage.

Among the persons at the YMCA conference on Negro
health and housing were representatives from the Armour,
Swift, and Morris meat packing plants, the Aluminum
Ore Corporation, and the American Steel Company. They
appointed a committee which subsequently never convened
and nothing further was accomplished.[45] The group had
recommended the employment of a Negro YMCA worker
but appropriated no funds for his salary. Some factory
managers such as Fox doubted that much could have been
done—many Negro social problems were deemed to be
based upon a lack of intelligence.[46] Near the end of the
conference there was a discussion about building segregated Negro housing; however, as already mentioned, this
proposal was not given serious attention because substantial financial contributions would have been required of the
conferees.

Since the corporation executives benefited from the
migration, few of them wanted limitations placed upon the
flow, and during the tense weeks of May, 1917, they took
no action to restore calmness and avert racial violence.
Their behavior actually aggravated a dangerous situation.
It is interesting that a week before the May riots, at a
board meeting of the East St. Louis Chamber of Commerce, vice-president Maurice V. Joyce introduced a resolution complaining that some unknown individual or
individuals had misused the name and prestige of the organization to entice Negroes. He called upon the board
to denounce the alleged misrepresentation as well as the
importation of migrants. However, representatives of in-

dustries employing Negro labor played an important role
in the decision to table the resolution, which was later withdrawn by its sponsor.[47] When white laborers learned about
the Chamber's action, they were more convinced than ever
that the organization was directly promoting the migration of Negroes.[48]

After the May disorders the members of the Chamber
still saw no relationship between their conduct and the
race riot. The militia was simply called in and the industrial leaders pleaded with Negro refugees to return to
work. The police department was not even strengthened,
despite its having been ineffective in coping with rioters.
Only the July riot cracked the complacency of most business and industrial leaders, but there was still some resistance to financing thorough police reforms. Although
soldiers were needed on European battlefields, the War
Department was pressured to keep the national guardsmen
indefinitely in East St. Louis, and officers on the scene
concluded that local businessmen were not trying very hard
to assume responsibility for adequate law enforcement.[49]
As already indicated, the businessmen decided to pay for
limited police improvements, and as an inexpensive pana-
cea for the overwhelming social and economic problems
besetting East St. Louis, they recommended that the Mollman administration should be replaced by a commission
form of government.[50]

Until the Congressional Investigating Committee arrived in East St. Louis, business leaders had done almost
nothing to remedy either the working or living conditions
of Negro and white laborers.[51] The legislators were scath-
ing in their criticism: "The greed that made crooks of
the politicians made money grabbers of the manufacturers . . ." [52] Apparently the nationally publicized condemnation wounded local pride and the East St. Louis
Chamber of Commerce was somewhat embarrassed by the
resulting notoriety. Shortly after the Congressional hearings the Chamber received a letter from J. Lionberger

Davis, a St. Louis banker and an official of the Alien Property Custodian's Bureau: [53]

> I did not realize when I was at home how widespread the prejudice against East St. Louis, on account of the riots, had become, but since I have been in Washington I appreciate the serious nature of the impression made on the minds of thoughtful people throughout the country. Anything you can do to prevent such an occurrence in the future, would, in my opinion, be of incalculable benefit to East St. Louis and also to St. Louis.

Davis suggested that local businessmen should participate with philanthropist Julius Rosenwald and the National Urban League in another social welfare survey of East St. Louis Negroes, leading to a program of amelioration: [54]

> I hope very much that your Chamber will look favorably upon the plan to have the living and working conditions of the negroes in East St. Louis improved with a view of eliminating the causes which brought about the very unfortunate situation in your community last summer. . . . I hope very much that you will take hold of this matter . . .

A few months later the Rotary Club was instrumental in establishing a local branch of the Urban League, which was the only social agency in the city working exclusively with Negroes. The first year's budget was about $5,400; $1,000 of which came from Rosenwald. A full-time executive secretary arrived and turned his attention to health, education, and recreation.[55] The industrialists, acting almost as if the Negroes had caused the riot, attempted to discourage them from congregating in saloons and suggested the erection of "respectable places" such as ice cream parlors or movie theaters. Even these efforts ran into trouble. For example, after a license was issued to open a Negro movie theater, 1700 whites signed a petition of objection: [56]

Principal among the objections to the theater for the colored people at this point is the statement that it brings large numbers of colored people together downtown at night, fills the street cars with colored people and that these conditions give offense to the white people of the neighborhood and create a situation that may lead to the repetition of the race riot troubles.

Between 1918 and 1919 the Urban League received $1,675 from the War Civics Committee, an organization of local businessmen and corporation executives which made some contributions to social welfare in the city. The Committee was established in 1918 under the auspices of the U.S. War Department, after federal officials had stressed that civic turmoil and disorganization interfered with war production. From 1918 to 1920 about $124,000 was expended. The War Civics Committee financed such agencies as day nurseries and the visiting nurses. There was special interest in strengthening existing activities in the YMCA and YWCA.[57] If the "Y" program for whites had been underdeveloped before the riot, the program for Negroes was simply non-existent. In January, 1917, a local YMCA official recognized "there is a great need of something for the Colored People of the city." [58] However, not until one full year after the race riot was a director (a school principal and a Negro) hired to take charge of colored recreation work, and his appointment was only for the summer of 1918.[59] Several months later, with the aid of funds provided by the War Civics Committee, a segregated branch of the YMCA was opened.[60] Far less attention was given to Negro YWCA activities, although after World War I, a colored women's recreation center was established with funds largely furnished by the War Civics Committee.

The work of the Committee ended in December, 1920, and although the welfare activities were to have been absorbed by the Chamber of Commerce, interest and support waned, particularly for the colored work. Within a short time both the Negro YWCA [61] and the local branch of the Urban League passed out of existence.[62]

Thus the unskilled, unorganized, and lower income white and Negro laborers faced the post-World War I decade in only a slightly improved condition over what had existed prior to the race riot. There were, however, two important differences: the determination that East St. Louis could not afford racial violence; and the loss of a large portion of the Negro population, fearful of returning after the July riot.

12
Negro Migration:
A Re-examination

SINCE the labor leaders had charged that the riot occurred because employers enticed hordes of Negroes, it is important to consider how many migrants actually arrived and what evidence, if any, existed to substantiate the accusation that they were imported. The riot erupted in an intercensus year and a dispute inevitably arose regarding the size of the East St. Louis Negro population. Unfortunately, no objective efforts were made in any of the investigations after the riots to determine the amount of growth since the 1910 census. Apparently the 1910 statistics were not even consulted. For example, during the Illinois Council of Defense hearings, Dr. Le Roy Bundy testified that according to his recollection, the decennial census had indicated there were about fifteen thousand Negroes in East St. Louis.[1] His statement went unchallenged, and there was no awareness that the actual 1910 enumeration had been 5,882.

All the investigations after the riots suggested that there had been rapid gains between 1910 and 1915 and an

enormous growth during the two years before 1917. For
instance, the Labor Committee of the Illinois State Council
of Defense concluded that the "long time" Negro population was between ten thousand and fifteen thousand, and
since mid-1916 an additional six thousand to fifteen thousand moved into the city.[2] The St. Clair County Grand
Jury guessed that until 1915 there were fifteen thousand
Negroes, but in the two following years about eight thousand Negroes supposedly arrived.[3] The Congressional Investigating Committee suggested that between ten thousand and twelve thousand Negroes came to East St. Louis
during the first several months of 1917.[4] According to
all these estimates, Negroes constituted close to one-third
of the city's total population.[5]

Population estimates were frequently inconsistent. In
April, 1917, Mayor Mollman said that two thousand Negroes were arriving weekly,[6] and a month later he announced that during the previous several weeks, six
thousand migrants moved in.[7] Shortly afterwards he stated
that in the preceding eight or ten months, between five
thousand and six thousand colored people arrived.[8] In a
fourth pronouncement, Mollman decided that about three
to six thousand Negroes were in the migrant category.[9]
Newspapers showed the same variation. On July 5, 1917,
the *St. Louis Globe-Democrat* considered that the Negro
population numbered more than twenty thousand before
the race riot; on July 8th the newspaper estimated that
about fifteen thousand Negroes had lived in East St. Louis.
A few factory managers, subjected to attack for importation of Negroes, constituted almost the only individuals
who thought these figures were too high. Thus Robert E.
Conway, superintendent of the Armour plant, suggested
that between 1916 and 1917 about four thousand or five
thousand came,[10] while F. A. Hunter, head of the Swift
Company, considered that the migration was even less than
that.[11]

What kind of evidence existed for these varying figures? East St. Louisans quoted each other as sources ("people kept saying . . ."), and since labor organizers gave the highest estimates, they attracted the most attention.[12] Citizens who disagreed were ignored by those "in a position to know." Members of the Central Trades and Labor Union said they had kept a daily vigil at the Relay Railroad Depot and that in the months before the riot, Negro arrivals averaged one hundred on weekdays and five hundred on Sundays.[13]

However, Frank Cunningham, who was in charge of the depot, challenged that estimate pointing out that for every migrant passenger there had been ten or twelve local Negroes waiting at the station to welcome him. Cunningham suggested that the "reception committees" were mistaken for the arrivals. While he agreed that during 1917 extra coaches were used to accommodate the heavy Negro travel, he denied there had been trainloads.[14] The impression which Cunningham's testimony made upon the Congressional Committee was indicated in the tone of the questions directed by Congressman Foster to G. E. Popkess, a St. Louis reporter who thought that in the months before the riot the East St. Louis Negro population increased by seven to eight thousand—"that has been the estimate that has been made by men who were in a position to know." [15]

Mr. Foster: It was generally known that trainloads of
              negroes came up here, wasn't it, from last
              fall till May?
Mr. Popkess: Oh, yes.
Mr. Foster: Everybody seemed to know that except
              [Cunningham]? [16]

At these hearings, superintendents of the large East St. Louis corporations testified that the percentage of their Negro labor force remained fairly stable between 1916 and 1917, but that the number of Negro employees increased slightly.[17] The legislators, instead of considering the possibility that the migration had been exaggerated, misunderstood the employers' testimony, implying that these witnesses were guilty of distortion. For instance, Congressman Raker asked an executive of the American Steel Foundry Company, "Isn't it kind of strange with all this increase of colored labor that none of your firms have increased your percentage in the employment of colored people at all in these factories?" [18] If the enormous increases in Negro employment did not exist, it was doubtful that a migratory flood had occurred—but that possibility was not explored by the legislators. Why should the undocumented and unverified estimates of union leaders have been believed instead of the personnel reports of corporation executives who, if guilty of fabrication, risked exposure since records could have been subpoenaed by the Congressmen?

Almost certainly the legislators came to East St. Louis with preconceived notions which reflected anxieties in the nation about the Negro movement to the North and Midwest. All over the country the subject had been widely discussed, and as early as June, 1916, the U.S. Department of Labor expressed concern about this "great migratory stream." [19] A few months later the U.S. Attorney General's office alerted the public to the colonization "conspiracy." Furthermore, in February and March of 1917 both the white and Negro press carried predictions that the spring would bring another exodus from the South, and "there is some evidence that the very discussion stimulated many to go North who otherwise would not have reached the decision to move." [20] The migration, while probably not as great as many feared, was divided among many cities.[21] However, some communities, in bracing for an unwanted invasion, concluded that far more than a proportional share of the migrants had been dumped on their doorsteps.[22] By the time members of the Congressional Committee arrived in East St. Louis, they were conditioned to believe that local union men were right in regarding their city as among the most "dumped-upon" in the nation.

In considering the size of the East St. Louis Negro population, the Congressmen might have been more objective were it not for the fact that the union estimates were shared by prominent local citizens such as the *Journal* publisher,[23] the U.S. Attorney,[24] and the realtors of the community.[25] Furthermore, a large Negro migration had actually occurred; even local employers admitted that. Since there were more Negro residents than previously, they were noticed on the streets and whites who regarded them as threats exaggerated their number. For example, one East St. Louisan testified that at busy downtown intersections such as Collinsville Avenue and Broadway, Negroes often outnumbered whites. Another citizen declared, "The streets were full of [Negroes] . . . when you would go down on Collinsville Avenue in the evening, you wouldn't think you were in the home town, you would meet so many people, colored people and white people, and new people coming into town, with their bags and belongings with them." [26]

White residents failed to differentiate between Negroes who came *to* East St. Louis and those who came *through* East St. Louis. The city was a northern terminus for several railroads operating in the South; it was also a gateway to the North and West. The Louisville and Nashville Railroad tapped Kentucky and Tennessee; the Mobile and Ohio Railroad tapped Mississippi; and East St. Louis was the transfer point for many Negro travellers en route to other cities. Some of these "floaters" stayed a day or two, receiving railroad passes from the Illinois Free Employment Bureau which shipped them out as section hands, track laborers, and roundhouse workers.

They went to various communities in the state, such as Chicago, Bloomington, Decatur, and Joliet; others were sent as far away as Detroit and Buffalo.[27] Some travelled in groups of fifty or more, attracting considerable atten-

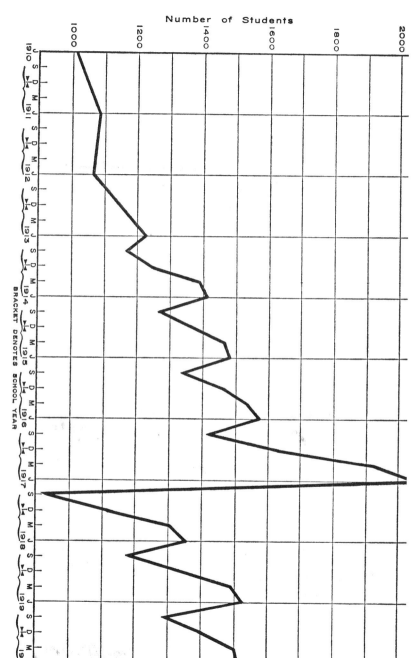

5 Negro enrollment in East St. Louis Schools, 1910-1920

tion during their brief stopover in East St. Louis. Between the May and July riots, Harry Kerr, an AFofL district organizer, noticed a group downtown at Missouri and Collinsville Avenues. He asked the night chief of police about them and the latter automatically concluded that they were planning to swell the local Negro population. After further inquiry, Kerr learned that they were actually going from Tuscaloosa, Alabama to Gary, Indiana; he said he watched with apprehension because other citizens might have made the same mistake as the policeman and attacked them.[28]

The confusion between the "floaters" and those migrants who became residents was understandable because the local press published nothing about the transhipment of Negroes, which had been a large operation since at least 1914. Between 1914 and 1916 the industrial upsurge had not yet affected East St. Louis. In those two years as many as seventy-five hundred colored persons may have passed through the city, obtaining jobs elsewhere as a result of the East St. Louis branch of the Illinois Free Employment Bureau.[29] After 1916, some colored transients were able to find jobs without moving on because East St. Louis began to share in wartime prosperity.[30]

Since an important variable was the size of the local Negro population at the time of the July riot, it was unfortunate that the Congressional Investigating Committee did not use its resources to present a carefully prepared estimate.[31] In addition to subpoenaing personnel records of local employers, the legislators could have used World War I draft registrations, voter registrations, and school enrollment statistics. A population projection based upon a combination of these data, although subject to error, would have possessed obvious superiority over the complete guesswork of witnesses.

The present writer prepared his own estimate of the 1917 Negro population based in part upon the school records. (East St. Louis maintained its segregated school system until 1950,[32] and the Board of Education kept monthly reports on Negro school enrollments).[33] Fig. 5 shows almost no change in the Negro school enrollment from 1910 until 1912. The increase between June, 1912 and June, 1914 was twice as large as the gain between June, 1914 and June, 1916. However, there was a growth of over thirty percent in the Negro school population during the year before the July riot. By September, 1917 the Negro school enrollment had dropped from 2,064 to 928. Since Fig. 5 indicates that September enrollments invariably dropped somewhat each year from the level they had been in June, most but not all of the decline in the autumn of 1917 may be attributed to the exodus after the riot. The annual enrollment loss was caused by at least three factors: some East St. Louis families left the city for the summer probably to work on farms, returning in the fall several weeks after school had resumed; others left permanently to accept higher paying jobs elsewhere, with their places in East St. Louis taken later by new residents; and school attendance laws were probably inadequately enforced until many weeks after the term began.

During the school year after the race riots Negro enrollments slowly rose each month, but by June, 1918, the number of Negro schoolchildren was still about thirty-five percent lower than it had been the year previous. Although the upswing continued between 1918 and 1920, the figures for June, 1920 were only slightly higher than the level of June, 1915. Fig. 5 indicates the Negro school population at the conclusion of each school year between 1910 and 1920.

The arithmetical progression method of estimation may be used to project the total East St. Louis Negro population from the colored school enrollment data by assuming a linear change in the ratio from 1910 to 1920.[34] According to the estimate in Table 2 there were 10,617 Negroes in East St. Louis in mid-1917, an increase of nearly 2,400 over the previous year.

TABLE 2

Estimates of Negro Population in East St. Louis, 1911–19 *

YEAR	ESTIMATE
1910	5882 (actual census enumeration)
1911	6182
1912	5975
1913	6735
1914	7646
1915	7910
1916	8237
1917	10,617
1918	6842
1919	7615
1920	7437 (actual census enumeration)

* Compiled from school enrollment data. Limitations exist which make refined analysis of these data unwarranted. From 1910 to 1913 no monthly school enrollments for Negroes are available and during that period information was tabulated in June at the conclusion of the school year. Consequently, for interpolations during the decade, the school populations in June were used uniformly and these were then related to the 1910 and 1920 censuses. However, the reader is cautioned to bear in mind that the 1910 census was taken in April while the 1920 census was taken in January.

However, the arithmetical progression method does not deal with the possibility that there was a particularly large migration of Negro persons without school-age children. Such a migration may have been composed primarily of young, unmarried males, but no objective evidence was ever introduced in any of the investigations after the riot to substantiate or refute this possibility. On an impressionistic level, several contemporary accounts indicated that migrants were mainly "discontented tenant farmers and unsettled young men from farms and small towns," but even the East St. Louis labor union officials, who supposedly kept vigil at the Relay Railroad Depot, noted that in the months before the riot many of the new arrivals were whole families, some with eight and ten children.[35] Nevertheless, on the basis of general demographic information,[36] researchers have usually found that areas showing gains through migration tend to show an excess of late adolescents and young adults. Furthermore, male migrants predominate when the move involves long geographical distances, and when the move is made to cities particularly characterized by heavy, hazardous industries. In 1917 these factors were applicable to East St. Louis.

A recent examination of 1917 draft registration records indicates that a pattern of selective migration occurred in East St. Louis, thereby necessitating an upward revision of the estimates in Table 2. On June 5, 1917, all males from twenty-one to thirty years of age were obliged by law to register, and of the 9,011 young men who were counted, 2,281 were Negroes.[37] These Negro registration figures were actually almost eleven hundred larger than would have been expected according to the projected estimate constructed from Negro school enrollments in 1917. If, in addition to the excess of young adult males over the estimates in Table 2, a generous allowance is also made for excesses in other age and sex groups (young adult females, pre-school children, and old people), there may have been a total of twenty-five hundred Negroes above the projection constructed from Negro school enrollments of 1917.

These twenty-five hundred persons could have been added to the total Negro population any time between 1910 and 1917. Even if it is assumed that all of them were migrants (excluding natural increases of births over deaths) who arrived in East St. Louis during the year before the riot (an impossible assumption), the total 1916-1917 Negro migration would have been approximately five thousand, a figure substantially lower than the ones given by East St. Louis labor leaders.

Since this was still a considerable amount of Negro migration, what brought these people to East St. Louis? Did they come on their own, or were most of them actually imported by the industrialists as union organizers had charged? As indicated earlier, the Labor Committee of the Illinois Council of Defense believed that East St. Louis employers deliberately conspired to attract a large artificial movement of population; although the industrialists issued denials, the Council contended that they "were the chief beneficiaries of the surplus of labor [and therefore] the force of motive points in their direction." [38] The Congressional Investigating Committee took a similar position.[39] Actually these conclusions went beyond the evidence which witnesses presented.

Before examining the testimony upon which these statements were based, it should be emphasized that there was nothing illegal in bringing Negro laborers to East St. Louis. However, since the influx was a crucial factor in creating and aggravating social problems which paved the way for the riots, it is necessary to determine if local industrial corporations, in pursuit of higher profits and in disregard of public opinion, sponsored the migration. Because the importation of Negro labor was unpopular in East St. Louis and elsewhere, if local industrialists were involved they would hardly have come forward to declare that as a group they arranged the population movement. Two kinds of evidence were required to make a case against them—the distribution of circulars or the purchase of advertisements in Southern newspapers, and the employment of labor agents who toured the South. Proof of the first point should have been easier to obtain than of the second, but it should be cautioned that the discovery of evidence which linked a few employers was hardly sufficient to show the involvement of East St. Louis industrialists as a group.

The subject of advertising was discussed at length in the hearings of the Council of Defense, and despite the

fact that the campaign was supposed to have been so
extensive, not one newspaper clipping or circular was ever
introduced by any witness. However, as previously indicated, Maurice V. Joyce, an officer of the East St. Louis
Chamber of Commerce, testified that a week before the
May 28 riots, he informed the organization that "certain
persons or interests" were unscrupulously circulating job
advertisements in the South giving the impression of the
Chamber's sponsorship.[40] Joyce admitted that he never saw
a single ad. His information was based entirely on rumors
particularly transmitted to him by John B. Altrogge, publisher of the *East St. Louis Mail*. Altrogge was also unable
to provide one copy of the advertisements he had allegedly
seen. The Labor Committee asked him to search carefully
for the evidence, but in testimony on the following day he
reported that the documents were lost or mislaid.[41] It does
seem strange that although Altrogge declared that the
Mail's articles about the influx had been inspired by the
advertisements, not only was he unable to produce one such
ad, but he could not name a single Southern newspaper
which for pay had exhorted Negroes to go to East St.
Louis.

Robert Conway, manager of the Armour packing
plant, testified that he had heard of a white man who allegedly saw one advertisement, but the fellow eventually
showed the witness only a New Orleans newspaper clipping
which reported that Southern Negroes were heading to
East St. Louis.[42] Negro migrants were questioned at the
hearings and several stated that they had seen advertisements describing jobs in East St. Louis and elsewhere.[43]
Others said that they had relatives in East St. Louis or had
read newspaper stories discussing higher-paying jobs in
the North.[44] These statements hardly constituted proof of
extensive advertising, and several months later, when members of the Congressional Committee held hearings, they
did not uncover much more evidence than did the Council
of Defense investigation. However, executives of the Mis-

souri Malleable Iron Company appeared as witnesses. They acknowledged that early in 1917 they had purchased several newspaper ads in a few Southern cities.[45]

If this first charge could not be sustained, what proof was there to show that local employers sent a corps of labor agents into the South? According to rumors, agents were particularly employed by railroads and meat-packing plants, but in almost every case "unidentified informants" had been the sources. Absurd and inflammatory accusations were frequently made. For example, John Altrogge had told *Mail* readers that labor agents, in enticing migrants, were involved in a "conspiracy on the part of some foreign government to denude the cotton fields of labor and thus hold down the munitions manufacturer[s]." The *Belleville News-Democrat* added that three key arguments had been used to induce unwilling Negroes to leave the South:[46] they could escape the army draft by coming North; they could get plenty of liquor in the North; and they would have all the white women they wanted after the East St. Louis males went off to France to fight.

Despite such often-repeated nonsense, it was true that a few East St. Louis corporations employed labor agents from time to time, but their use was not so widespread as the unions wanted the public to believe. As already mentioned, executives of Armour's and Swift's said that in 1916-17 they imported about 100 Negroes. During the Congressional hearings several colored witnesses dramatically testified that a white employee of the Mobile and Ohio Railroad brought them on a gang pass from Jackson, Tennessee.[47] The agent was identified, summoned to the hearing room, and admitted that twice a month he went to Tennessee, returning from each trip with as many as fifteen colored men.[48] He also said that the Illinois Central Railroad handled many Negro migrants.[49]

Of course, even if only a few labor agents operated from East St. Louis, there were others from various cities who went South to recruit,[50] and as indicated earlier, some

Negroes who passed through East St. Louis surely must have settled there. Furthermore, several railroads, in establishing reduced excursion rates, encouraged the migration even if they did not promote it.[51]

However, the Congressional Investigating Committee not only lacked evidence for the accusation that ten thousand or more Negroes were imported to East St. Louis, but the legislators also erred in suggesting that agents tricked Negroes by enticing them to abandon profitable employment in the South.[52] Although agents certainly exaggerated the advantage of life in the North, the role these men played in the migration movement was also exaggerated.[53] The basic driving causes of the movement were found in the fact that the South was not profitable for many Negroes. In 1914-16, farm laborers often received fifty to sixty cents a day during a severe labor depression which was aggravated by floods and the boll weevil. Even by 1917, when the migration forced white planters to raise wages, the pay scale was only 75 cents to $1.25 a day. In addition, housing on plantations was poor, interest rates were exorbitant, and crop settlements were unfair.[54]

Dissatisfied Southern Negroes became avid readers of the militant *Chicago Defender* and other race papers which passed from hand to hand. These publications announced that the North offered political, legal, and educational rights. "To die from the bite of frost is far more glorious than at the hands of the mob." [55] However, readers soon learned that there was no need to die from frostbite, since Northern factories, booming with European war contracts, required Negro labor to offset the sharp decline in the number of unskilled immigrants arriving in America.

Friends and relatives in the North also sent letters to Southern Negroes encouraging them to leave—many of these Northern residents had been born in the South and migrated in previous years. The migration of 1916-17 should not have been an occasion for surprise because, as

Professor Henderson H. Donald pointed out, the stream had been flowing from South to North for decades.[56] In his monograph Donald underscored the substantial proportional growth since 1880 among the Negro populations of nine cities in the North and Midwest—Boston, New York, Philadelphia, Chicago, Cincinnati, Evansville, Indianapolis, Pittsburgh, and St. Louis. For these communities as a whole, there had been the following percentage increases: 1880-90, 36 per cent; 1890-1900, 74 per cent; 1900-10, 37 per cent; and 1910-20, 50 per cent. In East St. Louis the Negro population increased from 1,799 in 1900, to 5,882 in 1910, and 3,907 of them were born outside of Illinois.[57] Thus, the presence of these residents was undoubtedly an important factor in stimulating the 1916-17 migration.

Did the migrants take "white men's jobs" as the union organizers had charged? An examination of East St. Louis census statistics for the white population casts considerable doubt on the validity of that accusation. In 1910 there were 52,646 whites while a decade later the number had increased to 59,330.[58] The net gain of 6,684 during the two census periods was distributed mainly in two age groups—the five-to-fourteen year olds (2,233) and the over-forty-five year olds (3,466). Obviously, those in the first category made no contribution to the labor force, while some in the second were too old to obtain jobs. Between 1910 and 1920 there was actually a net loss of 1,156 white males in the 15-44 age group.

When foreign born whites are examined separately (see Table 3), some interesting findings result. Between 1910 and 1920, there was a loss of 239 in the number of males and females under fifteen years of age; however, in the 15-44 year old category, there was a decrease of 2,443 (almost all were males) which, of course, affected the labor force. The emigration evidently occurred before the American entry in World War I when Southern and Eastern European laborers departed either to take higher-paying

jobs elsewhere in the United States or to return to their
mother countries.

TABLE 3

Foreign Born Whites in East St. Louis, 1910 and 1920 *

	1910		1920	
AGE	MALE	FEMALE	MALE	FEMALE
Under 5	55	45	7	3
5–9	118	110	31	30
10–14	89	79	89	97
15–19	287	170	114	132
20–44	4533	1609	2364	1546
45 and over	1374	907	1460	904
Unknown	23	1	4	1
Totals	6479	2921	4069	2713

* Adapted from *Thirteenth Census of the United States*, 1910, II, p.
480; *Fourteenth Census of the United States*, 1920, III, p. 249.

Some native-born whites also departed to find better
jobs in other cities, and although their places were probably filled by newly-arrived white migrants, the booming
East St. Louis factories of 1916-17 faced a shortage of
unskilled white labor. Negro manpower was needed to supplement the whites. However, as a propaganda weapon
union organizers claimed that large numbers of whites were
laid off and replaced by the Negro migrants. Only under
prodding at the Congressional hearings did union officials
admit reluctantly that a shortage of white labor had
actually existed in 1917: [59]

> Shortage of labor forced [wages] up more than anything
> else. They [the employers] couldn't get competent men,
> and the men were quitting and going places where other
> people were raising the wages, and they had to raise their
> own men before they left them . . . when [employers] got

bigger [war production] orders they had to give the men
more wages or they would leave and go some place else.

In the month before the July riot the unemployed
whites in the labor force were workers who had been fired
for union activities, a small group of hard-core strikers
at the Aluminum Ore plant, and old men who had been
passed over in the heavy industries. It should be emphasized that for whites of East St. Louis the basic problem
in 1917 was employment security rather than unemploy-
ment. Not only had the migration of Negroes adversely
affected the wage scale and helped to block unionization
of unskilled workers, but by the late spring of 1917 it
became increasingly apparent to both company officials
and union organizers that East St. Louis had an oversup-
ply of Negro labor.[60] The need for Negro labor had seemingly resulted in the arrival of a larger number than was
absorbed by the local economy. In order to impress whites
that they were not indispensable, the employers of large
industries threatened to use this reservoir of Negro labor.
More than ever before, management was involved in the
dangerous game of playing off one group against the
other.

The Negro surplus may have consisted of as many as
several hundred males, but the number was obviously
limited by the fact that these people were not going to stay
in East St. Louis unless jobs quickly materialized. Barring
an even greater expansion of the local economy, there were
no jobs for them, provided the white workers behaved
themselves. Out of this economic (and demographic)
squeeze arose the union organizers' charge of importation
and the exaggeration of the size of the Negro migration.
In this context the foundation for the riot was laid.

13
A Political Tradition

REGARDLESS of the economic frustrations and race prejudice of the populace, the July riot could not have occurred if people had believed there was law instead of "rotten" politics in East St. Louis.[1] In August, 1917, the St. Clair County Grand Jury declared that the race riot was the result of a "wicked and malicious plot" by unnamed political bosses.[2] Rumors circulated that a prominent politician might be indicted, and Attorney General Brundage indicated that prosecutions were being considered for "all the big, white politicians." Subsequently, Mayor Mollman's indictment was announced, but knowledgeable residents regarded him as only a "little potato."[3]

Actually no premeditated plot was ever proven, although politics, besides reflecting racial tensions, also created them. Politics was a big industry in East St. Louis, and as already mentioned, some Negroes wanted to play the white man's game of exchanging votes for money and power. Resenting such aspirations of the migrants who had been a voteless group in the South, whites accused politicians of spoiling Negroes by encouraging pretensions to equality. Because Negroes were becoming a potentially powerful political bloc by 1915, racist propaganda was used against them in subsequent elections.

The behavior of the rioters and the failure of municipal officials to preserve peace were the culminations of a long period of misgovernment. The amount of lawlessness permitted by various mayors and aldermen "put an ordinary western frontier place on the retired list." [4] For much of East St. Louis history the community was governed by political administrations which, corrupt and graft-ridden, bent the law to suit themselves. Persons occupying high places in the city government furnished the models and preserved the tradition.

Even in the early nineteenth century, East St. Louis had the reputation of being an isolated settlement "where the law did not reach." Distinguished St. Louisans rowed across the Mississippi to the "Bloody Island" to fight duels there. Criminals later made East St. Louis their retreat, and after the community was settled, politics became a lucrative source of revenue, with corrupt elections often the method of capturing offices. In these political contests blood was sometimes shed—during the 1870's a riot took several lives. Order was restored only by the arrival of the Illinois militia. A decade later the treasury was raided and as municipal indebtedness soared, officials burned down the City Hall in order to destroy financial books and records.

Almost as soon as the building was reconstructed the vault was dynamited to "make it appear that tens of thousands of dollars of money and bonds had been stolen, when they really had been previously appropriated by officials." [5] Shortly afterwards a former mayor was assassinated: [6]

> During this period public records were falsified and lost . . . bogus scrip was issued by the thousands of dollars, contracts were made but not kept, and money was spent

for work never completed. Funds collected for specific
purposes were misappropriated and stolen, the public
school fund which came to the city treasury was taken to
pay illegal claims, the police force was a synonym for
cruelty, oppression, roguery and robbery, and peaceful
citizens and travellers stood in dread of the force from
the chief down to the lowest ranking patrolman.

A generation later the stakes had become higher; the
Congressional Investigating Committee commented on
local developments between 1912 and 1917: [7]

> The looting of the city and county treasury has grown
> into a habit in East St. Louis. More than $250,000 has
> been stolen by various defaulting officials in the last five
> years. In one instance the school fund was robbed of
> $45,000, but the prosecution of the thief has gone on
> listlessly for several years without any real effort to con-
> vict him. He was not arraigned for trial until after [the
> Congressional] committee had left East St. Louis. He
> then pleaded guilty. Everybody knows who were protect-
> ing him, but so many similar thefts have been overlooked
> and there is but little public sentiment against him.

The legislators were unduly pessimistic, not realizing that
they had created sufficient public sentiment to send both
the school treasurer and the county treasurer to prison—
the latter was convicted of embezzling $91,000 of public
funds.[8]

In the city government there were many varieties of
irregularities which hardly engendered a respect for law
and certainly helped to bankrupt the treasury. For example, city treasurers in their capacity as tax collectors
were allowed by Illinois statutes to skim off two percent of
the receipts until their annual income amounted to $1500.
However, every treasurer for almost a quarter of a century
after 1888 ignored the $1500 limit and *kept two percent
of all tax collections*, thereby costing the city between

$100,000 and $150,000.[9] Similar perquisites accompanied other offices. East St. Louis school treasurers supplemented their salaries by depositing education funds in banks, and then pocketing the thousands of dollars in interest:[10]

> To perpetuate these fraudulent conditions the worst of tactics and fraud is and long has been practiced. The would-be school treasurer picks out candidates for school trustees, conducts their campaigns, pays expenses, buys votes to elect them, and when elected pays them such stipends as may be agreed upon for voting for and choosing him as school treasurer.

In 1913 the *St. Louis Post-Dispatch* sent a reporting team to East St. Louis and charged that City Councilmen were accepting bribes to pass municipal ordinances, collecting money illegally even though they did not attend Council meetings, and contracting to furnish goods and services to the city in violation of Illinois law. The newspaper noted that St. Clair County's prosecuting attorney, Charles Webb, received a sworn statement from Councilman Joseph A. Fansler, wherein the latter confessed that he and five other aldermen were paid $500 each for approving an ordinance benefiting the East St. Louis Interurban Railway Company. He also said that several Councilmen received $3,000 from the Alton and Southern Railway after the corporation obtained a franchise. The Aluminum Ore Company was identified as the "real backer" of that franchise. According to Fansler, former Mayor Charles S. Lambert and the City Attorney had been involved in these negotiations. Later, when his confession had been made public, Fansler repudiated it saying that two aldermen threatened his life.[11]

Under the direction of prosecutor Webb, the St. Clair County Grand Jury accused many top members of the Lambert administration of defrauding the city. Indictments were drawn against the ex-Mayor, City Treasurer, City Comptroller, Chief of Detectives, Health Commissioner, Superintendent of Streets, in addition to fourteen of the sixteen members of the 1912 City Council.[12] Webb met defeat in the next election, no court convictions were sustained, but much information came to light about a city government of "irregularities, extravagances, and laxity in business methods."

At a City Council meeting shortly before Mayor Lambert left office in 1913, members of the Finance Committee (none was an accountant) announced they had examined the records of receipts and disbursements in the offices of the City Treasurer and City Comptroller. In the committee's opinion, all vouchers and warrants were legally and properly paid and all transfers of funds legally and properly made. Nothing could have been further from the truth, but the City Council passed a resolution to destroy the financial records of the Lambert administration.[13] As a result of pressures largely generated by the *Post-Dispatch* and the *Journal*, John Chamberlin the newly elected Mayor, ordered Comptroller William Rodenberger to preserve the documents. After an accounting firm made a preliminary investigation "amazingly chaotic conditions" were uncovered. Thereupon, funds were not appropriated for a complete audit, but enough evidence was found to worry many people. A few days after Rodenberger declined to surrender the financial record books to State's Attorney Webb, "a person or persons unknown" stole several of them from the comptroller's vault. Among the disappearing documents were a register with the records of every bond transaction since 1902, and two ledger books containing a five year record of all receipts and disbursements.[14]

The preliminary examination of the vouchers had indicated the impossibility of learning why large sums of money were spent or who received it (since warrants often lacked endorsements). Fred Gerold, the City Treasurer, admitted that various municipal budgets were scrambled and that funds earmarked for one account were used to pay another. For example, the *Journal* noted, "In 1912-13 the city council appropriated $34,000 for the Election Board and Gerold was custodian. Nearly $6100 was missing and Gerold said he diverted it to another account, despite the state criminal code forbidding diversion of election board funds." [15] No one knew which accounts were short, and according to the *Journal*, Gerold said that when he became treasurer he inherited a $50,000 "deficiency in the books." [16]

While his friends agreed that the treasurer's bookkeeping system was in disarray, others retorted "there is a certain kind of bookkeeping to all rascalities." [17] More irregularities were uncovered. For example, in one case a contractor received $3,741 in street improvement bonds for building a sidewalk; however, someone in Gerold's office also entered this transaction in the books as if a treasurer's check had been paid for the construction. In effect, Gerold "took credit for [$3,741] when he had not paid a cent out of the treasury, thus putting that sum into [his] pocket." [18] After accountants discovered what had happened, he blamed a clerk and made good the full amount of the discrepancy. The *Journal* declared that without the scrutiny of the accounting firm, the East St. Louis treasury would have lost $3,741. [19] In another transaction, the city had been ordered to pay a $4,729 judgment to a citizen and a treasurer's receipt was issued for $5,729. After the recipient noticed the error the proper amount of money was paid, but the treasurer's office was credited with the amount of the original receipt which was, of course, $1,000 more than the actual disbursement. [20] A third case involved an expense account which financed a City Council junket to a municipal government convention in New York—although two aldermen did not go on the trip, Gerold was accused of "withholding . . . for his own use" $800 which had been designated as their expense money. [21]

The manner in which East St. Louis financial affairs were handled may perhaps be seen best by considering the redemption of street improvement bonds. An accounting audit revealed that during a period when the treasury was so low that municipal employee payrolls could not be met, the treasurer's office actually redeemed the same bonds twice. The bonds were originally returned for payment to Gerold's predecessor who apparently tossed them uncancelled into a box. During the Lambert administration some were removed and redeemed a second time. According to the accounting firm's report, as published in the *Journal:* [22]

> Our audit disclosed that the city has been defrauded [of $20,000] as a result of duplicate or excessive payments of special improvement [bonds and interest coupons] . . . the items of irregularities mentioned are chargeable to E. Fred Gerold . . . Vouchers on file purporting to represent the payment of coupons and bonds are in favor of E. Fred Gerold and the vouchers do not show the name of the individual or company who presented the coupons or bonds for payment, nor any reference to the ex-treasurer's check or other evidence whereby the transaction can be traced and verified. The dates of cancellation on coupons and bonds which have been paid correspond to the dates of the vouchers in favor of E. Fred Gerold and on their face this would indicate that Mr. Gerold redeemed such coupons and bonds.

It was impossible to complete a full analysis of many street improvement accounts because the record books had not been recovered. In the opinion of the accountants, "The vouchers which are missing were abstracted from the files either to conceal the irregular transactions or to raise a doubt as to the individual responsibility in case of detection of the irregularities." [23] The St. Clair County Grand Jury [24] indicted Gerold for withholding $50,000 of the city's money. [25]

During the trial he admitted that some funds had been improperly credited and he made restitution in the three transactions discussed on the previous pages. Although denying guilt in the duplicate payment of street improvement bonds, he agreed that on one occasion he took credit a second time for three $500 bonds. Gerold explained that an error had occurred because his books were $1500 short and a clerk assumed that the three bonds should have been added to the treasurer's account.[26] Gerold received a one-to-ten year prison term. Shortly afterwards the Illinois Supreme Court reversed the conviction, ruling that no intentional criminal violations or guilty knowledge was proven, although, of course, there was abundant evidence to show that the bookkeeping system used by the treasurer (and his predecessors) was "extremely defective." [27]

In another legal action the following year, Gerold went on trial for conspiracy to defraud the city of $100,000. Among the co-defendants were former Mayor Lambert, two city comptrollers, an alderman, and a deputy health commissioner. One of the defense attorneys was Hubert Schaumleffel, who became county prosecutor after defeating Charles Webb in an election the following year. All the defendants were acquitted.[28]

Although Mayor Lambert and most of his associates were Republicans, local elections in theory were non-partisan, and Lambert actually ran on the Progessive Citizens Independent ticket. The "non-partisan" system allowed Republican and Democratic leaders to unite behind certain candidates, with the victors rewarding supporters regardless of party affiliation. Politicians showed such dexterity and nimbleness in cutting across party lines that observers commented, "If Barnum wanted to get some tumblers, he could get them right in East St. Louis. . . . It wasn't a question of a man's politics; it was a question of his adaptability to be used in the situation." [29] For example, in the 1913 mayoralty race, John Chamberlin a Republican, was supported by Democratic leaders Thomas Canavan and Locke Tarlton. These two men were consulted on some political appointments and Canavan served as Commissioner of Public Works. In the 1915 election the Democrats received their turn at running City Hall; Tarlton sponsored the candidacy of Fred Mollman, collecting IOU's from Republican leaders.

Social relationships, and particularly the promise of patronage and privilege, were the important factors in creating alliances. Intra-party feuds also resulted in new alignments. As a case in point, Republican politicians such as Lambert and Gerold joined Tarlton because they accused Mayor Chamberlin of deserting them during their legal troubles. Chamberlin had also lost the support of some previous Republican backers because in his two year term as Mayor there seemed to be less mismanagement and corruption than in previous administrations.

After Mollman defeated Chamberlin in 1915, Locke Tarlton became the undisputed political boss of East St. Louis, and according to the Congressional Investigating Committee, used his power to enrich himself and his friends: [30]

> Much of the energy, some of the brains, and nearly all of the audacity of the gang that in recent years had held East St. Louis in its merciless grasp were centered in Locke Tarlton. It was his cunning mind that helped devise the schemes by which he and his associates were enriched. It was his practiced hand that carried them out. He made Mayor Mollman believe he was his creator; that he had elevated him to high station; and that his blind obedience to orders would mean rich political rewards in the future.

Tarlton was not only chairman of the St. Clair County Democratic Central Committee, but was also elected President of the East Side Levee and Sanitary District, which was established to protect Southern Illinois communities against the flooding of the Mississippi. A levee district tax financed drainage and sanitary projects, and through the handling of these funds Tarlton's influence grew. National politics seemed of secondary importance as long as "the right men [were] on the Levee Board." [31] The Congressional Committee asserted: [32]

> As president of the levee board, Tarlton deposited millions in a local bank and exacted no interest from it. The taxpayers suffered, while the bank lent the money and pocketed the proceeds. In further proof of the close relationship that existed between the levee board and the bank, [the] brother of the bank's president was elected attorney for the levee board.

In exchange for such favors it was said that the bank raised a "slush fund" for Tarlton's election campaigns. [33]

Some East St. Louis citizens made small fortunes when the Levee Board purchased land—the Congressional Investigating Committee charged that those who prospered were friends of the Board: [34]

> When the levee board needed a right of way over certain land that was owned by a widow, Dr. R. X. McCracken, the health commissioner appointed by Mayor Mollman, bought the land from the widow for $5,000 and sold it a few weeks later to his friends, the levee board for $20,000. The widow did not know when she sold the land that the levee board wanted it. McCracken's wife also sold land in the same locality to the levee board for $600 an acre, while adjoining land was purchased for $300 an acre.

There were also allegations that Tarlton, Canavan, and Jerry Sullivan (corporation counsel of East St. Louis) purchased "practically worthless" acreage which was covered by Horseshoe Lake in adjoining Madison County. Shortly afterwards, the Levee Board decided to drain the lake, underwriting other improvements such as the construction of canals. [35] According to the Congressional Committee: [36]

> Jerry Sullivan, the corporation counsel, who profited by the job which made the county drain a swamp which he

and his friends had very recently bought, evidently with the knowledge that it would soon be drained at public expense, was either an understudy for Tarlton and Canavan, or he was further back of the curtain. He tried to do in a lesser way what they did wholesale.

In the 1916 election Republican and Democratic chieftains traded votes for county offices. They united to reelect Tarlton and his fellow Democrats on the Levee Board while defeating the Democratic State's Attorney, Charles Webb. The office of prosecuting attorney was particularly important to East St. Louis politicians. The man who occupied the post played a major role in deciding whether or not to indict public officials, and without his cooperation East St. Louis could not have been a wide open town. Webb was considered completely untrustworthy after he supported indictments for many officials of the Lambert administration. His successor, Hubert Schaumleffel, was considered "broadminded"; although a Republican, he was a cog in the Tarlton-Canavan machine.[37]

The Congressional Committee reported that East St. Louis political contests were never devoid of election frauds: "One of the picturesque sights . . . was to see Locke Tarlton with a stack of $5 bills in his hands publicly paying the negroes who helped him win an election." [38] Considering the relatively small size of the Negro population in the city, Tarlton also required other sources of support. Although Negroes were not, as most East St. Louisans assumed, "the all dominant factor" [39] in his political organization, during closely contested elections they held a balance of power. Certainly the help of Negroes was assiduously sought in the 1915 mayoralty election when Tarlton engineered Mollman's victory by a scant twenty-seven votes.

Until nearly the end of that campaign Mayor Chamberlin possessed a good chance of reelection despite the fact that many fellow Republicans were supporting Mollman. The latter was portrayed by the *Journal* as a "good man" but a tool of "questionable associations." [40] Shortly before election day the newspaper announced that several political leaders such as Lambert and former City Comptroller William Rodenberger (only recently acquitted of "embezzling [sic] the financial record books") [41] "launched into the campaign management in full force, with instructions to marshal the [Negro] vote which may be controlled by the use of money for the Mollman crowd." According to the *Journal*, funds were being raised among the "wide open town fraternity." [42] Two years later, after Dr. Le Roy Bundy was extradicted to stand trial for his alleged role in the race riots, he confessed to involvement in the sale of Negro votes—he also credited Locke Tarlton with spending large sums of money in 1915 to handle Negro precincts for Mollman. [43]

Bundy said that his own activities were stepped up during the Levee Board election the following year. He stated that for "organizational expenses" Tarlton gave him at least $1500 to $1800. According to the Negro dentist, on the night before the election he received the payoff at Tarlton's office, and among those present were Tarlton, Canavan, and Mollman. He indicated that Negroes supporting the "right" candidates received five dollars for being workers, and to insure Tarlton's investment a flash system was used at the polling stations. (Friendly voters folded their ballots outside the booths so that precinct captains could get a "flash" on how they voted).

The Negro dentist asserted that saloonkeepers helped to build up a political war chest from which funds were disbursed. Some contributed voluntarily, while others were threatened with revocation of licenses. Bundy confessed that Negro tavernkeepers gave him $35 to $50 on the various occasions he acted as Tarlton's collector. Tarlton and his men were reelected to the lucrative Levee Board, and the *St. Louis Post-Dispatch* declared that "the Democratic Levee Board candidates almost invariably ran behind the other Democratic candidates in the white Democratic precincts and ran ahead of them in the negro Republican precincts." [44]

However, in that 1916 election Bundy and his Negro followers did not desert the national Republican ticket, despite their disgust with the St. Clair County Republican organization whom they accused of taking Negro loyalty for granted. Declaring that local Republicans were penurious both in financing campaigns for Negro votes and in distributing political jobs, Bundy established his St. Clair County [Negro] Republican League. It was quite true that local white Republicans had not been generous in granting patronage to Negroes, although in 1916 among colored county employees were a deputy sheriff, an assistant county physician, and an assistant state's attorney. As previously mentioned, Bundy and his followers were demanding political equality: if they could not have jobs in exchange for votes, they wanted money. And where possible they wanted jobs and money, like other East St. Louisans.

Local Negroes also sought further evidences of status and recognition, much to the consternation of the county Republican party: [45]

> East St. Louis is not going to have a Woman's Hughes-Fairbanks Club, as had been planned by Republican leaders among the women, because some of the women decline to meet with negro women, according to rumors. If the negro women are not admitted to the club it is feared they will not vote the Republican ticket. Mabel Craig Stillman of Chicago was in East St. Louis this week [October, 1916] to aid in forming the club. The postponement was caused, Republicans say, by a scarcity of speakers. They explain the postponement was not caused by the negro problem.

Since the St. Clair County [Negro] Republican League's demands for autonomy and money were ignored,

Bundy advocated ticket-splitting especially after Locke Tarlton proved to be receptive. However, neither Bundy nor others of the race had a champion in Tarlton, who was not hesitant about using the Negro dentist as a dupe in the Democratic party's efforts to link Negroes with the mythical colonization conspiracy.

In October of 1916 Bundy had received a letter from Edward Green, a Chicago Negro Republican official, warning that the *Chicago Daily News* had sent two Negroes to East St. Louis to find proof of colonization frauds. The Green letter was intended to put Bundy on his guard, since it was feared that the colored investigators planned to manufacture evidence. Tarlton and a *News* reporter apparently saw a copy of the letter and they said that Green ordered Bundy to have the investigators arrested before evidence of Negro colonization could be uncovered in East St. Louis.

The accusation was absurd, but after Bundy was en route to see Green in Chicago, the Cook County State's Attorney, Maclay Hoyne, received a telegram from East St. Louis, identifying the Negro dentist as leading the colonization drive. Hoyne, a candidate for reelection who was also using the colonization charge against Republicans, took Bundy into custody at a Chicago railroad station. However, after the arrest Hoyne was obliged to disclose publicly that there was no evidence against the East St. Louis political leader. Despite that statement the *News* and the *Journal* made it appear that Bundy was not only guilty but cagily refused to admit it.[46]

Whatever may have been Bundy's personal feelings about the Chicago arrest, he and his St. Clair County Republican League remained in Tarlton's camp, and one year later supported Mayor Mollman's 1917 bid for reelection.[47] Among other lures, Mollman promised to hire several uniformed Negro policemen and build a fire station in the ghetto. The Congressional Investigating Committee charged that after Mollman offered the carrot, State's Attorney Hubert Schaumleffel held the stick, threatening Negroes into voting for the Mayor.[48]

During the 1917 mayoralty campaign racist propaganda was evident, although not as extensive or inflammatory as in the 1916 colonization election. Mollman was, of course, assured of much support among Negroes,[49] and his strategy was to seek votes of white church people. Sponsoring a "morality drive" in which some Negroes were apprehended while frequenting "low" saloons, he publicized these arrests to show his independence of a race which had brought him victory in 1915. However, Mollman was outdone in using the race issue for political purposes when his opponent, John Domhoff, asserted that Negro vice resorts were not really being molested: "Is morality a question of color?"[50] Domhoff's backers also capitalized on an epidemic of smallpox in the city, charging without foundation that although two of Mollman's colored supporters were infected, for political reasons they were not sent to the "Pest House."[51] Domhoff apparently believed that citizens would vote for him to protect their health and safety,[52] but Mollman was easily reelected.

According to Dr. Le Roy Bundy's own admission, no Negro worked harder than he did to buy votes for Mayor Mollman and Locke Tarlton. Bundy's 9,000 word confession about his relationship with Tarlton between 1915 and 1917 was signed about the time that the Congressional Investigating Committee was preparing to leave East St. Louis, and it created quite a flutter among both whites and Negroes in the city. Negroes jubilantly predicted that at last the white higher ups would hear the sound of penitentiary gates closing behind them.[53] Mollman repudiated Bundy's statements, charging that the confession was only a device to obtain leniency at the dentist's murder trial.[54]

As usual, Republican state officials and Democratic federal officials loudly threatened to punish all persons guilty of vote buying or selling, but a notable lack of enthusiasm developed; perhaps because Bundy had implicated ranking local Republicans as well as Democrats. At first, U.S. Attorney Charles Karch promised a federal investigation and talked of convening a special grand jury to issue scores of indictments. In his opinion conditions in East St. Louis were worse than Bundy revealed.[55] Illinois Attorney General Brundage indicated that perhaps 1200 people would be indicted, including important citizens.[56] The following day he promised those who had bartered their votes that they would receive "immunity baths" in exchange for evidence against the higher ups.[57] The *St. Louis Republic* reported that scores of Negroes accepted Brundage's offer, and the press expected the St. Clair County Grand Jury to return many indictments. Brundage had given vigorous assurances that state authorities would prosecute unless the federal government wanted the privilege.

However, within a few days the *Republic* announced that Illinois Republican leaders were trying "to white wash the election fraud charges made by Bundy." [58] Brundage, who said earlier that election frauds were a direct cause of the race riot,[59] had indeed decided to drop the investigation. Inviting the federal government to prosecute, he told newsmen that Illinois statutes provided penalties only for men who sold their votes but not for those who purchased them.[60] By this time, the U.S. attorney had also lost his fervor, stating that bribers should be penalized under local ordinances.[61] The city attorney replied that since he lacked the power to prosecute, state officials were invited to initiate legal proceedings. With a straight face State's Attorney Hubert Schaumleffel suggested that federal authorities ought to handle the prosecution.[62]

Local newspapers were divided in accepting Bundy's confession. The *Belleville News-Democrat* considered that "the wily coon" was involved in a political plot to destroy Mayor Mollman and the Tarlton machine. Although terming the dentist's confession irrelevant, the editor agreed that it amounted to typical East St. Louis and Illinois campaign methods.[63] The *St. Louis Republic* concluded that Bundy was equivocating and had not told the complete story about colonization.[64] For, while Bundy implicated himself in voting frauds, he denied categorically that Negroes had been colonized. The *Globe-Democrat*, recognizing that the colonization accusation was utterly false, asked the Congressional Investigating Committee to determine "why high officials and campaign managers helped spread these baseless charges." [65] The *Post-Dispatch* also demanded a Congressional inquiry on the whole subject of voting fraud in order to present facts to the public, thereby creating unalterable pressures for court trials.[66] The *East St. Louis Journal* was disturbed by Negro threats to the democratic process,[67] but the *Globe-Democrat* reminded everyone that Negroes were hardly the only ones who bought and sold votes.[68]

What accounted for the tolerance of East St. Louis corporation managers and businessmen who were familiar with the city's long history of election frauds, corruption, and misgovernment? Why did they abdicate responsibility for reforming the political system? Was it simply because many of these men did not live in the community, that East St. Louis was, in the words of Sherwood Anderson "nobody's home . . . the most perfect example, at least in America, of what happens under absentee ownership"?

An examination of the fiscal and tax structure in the city makes it clear that the status quo was beneficial to their financial interests, and non-interference was the price for privilege. Although bookkeeping methods in the treasurer's and comptroller's offices had somewhat improved by 1917, politics kept the city in desperate financial straits. The bankrupt municipal government "seems to be going from bad to worse." [69] Its annual income was less than $400,000 but over $450,000 was needed to provide even minimal municipal services.[70] There was a bonded indebtedness of over $700,000, although no sinking fund for the retirement of bonds—they were taken up from the proceeds of new bond issues.[71] East St. Louis was unable to function without borrowing bank money (at five to six percent interest) against anticipated revenues. Since those revenues were based upon inadequate property appraisals, the municipality was engaged in a perpetual spiral of indebtedness, complicated by the cost of interest (nearly $8,000 in 1917). Ironically, the city treasury had about $130,000 in street improvement funds on deposit, without drawing interest, at the same bank from which money was borrowed.[72]

As scrambled and precarious as was East St. Louis's financial condition at the time of the riots, sheer chaos prevailed during the several years preceding. The local government "couldn't buy even a bale of hay," [73] while for months at a stretch electric and water bills went unpaid. Municipal employees received no paychecks and the firemen threatened to quit. East St. Louis issued anticipation warrants based on estimated tax proceeds for the following year, but more warrants were floated than allowed by law.[74] Their value was discounted by as much as twenty percent —city employees receiving them in lieu of cash were thus forced to take what amounted to pay reductions. For many, graft became a virtual necessity. The credit reputation of the municipality was so compromised that banks refused to lend money and politician-saloonkeepers acted as financial agents.[75]

At first glance it seems difficult to understand why East St. Louis, the railroad and manufacturing center of southern Illinois, should have been in such financial trouble. However, the basic problem was that local politics determined the amount and sources of municipal revenue. Wealthy individuals and corporations were allowed to escape paying a fair share of taxes, while the largest source of revenue was derived from saloon license fees.[76] Since each tavern was charged $500 a year until 1917 when licenses increased to $750,[77] East St. Louis collected nearly one half of its municipal income from these establishments. A few years before the riot, the City Council in seeking a way out of recurrent financial crises, considered requiring saloonkeepers to purchase licenses a full year in advance instead of quarterly. Typically, this action was taken about the time that thirty-three out of thirty-six real estate firms were delinquent in paying their license fees.[78]

A city comptroller observed that the larger property holders were always getting by "as cheap as they can." [79] For the big industrial corporations the cheap way was low property tax assessments. Having received such perquisites corporation executives closed their eyes to the way the city was governed. For other prominent businessmen substantial savings in taxes were obtained with one eye open and the other eye busily winking. The assessed property valuation in East St. Louis was approximately twelve millions dollars, or about one half the valuation in Illinois cities of similar size such as Peoria and Rockford.[80]

The tax base, once established, generally remained in force for a four year period, and in 1915 the city assessor, Michael O'Day, submitted very low appraisals for the large industrial corporations. These were increased slightly when the books reached county treasurer Fred Warning, but a real paring job was performed by the St. Clair County Board of Review.[81] After the Board completed its work, there was such a startling reduction in assessments that the total assessed valuation of East St. Louis property was actually lower than it had been almost a decade earlier.[82] Table 4 presents a few illustrations of the treatment accorded corporations.

The meat packing industry, employing the largest number of East St. Louis residents, was even more successful in saving money. Obtaining a charter from the state of Illinois the companies incorporated as a village called National City. [83] The municipality, containing only a few hundred inhabitants, had its own mayor, board of aldermen, and most particularly, a tax assessor (who worked

TABLE 4

1915 Property Values of some East St. Louis Corporations [84]

CORPORATIONS	East St. Louis Assessor O'Day	County Treasurer Warning	County Board of Review
Aluminum Ore Co.	$699,990	$799,990	$200,000
Missouri Malleable Iron Co.	465,000	519,000	132,000
Republic Iron & Steel Co.	21,330	63,990	16,788
East St. Louis Cotton Oil Co.	1,492	19,474	1,492
American Steel Foundries Co.	454,990	507,000	454,990

for one of the meat packers).[85] Although these plants were worth millions, Swift, Armour, and Morris were assessed at $42,873, $40,019, and $34,309, respectively.[86] The St. Clair County tax assessor increased the figures to $428,619, $420,057, and $402,927, but when the County Board of Review took a final look, the revised valuations were $54,110, $55,100, and $53,600.

The majority of members on the Board of Review were appointed by County Judge Joseph B. Messick, described by the *Journal* as "dominant in property assessment [as well as] taxation. . . . Judge Messick is a professional politician, pure and simple, and always has been. As such he became one of the most influential and successful lobbyists and corporation servers in the whole state of Illinois and is still such." [87] The Congressional Investigating Committee found that his son, a lawyer, also regarded corporations to be in need of help: [88]

. . . his profound (?) knowledge of the law appealed to some of the great corporations of St. Clair County, and

they at once employed him as attorney to appear before
his father's board of review to secure for them a reduction in their assessment. Young Messick rapidly developed an insight into assessment values, and proved
conclusively that from their standpoint his selection was
wise. . . .

The meat packers tried to rationalize the existence of
their little independent municipality by claiming that
National City retained its separate status because of "the
kind of politics in East St. Louis." [89] Actually, these companies allowed the community to be misgoverned; furthermore, the owners of National City managed to forget they
were independent when a fire broke out, as they had no
hesitation about calling East St. Louis hose companies to
help extinguish it.[90]

East St. Louis City Treasurer, Stephen J. Cashel, told
the Congressional Investigating Committee that if corporations had not used the assessment dodge, the municipal
government could have obtained enough revenue to operate without being financially embarrassed. Congressman
Cooper incredulously replied, "Financially embarrassed!
It has been robbed!" [91] Of course, the executives denied
that their companies escaped paying a fair share of taxes,
and although they had previously complained about the
large number of saloons, they pretended to be unaware that
saloon license receipts represented the largest source of
city revenue.[92]

The corporations set the example in tax dodging and
a large number of prominent property owners discovered
variations of the same game. For example, after the city
made improvements on property such as street construction or other repairs, many businessmen neglected to pay
special tax assessments. The amount of money which they
owed was fixed by the Board of Local Improvements,
whose chairman was Tom Canavan; the County Court,
under Judge Messick, helped to confirm these assessments.

According to law the city was supposed to take the property of tax delinquents, but the Congressional Investigating Committee was told that transfer of title was not completed for prominent citizens.[93] As a result of the combined effects of all these privileges, the burden of increased real estate valuations fell upon small householders.

After Mollman became Mayor he seemingly favored raising property valuations from twelve million to twenty million dollars.[94] Since no significant action resulted by the end of 1916, budget cuts were ordered in municipal agencies, including the police department. Shortly before the race riots Mollman admitted that the police and fire departments' budgets were very low, but he proposed to meet "all ordinary needs" of these agencies by increasing saloon license fees.[95] The City Council postponed action and the increase was not effective until July 1, the day before the riot.

After the July violence the business interests showed no inclination to change the methods of taxation.[96] At the end of 1917 the assessed valuation on taxable property in East St. Louis was only thirteen million dollars,[97] representing only a slight gain compared to two years before. The small increases provided an additional $8,000 a year in revenue. However, the city was actually in worse financial shape than previously, because during the "moral crusade" which followed the riot, many saloons were forced out of business, resulting in a loss of license fees.

During the hearings of the Congressional Committee, East St. Louisans voted on whether or not to preserve the mayoralty system.[98] The election must have been a conflict experience for some blue-collar workers who had not by then completely surrendered to apathy. While wishing to repudiate misgovernment at City Hall which the Congressional investigation exposed, they hated even more the industrial corporations that were doing everything possible (providing transportation and even baby sitters) to insure a large turnout in favor of the commission plan.

The dilemma was solved by staying home on election day, and the commission system won 4784 to 2454. The *Globe-Democrat* remarked, "considering it was a beautiful day, the light vote indicates a slight interest in the result." Negroes particularly supported the new form of government in some precincts by five to one, since they feared that the Mollman regime would not protect them in the event of another race riot.[99] Commission government went into effect in May, 1919, after Mollman served out his term. In February of that year East St. Louisans voted for new commissioners, and Mollman as well as most of his intimates were defeated.[100]

However, not only did the commission form of government fail to change the tax system favoring large corporations, but it also did not curb vice and corruption. The new commissioner of police was denounced as "absolutely inefficient," [101] and the post-World War I era ushered in bootlegging as well as the older diversions of organized gambling and prostitution. The following chapter focuses in greater detail on vice and its relationship to politics and the race riot.

14
A Wide Open Town

THE East St. Louis system of misgovernment and irregularity, which served in the place if not the function of city government, had shown citizens how little the law was to be respected in the community. Even more indelibly, organized vice activities under the protection of politicians taught disregard and contempt for law. Political leaders, who corrupted the police, municipal judges and juries, could hardly have been expected in 1917 to impose the controls necessary to prevent race tensions from erupting into violence.

During the years before the race riot, East St. Louis had a national reputation as a wide open, wild and woolly gambling town. For the convenience of patrons, politicians, and the police, activities were centralized in the Valley; a congested district of saloons, gambling parlors, and houses of prostitution.[1] The Valley was located within the shadow of City Hall, making it easy for public officials to observe conditions.[2] The area attracted not only local residents and tourists, but also St. Louisans escaping the enforcement of Missouri Sunday blue laws. Many merchants in East St. Louis considered that their "vice oasis" stimulated "legitimate business." [3]

Since the tax structure was so dependent on saloon license fees, these establishments not only remained open on Sundays, but were also permitted to violate curfews during the rest of the week. Many places featured gambling and assignation rooms; East St. Louis probably had more saloons than any city of its size in the country. At the beginning of 1917 there were 376 licensed thirst emporiums, and an undetermined number operating without licenses. The community catered to all tastes and interests—even the poor could have their barrel houses selling "nickel shots."

Hundreds of Negro and white prostitutes inhabited the Valley. Known both as women of the night and women of the day, they usually worked in shifts around the clock. During the evenings the girls walked along Missouri Avenue soliciting trade; when business was slow, attention was attracted by knocking on barroom windows—a practice resented by prostitutes inside. Protected by politicians and police, they were periodically arrested but a small fine amounted to a license to operate. One prostitute, known as "Mother of the Valley" because her professional career spanned several decades, was arrested over one hundred times; in all paying several thousand dollars' worth of fines and court costs. "Mother" and the rest of the girls regarded policemen "as a sort of father and big brother." [4]

During the Lambert administration (1911-13), it was said that Valley activities "reached such gigantic proportions as to be unprecedented in this city." The "East Side Monte Carlo" was a "gamblers mecca . . . a clearing house for the St. Louis racing business." According to the *East St. Louis Journal*, *East St. Louis Gazette*, *St. Louis Post-Dispatch*, and *St. Louis Star*, politicians made deals with St. Louis professionals and "relatives of members of the city administration . . . are in the employ of the gamblers." [5] Slot machines were installed around town, while dice games operated openly in saloons, cigar stores, and pool rooms.[6] The *Gazette* published a list of establishments protected by the police which featured craps, faro, roulette, and chuck-a-luck.[7] Politicians were so angered by the newspaper publicity that they barred unfriendly reporters from the police station.[8]

The police chief, believing he was used as a scapegoat, finally threatened to "clamp the lid on." [9] He was fired. Under pressure Mayor Lambert appointed a police commission which attempted to stamp out some vice activities, and in March, 1912 he announced, "Gambling has been stopped, despite the protests of some of those who helped to elect me." [10] However, the *Journal* printed an account of a conversation between the head of the police commission and the new police chief: [11]

> "We have the names of gambling places and they must be put out of business."
>
> "We will get some of our friends, Mr. President, if we do as you say."

The Commissioners resigned after publicly accusing Lambert of tying their hands: [12]

> As maintained now the police department is a travesty on the law and an outrage upon the good citizens of East St. Louis and an infamy with which we refuse to be any longer connected.

Since East St. Louis officials were not cleaning up vice conditions, State's Attorney Charles Webb personally conducted a series of raids in the Valley. On each foray he was careful not to notify the local police department. As a result of Webb's determination a special grand jury returned nearly three hundred indictments against gamblers; among whom were a former police chief and an alderman.[13] There is no evidence that Webb's campaign proved to be more than a temporary inconvenience, but he continued the raids despite threats to his personal safety.[14] In April, 1913, "every dive in the Valley [was still] running wide open." On one evening Webb's deputies arrested more than two hundred persons while East St. Louis police stood around watching. Later that same evening the local lawmen even staged a few raids.[15]

During the 1913 mayoralty election John Chamberlin ran on the slogan, "Make East St. Louis a little more like home and a little less like hell." Citizens predicted he would win because of Lambert administration support, but there were doubts that the lid would be clamped on. However, as already mentioned, a few months after Chamberlin's victory at the polls, the city was rocked by misgovernment scandals of the preceding administration and Chamberlin decided to break with old friends. Although Chamberlin's success in controlling vice was questionable, he made enough of an effort to insure his defeat at the following election. He hired the Burns Detective Agency, whose operatives reported what every citizen over twelve years of age already knew—that vice of any sort was easily available in East St. Louis. When the Mayor attempted to fire the police chief for "pernicious inactivity," politicians blocked him.[16]

Shortly before his attempt at reelection in 1915, Chamberlin decided that the only hope of winning lay in shutting down the Valley. (During the next three decades it was closed countless times.) [17] By 1915 other cities such as St. Louis and Chicago had evidently closed their red-light districts (at least temporarily), and many East St. Louisans were saying they no longer believed that prostitutes and gamblers could be controlled by a vice ghetto. At last a substantial group of citizens seemed to agree that "the real reason for the municipal fostering of the Valley was to commercialize vice, afford graft, and [increase] political prestige and power." [18]

However, Chamberlin discovered that vice curbing efforts were actually unpopular among prominent business and professional men who owned real estate in the Valley. Prostitutes had paid $30 to $100 for a house that would have rented for $15 as a home. The "better class of citizens" eschewed direct dealings with their tenants by employing real estate agencies to collect rents.[19] In waging war on the vice district, Chamberlin had also alienated other citizens who, although not landlords of the Valley, nevertheless maintained business and political connections with saloonkeepers and gamblers there. On the rare occasions when members of the latter group were caught violating the law, they could count on respectable people to serve as character witnesses.[20]

In 1915 Chamberlin was defeated by Fred Mollman, who also ran on a law and order platform promising to drive vice from the city. Although the Valley reawakened, the new Mayor briefed newspapers on his "moral cleanup," and month after month Mollman and Police Chief Ransom Payne announced they were ordering the vice crowd to pack up and leave town. Although the licenses of a few saloons were revoked, such establishments often continued to operate.[21] There were also arrests, but according to rumors the morality squad was obstructing saloonkeepers who had voted for Chamberlin.

When some citizens strongly protested against horse betting and illegal card games, the Mollman administration knew exactly where to find the gamblers—"word [was] sent to them to close up [and] close tight."[22] Two months later, despite the Mayor's previous assurances that vice had been suppressed, the *Journal* reported that operations were conducted by persons "pretty high up in municipal affairs of this city." The places were "in some manner protected so that the regular officers cannot or do not make any arrests."[23] Mollman had a ready explanation, announcing that, because the gamblers had proved too wily for the regular beat policemen two experienced detectives were being assigned the case.

At this time craps games, poker games, and baseball derbies were still conducted in cigar stores, saloons, and club rooms. In June, 1916, *Journal* readers were again told that the "Lid Goes On All Kinds of Gambling." According to the personalized East St. Louis system of law enforcement, the police chief summoned the gamblers to receive the news. After reporters asked the reason for the sudden determination to act he replied that citizens were complaining again.[24] With little effort the police confiscated forty-nine slot machines, despite the fact that East St. Louisans had been assured for months that their community was completely free of these games.[25]

After Mollman solemnly warned once more that vice activities were going to be things of the past, the *Post-Dispatch* sent a reporting team to see how far the latest pledge was being kept. In a journalistic exposé persons and places were named—"they boasted that [since they] were protected . . . there was no danger of them being raided." The newspaper also quoted an alderman as stating that Mollman knew very well what was going on.[26] Before the article appeared, Paul Anderson, one of the newspapermen who had made the investigation, reported that he went to Mollman and Chief Payne, offering names and addresses of illegal establishments. Anderson said that Mollman cursed him, and from the time of the exposé in August, 1916, until the race riots the following year the *Post-Dispatch* journalist was barred from the police station.[27] It has already been shown that the Mollman administration had sufficient precedent for harassing diligent reporters. Furthermore, a year before the Anderson case Chief Payne refused to allow journalists to examine the arrest book at headquarters because they were "butting in."[28]

During the Mollman administration the vice districts of Peoria, Springfield, Decatur, and Danville were closed and the prostitutes hurried to East St. Louis. Some established residences in the Valley while others scattered all over the city. In spite of the Mayor's avowed wars on these women, they had nothing to fear: the *Journal* reported that "they are standing in front of their places dressed in scanty attire, enticing the men and pay no attention to police who order them to their room." [29]

The manipulation of the East St. Louis system of justice made a farce of the Mayor's moral uplift campaign. The system was devised to permit police to make token arrests; thus giving the impression of attempting to enforce the law. Since politicians controlled the police department, they determined not only which smalltime prostitutes and gamblers would be arrested, but also what dispositions would be made of the cases. At every step of the way money was paid by the lawbreakers, assuring their expeditious return to the Valley. According to the Congressional Investigating Committee, the overseers of the system were Mayor Mollman; Maurice Ahearn, secretary of the Board of Police and Fire Commissioners, and "the men higher up": [30]

> Tarlton and Canavan were "the men higher up." They knew . . . who could be depended upon to put things over, and the courts and the police were so organized that no real friend of the "gang" ever suffered . . . Whenever profitable vice was imperiled, Tarlton was always found ready to defend. The criminal element believed, as publicly expressed by them, "that he owned the mayor body and breeches;" and they looked to Tarlton to save them from interference by the police and from prosecution by the courts. He kept his compact faithfully. They never called for help in vain, and on election day the ranks of crime and its immediate beneficiaries, the saloon, the gambling den and the house of prostitution, paid him back with compound interest.

Operations were worked out smoothly, and after gamblers or prostitutes were apprehended, an influential person appeared at the police station to sign a bond for their

release. Sometimes for as little as fifty cents the night chief
of police released on bond defendants arrested during the
evening.[31] In the daytime a professional bondsman usually
handled the transaction—only men friendly to the Mollman administration received the business.[32] They had an
understanding with the justice of the peace that in case a
violator fled the bond was rarely forfeited.[33] Instead, they
agreed to pay a minimum fine and court costs.

Often, "straw bonds" were posted, since politics made
the justice so tolerant that securities were never checked.[34]
The bondsman usually arrived at the police station within
minutes after a prostitute or gambler was arrested. Since
it was so simple and inexpensive to obtain release, clients
resumed vice activities after only a brief interruption.[35]
Upon returning to the Valley they were not bothered by
the police, but even in the unlikely event of rearrest, a
hurried phone call to the same bondsman was all that was
necessary.

According to witnesses before the Congressional Investigating Committee, the Mayor and his associates also decided which justices of the peace would try cases; only
political friends received assignments.[36] The secretary of
the Board of Police and Fire Commissioners told the
judges "when to fine criminals, how much they should pay,
and . . . who were to go free." [37] Through political intervention charges were changed to less serious ones—for example, carrying a concealed weapon became disorderly
conduct. Many proceedings never even ended in a trial.
Some were dropped after being continued indefinitely,
while others were dismissed. In one instance police discovered burglar tools during a raid of an ex-convict's room in
a notorious hotel, but judicial proceedings were abruptly
halted after the proprietor "raised the dickens" with politicians.[38]

Defendants in vice cases were unafraid to go on trial,
since with cooperation from a justice of the peace, an
"irrigation jury" was employed. For one or two dollars a

constable selected talesmen from nearby saloons, and the appropriate verdict was rendered for fifty cents a juror. After adjournment the jury was "irrigated" at a tavern appropriately called the Court Bar.[39] In one trial of a woman charged with conducting a house of prostitution, two jurymen had arrest records and were "hangers on" in the Valley. There were complaints about these fixed juries and one tampering case was actually brought to trial. It was dismissed.[40]

A municipal judge was always enriched by the hearings he held. While it was true that he could not fine certain prostitutes or gamblers, court costs were levied and pocketed.[41] When fines were allowed, justices kept most of the money, although an occasional corporation counsel in East St. Louis history insisted on having the funds turned over to the treasurer's office.[42] Since municipal justices were able to save defendants a considerable amount of money, they were offered tokens of appreciation. One grateful prostitute presented her judge with a new desk and "when joked by his friends about this gift he remarked he was only sorry she had not given him an automobile instead." [43]

Occasionally, officials criticized the system while absolving themselves of responsibility. For example, Police Chief Payne complained that "for some reason or other," he was unable to obtain convictions against many defendants.[44] According to him, police officers were doing an excellent job, but the judges, bondsmen, and juries were frustrating justice and making his job difficult. The chief's job was even more "difficult" in 1917 when Mayor Mollman was pressured into taking action to enforce the Sunday closing law. This piece of state legislation had been enforced once in East St. Louis for a three month period about 1907.[45] Over the years the Women's Civic Federation and the Ministerial Association had protested against Sunday violations, but politicians responded with ridicule, particularly against the women.[46]

The saloonkeepers formed a powerful lobby, and in the old days they not only reminded each city administration how much the taverns were contributing legally and illegally, but they also possessed a potent threat: if saloons were forced to close on Sundays, free lunches would forever be discontinued. That argument was particularly unassailable to municipal employees, for whom free lunches were absolutely essential in an era when regular paychecks were not forthcoming from the bankrupt city treasury.[47]

However, by 1915 and 1916, the Southern Illinois Law Enforcement League, an affiliate of the Anti-Saloon League, was pressing harder than ever. Mollman replied that enforcement of the Sunday closing law would drive many saloons out of business causing a loss of license revenue.[48] League leaders did not suggest a change in the tax structure. Instead they unveiled their true aim—complete prohibition for the town. In December of 1916, Federal Judge Kenesaw Mountain Landis peremptorily called Mayor Mollman to the bench to tell why East St. Louis was the only remaining medium-sized city in Illinois which openly and completely flouted the Sunday closing law.[49] Facing reelection four months after the Landis rebuke, Mollman made political capital out of it. He announced that since tavernkeepers had been inconsiderate of "respectable public opinion," beginning January, 1917, all saloons would be closed on Sundays.[50] As in 1915, the Mayor enlisted "representative citizens" for the "moral elevation" campaign, complaining that outsiders have been led to believe that East St. Louis "is worse than the frontier villages of the far west." [51] Newspapers were told that ultimately 134 out of 376 saloons would not be allowed to renew their licenses.[52]

By February there were supposedly 303 licensed "emporiums," and while that figure may have been correct, citizens later told the Congressional Investigating Committee that some establishments were permitted to operate without a license. Other evasions of the law were also suspected. Although Mollman announced that henceforth he would follow the statute requiring American citizenship to obtain saloon licenses, the *Belleville News-Democrat* stated that one Antoni Junkniewicz "admitted Mollman advised him to have his saloon license put in the name of George B. Kaufer." [53]

The *Journal* supported the Mayor's efforts "to clean up the city," [54] while prominent ministers praised his statements as "trumpet calls." [55] With such encouragement Mollman declared (again) that he would crush gambling, which "is said to have sprung up in various parts of the city." [56] Besides the usual saloon gambling, in 1917 there were big "quiet" games in office buildings and hotels. Many citizens thought the gamblers were still being protected by the police. For example, W. A. Miller, head of the Railroad YMCA, reported a gambling establishment to a justice of the peace who told him to contact the chief of police who suggested that he check with the chief of detectives who referred him to the chief of police. [57] However, Mollman's energies seemed boundless two months before the election, and East St. Louis was treated to a reenactment of old routines. The police chief told reporters that gamblers were being summoned to his office and ordered to stop their games. [58] Some smalltime gamblers, particularly among the Negroes, were arrested for shooting craps, and a police drag net was spread to catch a few Negro numbers writers. Other petty dice players and drunks were charged with violations and in one Sunday mass raid, eight beer drinkers were arrested in a Negro flat. [59]

Mollman's opposition charged that protected saloons were allowed to engage in backdoor traffic on Sundays, and the *Journal* agreed that "reforms are not as thorough as friends of East St. Louis would desire." [60] But the newspaper and many ministers believed that since some reforms had been made, Mollman should be encouraged. [61] Besides, voters were told to remember that the Mayor's opponents, although calling themselves the Good Government party, had not driven vice from the city when they were in power.

One of Mollman's supporters was Rev. George Allison, pastor of the First Baptist Church.[62] His support of Mollman was a calculated risk because several fact-finding tours of the Valley convinced him that saloons which lost their licenses were able to get them restored or were allowed to reopen without them. He had seen teen-aged girls "go up those stairs." He knew a fifteen-year-old girl who was attacked by several men, after which a saloonkeeper locked her in a room, forcing his attentions upon her until the next morning. Mollman and Schaumleffel accused the clergymen of exaggerating.[63] However, Allison said later that to gain his political endorsement they promised that things would be different after the election.

Mollman was reelected by the biggest majority in East St. Louis history, but almost as soon as the votes were counted there were rumors that "things might loosen up a bit." [64] Allison tested the Mayor's intentions by disguising himself as a soldier for another tour of the saloons and "resorts." [65] Partly because of the minister's efforts, scores of prostitutes were arrested and Police Chief Payne issued another sweeping order demanding that women of questionable character leave town immediately.[66] Continuing his investigative activities, Allison gradually concluded that behind these well-publicized raids the old pattern prevailed. In a confrontation with the Mayor he charged that police and city officials were receiving payoffs from the prostitutes and saloonkeepers whose cases had been dismissed.[67]

According to Allison, Mayor Mollman presented all sorts of excuses for disregarding evidence of extensive vice operations. In spite of the evidence Mollman refused to shut down a saloon on Collinsville Avenue because it was a "watering place for crooks" and the police wanted to keep the clientele under surveillance.[68] That establishment remained open—months after the July riot it was still doing a flourishing business.[69] In the Baptist minister's report of his interview with Mollman, the latter declined to padlock the "notorious resort" in the Commercial Hotel "until after we collect the July license." [70] Because of Allison's persistence and the overwhelming evidence against the hotel, the Mayor finally agreed to revoke its saloon license.

Nevertheless, according to testimony presented at the Congressional Committee hearings, the hotel reopened after election day. [71] The Commercial's rental agent was the real estate firm of Canavan and Tarlton; Canavan (who was president of the Board of Local Improvements) later claimed that his company had no idea that the hotel was used for immoral purposes. [72] Allison told an entirely different story. The minister had hired private detectives who called upon Tarlton, pretending an interest in acquiring a lease to operate the hotel as it had been run in the past. Afterwards Allison met with Tarlton and Mollman, and when both denied there was anything wrong with the Commercial Hotel, the clergyman said he reminded them of the interview with the private detectives. [73] Thereupon, Tarlton reportedly commented, "Well, Reverend, the trouble about it is, the damned city is just like it has always been." [74]

Mollman also received complaints about the Commercial Hotel from other citizens. In the spring of 1917, shortly after a city detective was shot behind the establishment, the director of the Railroad YMCA (located across the street), sent a prophetic letter to the Mayor: "With the encouragement of the lawless element harbored by saloons licensed by the city to operate in a section of vice and crime not equalled in any city in the West, I predict that more blood of good citizens will be spilled as a price of these saloon licenses." [75] In June, Attorney General Brundage sent investigators to East St. Louis, ordering Mollman to take action against the Commercial and other "disreputable hotels" near City Hall. [76] On the night of July 1, 1917, the men in the Ford car who "shot up" a

Negro neighborhood arrived at the Commercial Hotel following the shooting.[77]

Since the East St. Louis vice interests were also flout-
ing the Illinois penal code, State's Attorney Hubert
Schaumleffel could have acted to suppress them. However,
according to the Congressional Investigating Committee,
he was [78]

> the ready servant of scheming politicians; at heart a
> sympathizer with criminals whom he should have prose-
> cuted relentlessly. A member of the Tarlton-Canavan cor-
> rupt machine, he rendered menial service to his masters.

Schaumleffel also protected illegal establishments a
short distance beyond the boundaries of East St. Louis.
Despite the Illinois statute prohibiting saloons from operating within two miles of any incorporated town, the *St.
Louis Star*, with very little effort, found twenty-five of
these unlicensed places in 1917. The Illinois Attorney General's office added another twenty-one to the list, and
Schaumleffel was ordered to padlock them. He told Attorney General Brundage that according to St. Clair County
tradition extending back at least thirty years, these
saloons had been allowed to remain open because the
county needed the one hundred dollar fines obtained from
arresting the owners once or twice a year.[79]

There were also many houses of prostitution and gambling parlors which made no attempt whatever to conceal
their existence. Their names suggested a defiance of law
reminiscent of a frontier mining town—"The Bucket of
Blood," "The Yellow Dog," and "The Monkey Cage." In
front of "Aunt Kate's Honkytonk" was a sign assuring
visitors, "Something Doing Every Hour." "Uncle John's
Pleasure Palace" told passersby to "Come In And Be
Suited." Witnesses at the Congressional hearings testified
that law enforcement officers had specific orders not to dis-
turb these places. Constables and deputy sheriffs were paid
to maintain order, and, when not functioning as bouncers,

some had a sideline as part-time procurers. Another lucrative duty was guiding tourists from one "Pleasure Palace" to another.[80]

In March, 1917, the *St. Louis Star* and the *Post-Dispatch* exposed an illegal cockfighting arena near East St. Louis—the entertainment lasting from Saturday night until Sunday morning. Many of the patrons included East St. Louis business and professional men. Although the local Humane Society protested against the cockfighting, the Society's president was also treasurer of the transportation company which furnished a special streetcar to take spectators to and from the arena. When newsmen asked him about the incongruity, he replied that his company could not be expected to know the uses to which its special cars were put.[81]

Under Illinois state law, operators of cockfights as well as the guests were liable, and the *Star* offered Schaumleffel the names of all who were connected with the fights. Incensed by the newspaper's temerity, the State's Attorney replied, "I don't pay any attention to newspaper talk. These St. Louis papers had better attend to their own damn business and stop trying to run this county. . . ." After newsmen complained that the cockfight promoters had threatened them, Schaumleffel reportedly replied, "It would be a damn good thing if they would shoot about a dozen of the goddamned reporters." Because the fights continued to operate without interference from St. Clair County officials, the *Star* went directly to Governor Lowden who ordered the arena closed. Nevertheless, the State's Attorney refused to prosecute the promoters, saying that he did not know their identities.[82]

In their public statements Schaumleffel and his political associates in East St. Louis continued to blame Negro migrants for creating vice and crime problems. Especially after the race riots most whites accepted that view, but some held the State's Attorney and other politicians responsible for having encouraged and protected the colored lawbreakers.[83] Critics complained that although white "disorderly resorts" were padlocked, the Negro ones remained open.[84]

Certainly Negro politicians, like their white counterparts, went to City Hall to plead the cause of constituents in trouble with the law, and certain Negroes benefited from the East St. Louis system of law enforcement. However, it is scarcely conceivable that more privileges were given to Negroes than to whites.[85] There is far more justification for the conclusion that Negro politicians had less influence than whites. The actual amount of pull exercised by colored political leaders was evidenced by the small number of political jobs they obtained, and by the fact that, during the months before the riots, they were unable to persuade Mayor Mollman to stop police discrimination or to gain police protection from the nightly beatings. Negro politicians did secure the release of bordello operators who had been arrested, but white politicians possessed sufficient influence to prevent the arrests of many whites in the first place.

Negro vice was small-time and simply not in the same league with the organized operations run by white overlords. Nor did Negroes commit crimes of gang violence directly connected with vice dominance, such as that detailed in the Congressional Investigating Committee's report: [86]

One of the worst crimes ever committed in St. Clair County was the abduction and murder of Alphonso Magarian, 3-year-old son of an Armenian baker. The father of the child complained to the police that a house of prostitution was being conducted next door to his home. Soon thereafter his child disappeared, no trace of it being found until nine days later, when the little headless body was discovered 100 yards away in the dump heap. Several pimps and two prostitutes from the house next door were arrested, and one of the women confessed

to having assisted in abducting the child. Many threats
had been made against her by friends of the accused. Before the trial her mangled corpse was found on the railroad track. A coroner's verdict of suicide was rendered,
but it is believed she was first murdered and then placed
on the track. Strong gang influence was used to save
the indicted men, one of whom was a relative of Health
Commissioner McCracken. State's Attorney Schaumleffel
conducted the prosecution, and again, as a matter of
course, there was a verdict of acquittal. The house of
prostitution complained of by the father of the murdered
child was in a building owned by Thomas Canavan, president of the board of local improvements, and Locke Tarlton, president of the levee board.

Aside from vice there were, of course, repeated charges
that the Negro migrants caused a crime wave of shootings
and robberies in 1917. Unfortunately, without adequate
crime statistics it is impossible to state definitely whether
there was a substantial increase in crimes by Negroes between 1916 and 1917. Before World War I the Illinois
legislature had created a central bureau of criminal statistics, but no funds were appropriated to finance the
agency.[87] A recent search indicates that 1916-17 records
of the East St. Louis Police Department have been lost or
destroyed. However, the present writer examined the *East
St. Louis Journal* for the period of April 1 to June 30
in each of the years 1916 and 1917, tabulating the number
of crimes of violence (murders, shootings, stabbings, and
holdups) attributed to Negroes. Since the paper usually
played up such news it is doubtful that it omitted felonies
for which Negroes were blamed. In the news columns Negroes were identified by race, a practice which magnified
Negro crime, and contributed to tension. For purposes of
the present tabulation, a shooting during a holdup counts
as two crimes—a shooting and a holdup.

From April through June, 1916, the *Journal* attributed

to Negroes eleven holdups, two stabbings, four shootings, and three murders. In every holdup the victim was white, but, with one exception, in all the other cases of violence Negroes were the victims. In that one exception the white man was shot during a robbery. During the second period, from April through June, 1917, Negroes were allegedly involved in twenty-six holdups, nine shootings, three stabbings, one assault to murder, and two murders. Once again, whites were the robbery victims, but in 1917 they were also the victims in several instances of violence, all of which were committed during holdups. In the three months before the July riot, Negroes allegedly killed two whites, shot six others, knifed one, and were accused of assaulting to murder one more.

Although more Negro crimes were listed in the second period than in the first, very likely some were hoaxes fabricated for the purpose of inciting whites to protest against the migrants. (We have already noted that on July 5, 1917, the *Journal* published two such hoaxes in which Negroes were accused of knifing two white women.) Furthermore, in other instances Negroes may have been wrongly blamed for crimes which actually occurred. During the late spring of 1917 a Negro was alleged to have shot a white detective behind the Commercial Hotel, but knowledgeable citizens, such as the Rev. George W. Allison, raised doubts about the publicized version of the shooting.[88]

Even if a real increase in Negro crimes is granted, its extent was greatly exaggerated. A newspaperman claimed that from September 1916 until mid-1917, Negroes murdered a white man "every other night or so." They became "so bold" that white women were afraid to go out at night because "many murders and assaults eminated [sic] from this element." [89] A union official estimated that in the ten months before the July riot, Negroes committed over 800 holdups, 27 murders, and 7 rapes.[90]

However, when the Military Board of Inquiry convened two weeks after the riot, the members concluded

there was "no evidence tending to show that the lawless
element among negroes is large or is abnormal . . . evidence
tends to show that the negro citizens of the community
and those who have come into East St. Louis within the
last six or eight months are law abiding working people. . . ." [91] The Board particularly questioned Mayor
Mollman about recent sex crimes which Negroes allegedly
committed against white females: [92]

> Q. Any sex outrages?
> A. No.
> Q. No complaints or prosecutions that white women were
>   outraged by colored men?
> A. No, sir.

It was ironic that in a city "where the law did not
reach," the whites should have said that Negroes were the
"lawless" ones, and after the July race riot that accusation
was one of the means of justifying the violence against
Negroes. The spector of the Negro criminal and merchant
of vice was used by East St. Louisans for their own purposes in 1916-17. The labor organizers had hoped it would
gain sympathy in their campaign to stop the Negro migration—the unionists said that unemployed Negro migrants
ran wild and the employed ones robbed or killed with guns
furnished by corporation managers. Politicians had
charged Negroes with criminality to gain the votes of
whites and divert attention from large-scale vice activities
operated under police protection.

A wild and wide open town was profitable to some East
St. Louisans. However, organized vice activities not only
reflected a lack of respect for law, they helped also to
create the lack. Regardless of what was written in the
statute books, citizens saw that influential persons disre-
garded the legal code. Laws were ignored for so long that
for some people they almost ceased to exist. Thus in all
seriousness, before the May riot an attorney could tell a

union gathering that there was no law against mob violence. So far as the Illinois legislature was concerned, he was inaccurate, of course, but the advocates of a "wide open" town had demonstrated only too well that men could select with impunity those articles in the legal code they would obey. On July 2, 1917, East St. Louis mobs obtained the same privilege.

15

A Summary of Patterns in Race Riots: East St. Louis, Chicago, Detroit

IF seriousness of a race riot is measured by its death toll, the East St. Louis riot, which took the lives of nine whites and about thirty-nine Negroes, was the most serious one in the United States during the twentieth century. Next were the Chicago riot of 1919 (fifteen whites and twenty-three Negroes) and the Detroit riot of 1943 (nine whites and twenty-five Negroes). In the three cities the racial violence resulted from: threats to the security of whites brought on by the Negroes' gains in economic, political, and social status; Negro resentment of the attempts to "kick him back into his place"; and the weakness of the "external forces of constraint"—the city government, especially the police department.[1]

During the years immediately preceding its race riot each city experienced large increases in Negro population primarily because of an influx from the South. Between 1910 and 1917 the East St. Louis Negro community grew from nearly 6,000 to perhaps as many as 13,000. In Chicago there were nearly 110,000 Negroes in 1920 compared to 44,000 a decade earlier. Detroit in 1940 had about 160,-000 Negro residents, but three years later there were an estimated 220,000 Negroes. The numerical increases in East St. Louis seem small compared with Chicago and Detroit, but largely as a result of the migration, the percentage of Negroes in the total East St. Louis population rose from 10 per cent to perhaps 18 per cent. Consequently, white East St. Louisans, to a greater degree than was true of whites in Chicago or Detroit, feared being overrun by Negroes.

In all three cities, unskilled whites manifested tension after they considered their jobs threatened by Negroes. There was also concern because migrants had overburdened the housing and transportation facilities. Everywhere, efforts of Negroes to improve their status were defined as arrogant assaults, and whites insisted on retaining competitive advantages enjoyed before the Negro migration.

Economic conflict was inevitable because the industrial corporations had employed Negroes not only to supplement white labor but also to crush strikes and destroy unions.[2] Negroes had helped to break the 1904 and 1916 strikes in the Chicago stockyards, and a generation later near Detroit, a strike erupted at the Ford River Rouge plant where Negro and white workers were "pitted against each other." However, nowhere was the relationship between labor strife and race rioting more clearly and directly evident than in East St. Louis. The July violence occurred shortly after the Aluminum Ore Company workers lost a strike that began when union sympathizers were replaced by Negroes.

Of course, labor leaders might have combatted industrialists by conducting an aggressive campaign to encourage Negro unionization. Until the late 1930's such gestures were insignificant because of Negro prejudice against unions as well as union prejudice against Negroes. By inclination and pressure the migrants trusted employer paternalism to protect them against the hostility of lower class whites. Even in the 1940's, many whites were unable to surrender their "depression psychology" and their fears that Negroes would displace them. For example, shortly before the Detroit race riot, there were several strikes when Negroes were hired, and at the Packard plant, 3,000 whites walked off their jobs in protest against the upgrading of three colored assembly line workers.

The East St. Louis and Detroit riots erupted in wartime, and the Chicago riot occurred in an immediate postwar period when even substandard housing was scarce.[3] Landlords raised rents, playing off one race against the other. Whites also resented increased contacts with Negroes after the black ghetto gradually expanded or "invasions" took place. Improvement Associations held indignation meetings, and, when warnings were ignored, violent measures were sometimes taken. During the two years before the Chicago riot, bombs wrecked an average of one Negro dwelling a month.

Slum neighborhoods were (and are) deficient in recreational facilities; this inadequacy became critical as a result of the migration. Disputes occurred when Negroes attempted to use parks, playgrounds, or bathing beaches which were controlled by whites.[4] Frequently, before the conflicts subsided, adult participants became involved. The Chicago riot began at a bathing beach and the Detroit riot started in an amusement park. Of the communities under study, only at East St. Louis were recreational facilities unimportant as sites of pre-riot clashes. In East St. Louis Negroes evidently still "knew their place" in regard to these facilities and had not yet challenged their complete exclusion from parks, playgrounds and theaters.

In all three cities, public transit systems were overtaxed. Crowded, uncomfortable streetcars were responsible for many incidents which, in the absence of racial prejudice, would have been endured with good humor or only

perfunctory grumbling. Jammed vehicles, with their jerk-
ing and jolting motions, furnished an excuse for hostile
and tense passengers of both races to interpret uninten-
tional pushes or shoves as racial insults. Many whites were
annoyed that they were obliged to stand, particularly when
any Negroes occupied seats. Shortly before the East St.
Louis riots, a sixty-six year old Negro was beaten into
insensibility by an embryonic race riot mob after refusing
to give his seat, it was stated, to an elderly lady.

Whites also complained that migrants took advantage
of Northern freedom by refusing to follow segregation
patterns prevalent in the region from which they came. It
was said that dirty Negroes sat all over the car, smelled
of body odor, and exhibited loud or boisterous behavior.[5]
Interestingly, in East St. Louis, Chicago, and Detroit,
there were almost no complaints that Negro passengers
molested white women, although the Chicago Commission
on Race Relations learned of cases where white males allegedly molested Negro women.

Many whites charged that the Negroes' challenge of
the old social order was caused by their political power,
which increased as a direct result of migration and residential segregation. There was resentment that at close elections (the mayoralty races in East St. Louis in 1915 and
in Chicago four years later), the Negro bloc was the
deciding factor.[6] Race prejudice was used as a political
weapon: during the colonization controversy preceding the
1916 Presidential election, East St. Louis and Chicago
Democrats employed it as a stick to insure a large turnout
of supporters at the polls gaining extra white supremacy
votes and to intimidate colored migrants from casting
ballots.

Whites resented sharing political rewards with Negroes, invariably exaggerating the number of important
political jobs allocated to colored people.[7] Despite a bargaining advantage Negroes were actually slow to exploit
their voting power. White politicians flattered them by

occasionally attending colored meetings or calling Negroes
to City Hall for "consultations," and even these innocuous
actions, in seeming to suggest equal treatment, angered
some whites. Politicians were blamed for Negro "arrogance." Before the riots, whites charged that because of
the ballot, Negroes had transformed from a subordinate
to an insubordinate race. Critics even suggested that if the
North had denied political participation to Negroes, the
migration would never have occurred.

Another accusation was that Negroes were responsible
for large-scale vice and obtained protection through political influence. Unquestionably, at least in East St. Louis
and Chicago, certain Negroes supported corrupt municipal administrations but so did other groups. Negroes had
their "gambling dens" and houses of prostitution, but a
considerable portion of the organized vice in Negro neighborhoods (or in close proximity to these districts) was
operated by whites for other whites, under the protection
of municipal officials and the police.[8]

Negro participation in politics, while of limited practical value until World War II, was an important propaganda weapon which Negro organizations used in their
conscious campaign to teach members of their race a new
conception of self. This new image challenged the traditional ideology of white supremacy and race inequality.
It was no coincidence that the major race riots occurred in
the World War I and World War II periods when equal
rights agencies, such as the N.A.A.C.P., and militant race
newspapers, such as the *Chicago Defender*, encouraged
Negroes to reject their role of a biologically and socially
inferior caste and refuse to accommodate themselves to a
subordinated, dominated, and isolated status.

There is no doubt that this self-conception motivated
some Negroes to test the availability of first class citizenship by "creating incidents." The new teachings, almost
as much as the presence of Negroes, provoked "violence-
proneness" and tensions among whites, who complained

that migrants were "intoxicated by new Northern freedom." At least in East St. Louis, several of the Negroes arrested after the riot were political leaders known to be vigorous advocates of equal rights. For whites, this was an erroneous doctrine which, in creating discontent, was a prelude to race war.

In East St. Louis, Chicago, and Detroit, each race riot was preceded by "a series of irritating events that dramatized race frictions upon a rising crescendo." [9] Before the East St. Louis riot, Negro workers at the Aluminum Ore plant were repeatedly beaten. In late May, a "preliminary riot" erupted after a union-sponsored meeting protesting the migration. A rise in the number of robberies committed by Negroes was also reported (and magnified by the press); at least some of these crimes may have been counter-attacks motivated by revenge.

In Chicago, many pre-riot incidents erupted in playgrounds and trolley cars. Negroes returning from work were also repeatedly waylaid by white gangs, and five weeks before the holocaust, two colored men, each traveling alone, were murdered without provocation.

After the killings, signs began appearing all over the South Side, announcing that the whites "intended to get all the niggers on July 4." These two crimes and the notices stimulated Negro efforts to prepare for the impending explosion. [10]

In Detroit, a year before the riot, a serious conflict occurred at the Sojourner Truth Housing Project when Negro tenants attempted to move into the development which had been constructed for them. Subsequent to this outbreak, fights between Negro and white teenagers increased in intensity near several high schools, and these events were followed by: a "battle" between white soldiers and Negroes; the strikes at the Packard plant protesting Negro hiring and upgrading; and clashes between white and Negro youths at the Eastwood Amusement Park. [11]

According to sociologists Alfred M. Lee and Norman

Humphrey, ". . . with respect to the symptoms of approaching riot, the incidents are not as significant in themselves as is the inescapable fact that they begin to increase in (a) frequency, (b) boldness, and (c) violence." [12] In East St. Louis and Chicago, observers, after examining the quality and quantity of these incidents, forecast the explosions. Similarly, over a year before the Detroit race riot, the Federal Office of Facts and Figures (later renamed the Office of War Information) issued a memorandum containing such a prediction. [13]

At each of these cities, the incidents both reflected and re-enforced the tensions among Negroes and whites until the spontaneous occurrence of the event which actually provoked the riot: [14]

> It may be submitted that given a sufficient level of social tension and/or a sufficiently low level of efficiency in the agencies of external control [primarily the police], any one of a large variety of types of incidents can provide the spark that sets off a major eruption of social violence.

In East St. Louis, white detectives were shot by a Negro mob after being, in all likelihood, mistaken for a group of whites who had fired into a Negro neighborhood earlier that evening. The riot erupted the following morning when whites learned about the killing. In Chicago, several Negroes were ejected from a beach which by tacit understanding had been reserved for whites; within less than an hour, a Negro teenager drowned after being attacked in the swimming area. A white policeman refused to arrest a white man allegedly involved in the drowning, and in anger and protest, a large group of Negroes crossed the imaginary line from their bathing area two blocks away. One of them was arrested by the same policeman who had failed to take any action a few moments earlier. The riot began after the officer was mobbed. [15]

The Detroit riot also erupted in a recreation area, when white and Negro teenagers clashed at the Belle Isle

Amusement Park. According to sociologist Allen Grimshaw, "some of the Negro boys who attacked whites in the
initial battles of that day were themselves reacting directly
to their own exclusion several days earlier from Eastwood
Park, a commercial recreation facility dominated by
whites." At Belle Isle, members of both races disseminated
the rumor that persons of the other group had attacked
a woman and her baby; after this false information was
relayed to a Negro night club, the patrons there were told
"to take care of a bunch of whites who killed a colored
woman and her baby at Belle Isle Park." [16]

Rumors contributed to the violence in all three cities.
During periods of tension and crisis, when "people were
jittery and willing to believe almost anything," rumors
were manufactured, rapidly circulated, and of course accepted uncritically by many citizens.[17] Grimshaw commented, a rumor "reaches individuals who are already
prejudiced and reinforces rather than changes or molds
attitudes. This reinforcement may tend to raise the level
of social tension and violence-proneness." [18]

Preceding the riots, particularly at East St. Louis and
Chicago, it was said that thousands of Negroes were imported by labor agents whom local industrialists sent to the
South.[19] After the social violence began, the whites circulated the rumor that their neighborhoods were in im-
minent danger of a massive Negro invasion force.[20] In
East St. Louis, it was erroneously reported that Negro
reinforcements were arriving from other cities, and in Detroit, a news commentator told radio listeners that according to the Michigan State Police, a large auto caravan of
armed Negroes was on the way from Chicago.[21] Many of
the rumors concerned atrocities allegedly committed by one
group upon the other. In Chicago it was said that the
breasts of Negro women were cut off, and that after scores
of Negroes were slaughtered they were hurled into Bubbly
Creek.[22] At East St. Louis, the creek story was repeated

among many others, e.g., Negroes were being hung from every lamppost or telephone pole in the city.

There is no doubt that during all three riots, newspapers contributed to social tension and "violence proneness" by publishing inflammatory rumors. For example, in Chicago, metropolitan newspapers reported that Negroes slaughtered a defenseless white woman carrying a child in her arms. The *Chicago Defender* erroneously announced the killing of a Negro woman and her baby. It has already been noted that a generation later, the same story helped to extend the Detroit riot.[23] The *Detroit Times* also reported that a Negro had murdered a white police sergeant, although the officer actually survived the assault.[24]

The three race riots occurred in warm weather during the summer months—Detroit in late June and East St. Louis and Chicago in July—when large crowds of people congregated out of doors. In each case the precipitating incident took place on a Sunday.[25] According to the typical riot pattern, a gathering crowd provided "the media through which hysterical, inciting rumors travel." During the overwrought confusion participants stimulated each other, raising the level of excitement. Although the crowds were large, most persons were spectators or bystanders furnishing encouragement and a sense of anonymity for the attacking gangs. The Chicago Commission on Race Relations noted, "without the spectators mob violence would probably have stopped short of murder in many cases." The actual rioting gangs were small, usually containing far less than fifty persons in each group (typically composed of teenagers or young men).

During the riots, all three cities exhibited similar ecological patterns. Regardless of where the precipitating event occurred, considerable violence broke out in downtown business sections, where whites invariably outnumbered Negroes. In these areas, the largest crowds of East St. Louis, Chicago, and Detroit gathered. In each city, a small active nucleus was encouraged to attack isolated

Negroes without risking immediate retaliation. Police were both unable and unwilling to protect the victims. At various transfer points in these districts, Negroes were stranded waiting for streetcars to return them to the safety of their neighborhoods, and some who were fortunate enough to board trolleys were pulled off, beaten, or killed.[26]

Violence invariably occurred in Negro slum neighborhoods. Principally in the early stages of the riots, Negro gangs in the black belt of East St. Louis and Chicago killed a few isolated whites. In Detroit's Paradise Valley, stones were hurled at cars driven by whites (who did not realize there was a race riot). Negro gangs also roamed the area, stopping streetcars and beating whites. Other Negro mobs broke into white stores, looting and destroying property.[27] Particularly in Chicago and Detroit, small groups of whites in automobiles made a few raids through Negro neighborhoods, firing into homes; the residents were prepared and returned the fire. Most police contingents were assigned to the black belt where gun battles took place between lawmen and the Negro mobs.

Whites, fearing a counterattack, did not make invasions into the heart of Negro territory. In Detroit, although a large mob was supposedly prepared to penetrate, they were actually not anxious to face an angry multitide of armed Negro residents. Most violence occurred on the edges of Negro territory and in a boundary zone separating a colored residential district from a lower class white area. In Detroit there were many casualties along Woodward Avenue, the main north-south thoroughfare, where isolated members of one race were beset by gangs of the other racial group. In East St. Louis, white mobs invaded Negro homes at Fourth and Broadway, near the downtown business district, and the residents who died there were isolated from other members of their race. The Negro victims at Eighth and Broadway in East St. Louis, which was "burned to an ash heap," lived on the edge of a colored neighborhood.

In Chicago, Wentworth Avenue was the boundary line separating the two races, and although there were clashes on that thoroughfare, most Negro casualties occurred further west in the white-dominated stockyards residential district. In that respect, the ecological pattern represented a special case because Negroes passed through a violently hostile Irish neighborhood to go from their homes to their jobs in the stockyards. During the first day of the riot, streetcars carrying colored passengers were attacked, and on the second day, after a strike suspended public transportation facilities, white gangs assaulted Negroes walking through hostile territory to the black belt. According to Grimshaw, "If in Chicago, it had not been for the transportation strike, it is doubtful that so large an amount of total social violence would have occurred within the stockyards area. More likely, a pattern similar to that of other cities would have occurred in which battles were concentrated along boundary lines between the two areas." [28]

In all three riots, more Negroes than whites were killed and seriously injured. The number of wounded Negroes was under-reported, since many were afraid to seek hospitalization and risk arrest for rioting. [29] Nevertheless, the majority of persons arrested were Negroes. Since there was obviously greater riot activity on the part of whites, prejudicial police attitudes accounted for the conclusion that "whites were not apprehended as readily as Negroes." [30]

The law enforcement officers invariably interfered when Negroes assaulted whites, but when Negroes were attacked, police frequently left the scene or adopted the role of interested spectators. Sometimes they were even participants. [31] There is no way of knowing how many police bullets killed Negroes during the violence of East St. Louis, but as many as seven Chicago Negroes and seventeen or eighteen Detroit Negroes were shot down by law enforcement officers. Municipal authorities adjudged such cases "justifiable homicides," and a portion undoubtedly were, i.e., where colored mobs looted property or fired on the police. However, the race prejudices of police officers inflated the Negro death toll.[32]

In all three communities, police bias and ineptness not only stimulated and re-enforced the racial tensions of the populace, but were also responsible for the failure to localize and promptly terminate the incident which precipitated the riot. At East St. Louis, law enforcement officers parked the bullet-riddled, blood-stained squad car of Sergeant Coppedge in front of police headquarters *in order to attract avenging mobs.* As indicated previously, a racist policeman played a prominent role in the Chicago bathing beach incident; the retaliatory violence of the Negroes would have been avoided if a sufficient number of police officers had been dispatched to the scene. Similarly, in Detroit, prompt police action could have stopped the clashes at the Belle Isle Amusement Park before they increased in number and intensity and spread to other parts of the city.

In each of these cities, police administrators later declared that riot control became an impossibility because their departments were seriously undermanned. Certainly, an understaffing problem existed: East St. Louis had only fifty-two patrolmen in a city of about 70,000; a Chicago grand jury reported that there was a shortage of at least 1,000 officers. A similar situation existed in Detroit. However, the more basic problem involved not the numbers but rather the unpreparedness, corruption, and prejudicial attitudes of the police officers. Despite the increasing incidence of interracial clashes, which should have functioned as a warning signal of an impending explosion, these police departments failed to develop an adequate riot control plan. At least in part, this lack of preparation was due to the often-expressed point of view: "the niggers deserve what they get."

During the months before the riots, police partisanship

was obvious to both whites and Negroes. MacClay Hoyne, the Cook County State's Attorney, frankly described a situation which characterized all cities experiencing major race riots: "There is no doubt that a great many police officers were grossly unfair in making arrests. They shut their eyes to offenses committed by white men while they were very vigorous in getting all the colored men they could get." [33] At East St. Louis, police were unavailable to protect Negroes subjected to nightly attacks by white gangs. In Chicago when Negroes were excluded from recreation facilities, patrolmen were frequently on the scene— to encourage the whites. [34] The police never apprehended persons responsible for bombing Negro homes. Nor did the law enforcement officers make an arrest when a white woman identified the man who murdered a Negro without provocation shortly before the riot. In Detroit, at the Sojourner Truth Housing Project disturbance, police encouraged white mobs by pointing guns at colored tenants trying to move into their new homes. [35]

It was for reasons such as these that Grimshaw, in his *Study in Social Violence*, suggested "that the occurrence or non-occurrence of violence depends less on the degree of social tension . . . than on the strength and attitude of police forces. . . . In every case where major rioting has occurred the social structure of the community has been characterized by weak patterns of external control." [36]

In East St. Louis, Chicago, and Detroit, military forces were sent to quell the riots. In Chicago (and to a lesser extent Detroit), there was an unconscionable delay before municipal authorities asked for military assistance. At Detroit and East St. Louis, even after requests by the Mayor, the troops were not available for duty until many lives were lost. With the exception of East St. Louis, when the soldiers finally arrived, they took vigorous action to stop the disorders and preserve the peace.

In Chicago, the police chief readily admitted that his men were inadequate to meet the emergency, but claiming that inexperienced militiamen would make the situation worse, he opposed requesting military re-enforcements. He was supported by Mayor Thompson until mounting pressure forced the latter to call the governor for help three days after the outbreak at the bathing beach.[37]

In Detroit, federal troops were on duty approximately twenty-four hours after the opening violence at Belle Isle. However, over thirty persons had already been killed. The delay was due to bureaucratic bungling. By half-past six on the morning after the Belle Isle disorders several persons had lost their lives, but the mayor considered "the situation under control." By nine o'clock, he overcame initial reluctance to ask for troops, but two hours later he learned that in the absence of martial law, no military assistance would be given. The governor refused to suspend state and local laws, and by four o'clock that afternoon, he and the mayor were in conference exploring the possibilities of employing federal troops without declaring "full" martial law. The debates were interminable and more hours passed; by late evening someone discovered that only President Roosevelt could issue the proclamation calling out the troops.[38]

At East St. Louis, the mayor requested the aid of militiamen almost immediately after the slaying of Sergeant Coppedge, but during the following seventeen hours, while the Negro death toll rose, only about 160 guardsmen arrived. Inexperienced, biased soldiers were commanded by an incompetent officer lacking any knowledge of riot control measures. He refused to call for re-enforcements and there was no interference with the mobs "as long as they killed nobody but Negroes."

In each city, after the violence was over, whites sought justification by blaming Negroes. More Negroes than whites were indicted and convicted for felonies growing out of the rioting.[39] Everywhere there were widespread rumors that Negroes were plotting a drive for revenge, while whites freely threatened "to finish the job next time."

Even among white and Negro community leaders a breakdown in communication resulted. The pattern was seen most clearly at East St. Louis where several Negro professional men were arrested. In Detroit social work agencies "were forced to sharply curtail their activities . . . and their effectiveness, particularly in the case of inter-racial agencies, suffered a sharp decline." [40] In Chicago, "after the restoration of order community activities were superficially the same as before the riot, but under the surface there remained a deepened bitterness of race feeling. . . ." [41]

However, despite the alienation, a reaction occurred when white community leaders realized the serious threat to law and order and the bad publicity that would result from another riot. Newspapers which had previously increased social tensions made concerted efforts to prevent a recurrence of the disorders. Governor's commissions of inquiry were appointed in all three cities in addition to the Congressional Committee which investigated in East St. Louis. [42]

The Military Board of Inquiry at East St. Louis ignored the conduct of the militiamen. The Detroit investigation was even more biased—conducted by the Detroit prosecuting attorney, the Attorney General of Michigan, the Commissioner of the Michigan State Police, and the Detroit Police Commissioner. Blaming the riot on Negro leaders, the report whitewashed the activities of law enforcement agencies and government officials. [43] The East St. Louis Congressional investigation and the Chicago inquiry were serious efforts to examine the background of the riots. The legislators' relatively short report on East St. Louis—containing some errors—has long been forgotten. [44] However, *The Negro in Chicago*, the volume published in 1922 by the Chicago Commission on Race Relations, is still "without question the best single source on social racial violence in the United States and quite likely is the best sociological study of a single case of social violence which is available." [45]

Race riots have led to some limited social reforms; for example, Mayors' commissions on interracial relations were established at Detroit and Chicago, and there were small improvements in Negro living conditions. [46] Because the East St. Louis riot provoked the disgust and anger of local business leaders, the mayoralty system was replaced by a commission form of government in that city. The Chamber of Commerce was finally aroused to support a social welfare program, with Negroes directly benefiting through the creation of an Urban League and a YMCA recreation center.

Nevertheless, memories of the holocausts were not effaced. Many years after the riots local white citizens have described them not so much as the product of race prejudice but as *the cause* of it. For example, in 1937, the Illinois YWCA held a state conference in East St. Louis, and for the "first time negro delegates were really asked to attend from other cities." Their presence created "problems" for the "Y" largely, it was said, because of the "race prejudice which has existed since the riot." [47]

A decade later, a Negro club composed of teenagers wanted to have a picnic at a public park with white youngsters from several clubs, and the recreation agency which sponsored the groups vetoed the idea because it might start another race riot. When East St. Louisans debated the question of school integration in the late 1940's, some opponents declared that the residue of prejudice from the race riot might start another one if the schools were desegregated.

Gunnar Myrdal discussed race riots in *An American Dilemma*, writing that because of "their devastation and relative fewness" they were "landmarks in history." [48] The violence in East St. Louis, Chicago, and Detroit, resulting from the status struggle between Negroes and whites, demonstrated how far from realization were the ideals

Myrdal described as "the American creed." Yet it must not be forgotten that the last major race riot took place over two decades ago, and since then there have been far-reaching demands for a redefinition in the relations between Negroes and whites. The Negro protest for equal status, although generating controversy, recrimination, and even conflict, has thus far occurred without a major race riot. This is itself a landmark of significance in American race relations.

* * * *

These words were, of course, written in 1963, at the height of the nonviolent direct action movement in black protest, and scarcely a year before outbreaks in New York, Rochester, and elsewhere, presaged the wave of civil disorders that were to mark the second half of the decade. Those conflagrations, so different from the civil disorders of the World War I era, reflected the significant changes that had occurred in patterns of race relations in the half-century following the East St. Louis riot.

Naturally, there has been an enormous outpouring of literature on interracial violence since this book was written. In view of the discussion of Chicago in this chapter, I would like to call the reader's attention especially to William M. Tuttle's very fine monograph entitled *Race Riot: Chicago in the Red Summer of 1919* (New York, 1970).

Kent, Ohio
July 2, 1981

Notes

Sources Consulted

Index

Chapter One

1. Allen D. Grimshaw, "A Study in Social Violence" (Doctoral dissertation, University of Pennsylvania, 1959), pp. 178–80. This scholarly work is a valuable contribution to the understanding of race riots. The present writer gratefully acknowledges a debt to Professor Grimshaw and recommends this unpublished work.

2. Oscar Leonard, "The East St. Louis Pogrom," *Survey,* XXXVIII (July 14, 1917), 331–33. See also, Arna Bontemps and Jack Conroy, *They Seek a City* (Garden City: Doubleday, 1945), p. 125. *St. Louis Star,* June 2, 1917.

3. Leonard, *op. cit.*

4. For illustrations see "Select Committee to Investigate Conditions in Illinois and Missouri Interfering with Interstate Commerce between the States" (Unpublished transcript of Congressional hearings concerning the 1917 East St. Louis riots and hereinafter referred to as Congressional Hearings), pp. 440, 657, 710, 1019, 1641.

5. Chicago Commission on Race Relations, *The Negro in Chicago* (Chicago: University of Chicago Press, 1922), pp. 234–35.

Chapter Two

1. *East St. Louis Daily Journal,* August 1, 1912.

2. "Select Committee Appointed By Senate To Investigate Causes Which Have Led To Migration Of Negroes From South To North, 46th Congress (1879)," *Journal of Negro History* IV (1919), 58–92. See also, Emmett J. Scott, *Negro Migration During the War* (New York: Oxford University Press, 1920) pp. 3–6. John Hope Franklin, *From Slavery to Freedom* (2nd ed.; New York: Alfred A. Knopf, 1956), pp. 392–93.

3. *East St. Louis Daily Journal,* November 4, 1910. For other examples of Negro complaints see *East St. Louis Daily Journal,* May 14, 1903 and November 9, 1908.

4.   *Ibid.,* October 9, 10, 11, 19, 22, and 24, 1916.

5.   *Ibid.,* October 24, 1916.

6.   *St. Louis Argus,* October 20, 1916. See also "Congressional Hearings," pp. 471–72.

7.   *East St. Louis Daily Journal,* September 28 and October 6, 1916.

8.   *Ibid.,* October 19, 1916.

9.   *Belleville News-Democrat,* October 31, 1916. This piece was reprinted in the *Journal* on the following day.

10.   *East St. Louis Daily Journal,* October 15, 1916. See also *Journal,* October 6, 1916.

11.   *Ibid.,* October 19, 20, 1916. *New York Times,* October 18, 1916.

12.   *East St. Louis Daily Journal,* November 2, 1916.

13.   *Ibid.,* October 9, 1916.

14.   *Ibid.,* October 20 and 29, 1916. See also "Congressional Hearings," pp. 3380–83.

15.   *East St. Louis Daily Journal,* October 22, 1916.

16.   *Ibid.,* November 1, 1916.

17.   "Congressional Hearings," pp. 4531–34, 4556.

18.   *East St. Louis Daily Journal,* October 10, 13, and November 1, 1916.

19.   *Ibid.,* October 31 and November 1, 1916.

20.   *Ibid.,* November 3, 1916.

21.   *St. Louis Globe-Democrat,* November 4, 1916. See also *Belleville Daily Advocate,* October 20, 1916. *Chicago Defender,* October 28, 1916. "Congressional Hearings," pp. 4531–34.

22.   *East St. Louis Daily Journal,* August 16, 1916. *Chicago Daily News,* October 11, 1916. *Chicago Defender,* October 28, 1916.

23.   *Belleville News-Democrat,* November 10, 1916, where Negro Republicans are referred to as "voting cattle."

24.   *Chicago Daily Tribune,* November 6, 1916.

25.   *Chicago Herald,* November 4, 1916.

26.   *Chicago Daily Tribune,* November 4, 1916.

27.   *Chicago Herald,* November 4, 1916. See also *St. Louis Republic,* November 4, 1916. *East St. Louis Daily Journal,* November 5, 1916.

28.   *Chicago Evening Post,* November 3, 1916. *Chicago Daily News,* November 3, 1916.

29.   *Chicago Daily News,* October 17, 1916. See also, *St. Louis Post-Dispatch,* October 23, 1916. *Chicago Evening Post,* November 4, 1916.

30.   *St. Louis Globe-Democrat,* October 30, 1916. See also statement by Alvin T. Hert, Manager of Western Republican Headquarters, reported in *New York Times,* November 7, 1916.

31.   For discussion of Election Day in East St. Louis see *East St. Louis Daily Journal,* November 7, 1916.

32.   *New York Times,* November 15, 1916.
33.   *Belleville Daily Advocate,* January 15, 1917.
34.   *Chicago Daily Tribune,* November 6, 1916. See also *Belleville Daily Advocate,* November 17, 1916.

Chapter Three

1.   "Hearings of Labor Subcommittee, Illinois State Council of Defense," p. 26. (This is an unpublished transcript of testimony taken in June of 1917 concerning the May riots and is hereafter referred to as Council of Defense Hearings.)
2.   "Congressional Hearings," pp. 1513–15.
3.   *Ibid.,* p. 1528.
4.   *East St. Louis Daily Journal,* December 13, 1916.
5.   "Congressional Hearings," pp. 2150–53, 2245, 2309–12. See also *Belleville News-Democrat,* April 19, 1917.
6.   *Ibid.,* p. 1507.
7.   *Ibid.,* pp. 2219–20, 2244.
8.   *Ibid.,* p. 2155.
9.   *Ibid.,* pp. 1957, 2168–69, 2231–32, 2241, 2262, 4307–08.
10.   *Ibid.,* p. 2315.
11.   *Ibid.,* pp. 2167–68, 2259.
12.   *Ibid.,* pp. 1594, 1793–97, 2169–72.
13.   *East St. Louis Daily Journal,* April 23, 1917. For newspaper discussion of the strike see *Journal,* April 19, 20, 22, 23, 24, 26, and May 6, 1917. *Belleville News-Democrat,* April 19, 1917. *St. Louis Republic,* April 20, 1917.
14.   *St. Louis Star,* April 23, 1917. *St. Louis Times,* April 27, 1917. See also "Congressional Hearings," p. 1559.
15.   *East St. Louis Daily Journal,* April 23, 1917.
16.   "Congressional Hearings," pp. 1558, 1595–97, 1660.
17.   *Ibid.,* pp. 3900–71, 4005–62. The legislators were infuriated at the possibility of unarmed strikers being shot with U.S. Government rifles. Congressman Henry A. Cooper asked Sorrels, "What difference is there between you and the worst member of the IWW when you furnish means of violence during industrial trouble?" Although the Congressional Committee evidently requested the Secretary of War to seek a Justice Department indictment against Sorrels, no action seems to have been taken. Months after the race riot, U.S. Attorney General Thomas W. Gregory received a confidential memorandum from the U.S. Attorney in East St. Louis, indicating that the Aluminum Ore Company still possessed the rifles and that the local laborers considered the situation to be proof of the Federal Government's partiality. The following week, W. C. Fitts, Assistant Attorney General, notified the Secretary of War that the guns constituted a community menace. (See the following, located in the National Archives, Washington, D. C.: Charles Karch to Attorney General

Gregory, November 28, 1917. W. C. Fitts to Secretary of War Baker, December 4, 1917.)

18.	*East St. Louis Daily Journal,* March 27 and April 23, 1917.

19.	"Congressional Hearings," p. 2455.

20.	*East St. Louis Daily Journal,* April 23, 1917. See also, *Journal,* April 20, 22, 24, and May 31, 1917. *St. Louis Times,* April 27, 1917. *Chicago Defender,* October 27, 1917.

21.	*East St. Louis Daily Journal,* April 22, 1917.

22.	"Congressional Hearings," pp. 2182, 2210–11, 4309.

23.	*East St. Louis Daily Journal,* April 26, 1917.

24.	"Congressional Hearings," p. 2237.

25.	*Ibid.,* pp. 1863, 1892, 2019–20.

26.	*Ibid.,* pp. 1863–64, 2056, 3119. "Council of Defense Hearings," pp. 59, 62–63. See also, *St. Louis Post-Dispatch,* July 3, 1917. *St. Louis Republic,* July 4, 1917. Henderson H. Donald, "The Negro Migration of 1916–18," *Journal of Negro History,* VI (1921), 438–39. Donald inaccurately wrote that the origin and cause of the July 2 race riot was the meat-packing plant strike.

27.	"Congressional Hearings," pp. 2018–19.

28.	For accounts of the strike in the local press see *St. Louis Globe-Democrat,* July 27, 30, 31, and August 1, 1916. *St. Louis Post-Dispatch,* July 27, 28, 29, 30, and 31, 1916. *St. Louis Republic,* July 28, 1916. *East St. Louis Daily Journal,* July 27, 28, 30, and 31, 1916.

29.	*St. Louis Post-Dispatch,* July 29, 1916.

30.	"Council of Defense Hearings," p. 98. See also *St. Louis Post-Dispatch,* July 27, 1916.

31.	*East St. Louis Daily Journal,* September 25 and 29, 1916.

32.	*St. Louis Argus,* August 18, 1916.

33.	"Congressional Hearings," pp. 68, 125, 437.

34.	"Council of Defense Hearings," p. 89.

35.	"Congressional Hearings," pp. 126, 151. See also *St. Louis Post-Dispatch,* November 1, 1917.

36.	"Congressional Hearings," p. 2022. See also "Council of Defense Hearings," p. 118.

37.	"Council of Defense Hearings," pp. 20–24, 110–12.

38.	"Congressional Hearings," pp. 2061, 2495.

39.	*St. Louis Republic,* May 18, 1917. See also *St. Louis Star,* May 5, 1917. *East St. Louis Daily Journal,* May 11, 1917. *Belleville News-Democrat,* May 18, 1917. "Congressional Hearings," p. 3121.

40.	*East St. Louis Daily Journal,* May 11, 1917. *St. Louis Post-Dispatch,* October 31, 1917.

41.	"Congressional Hearings," pp. 1869–70. The Springfield Riot occurred on August 14–15, 1908 in the capitol of Lincoln's state, costing the lives of several Negroes and whites. The vio-

lence took place after a white woman falsely reported that a
Negro raped her. The riot alarmed white liberals in New York
City and led directly to the formation of the N.A.A.C.P. (*The
Negro in Chicago, op. cit.*, pp. 67–71. See also James L. Croutha-
mel, "The Springfield Race Riot of 1908," *Journal of Negro
History*, XLV [1960], 164–81. Elliott M. Rudwick, *W.E.B.
Du Bois: A Study in Minority Group Leadership* [Philadelphia:
University of Pennsylvania Press, 1960], p. 120. Mary W.
Ovington, *How the National Association for the Advancement of
Colored People Began*, pamphlet, [1914].)
42.   "Congressional Hearings," p. 3122.
43.   *American Industry in War Time*, I (August 10, 1917),
6–7. R. H. Leavell, *et al.*, *Negro Migration in 1916–17*, United
States Department of Labor, Washington, 1919, p. 131.
44.   "Congressional Hearings," p. 2391.
45.   *St. Louis Republic*, May 24, 1917. *East St. Louis Daily
Journal*, May 24, 1917.
46.   "Congressional Hearings," p. 1473.
47.   *East St. Louis Daily Journal*, May 16, 1917. See also
Journal, May 17, 22, and 24, 1917. *St. Louis Star*, May 5 and 10,
1917. *St. Louis Republic*, May 18, 1917. *Belleville News-Democrat*, May 18, 1917.
48.   However, on one occasion the *Journal* decided to call for
a "humane and patriotic" solution to "the negro influx problem";
the editor observed that although migrants had been "openly recruited," there was still time for leaders of both races to make
plans for the prevention of friction. The *Journal* also published
a "reasonable and fair" plan proposed by a Negro minister. The
Rev. Edgar M. Pope opposed a segregation ordinance but suggested that the real estate association should construct a special
territory for Negroes in the Tudorville section of the city. Similar proposals were made by some white industrialists. (*East St.
Louis Daily Journal*, May 22, 24, and 25, 1917. See also "Congressional Hearings," pp. 165, 722.)
49.   *East St. Louis Daily Journal*, May 28, 1917.
50.   *St. Louis Republic*, May 28, 1917.
51.   "Congressional Hearings," p. 2134.
52.   *East St. Louis Daily Journal*, May 17, 1917. See also
Belleville News-Democrat, May 14, 1917.
53.   "Congressional Hearings," pp. 1872, 3125, 3869, 4364.
54.   *Ibid.*, pp. 3146, 3182.
55.   *East St. Louis Daily Journal*, May 14, 15, 16, 17, 18, 22,
and 25, 1917. See also *St. Louis Republic*, May 24, 1917. *St.
Louis Globe-Democrat*, May 25, 1917.

Chapter Four

1. "Congressional Hearings," pp. 3156, 3164, 3182.

2. The advertisement appeared in the *Journal* on May 25, 1917, announcing the meeting for that very evening, but it was postponed until the following Monday. See also "Proceedings Before Board of Inquiry," p. 30, hereafter referred to as Military Board Hearings. (This is an unpublished transcript of testimony taken at the hearings of the Board of Inquiry in July, 1917 in which the conduct of the Illinois militiamen on July 2 and 3 was investigated.)

3. "Congressional Hearings," pp. 1872, 2026, 2401–02, 3162.

4. *Ibid.*, p. 3169. See also "Council of Defense Hearings," pp. 6–13.

5. "Congressional Hearings," pp. 1916, 4310–13.

6. *Ibid.*, pp. 1916, 4316.

7. *Ibid.*, p. 1416. For newspaper discussion of the meeting and the violence following it, see the following for May 29, 1917: *East St. Louis Daily Journal, St. Louis Post-Dispatch, St. Louis Globe-Democrat, St. Louis Republic, St. Louis Star,* and *St. Louis Times.*

8. "Congressional Hearings," pp. 1418–19, 1458, 1807.

9. *Belleville News-Democrat,* May 29, 1917.

10. *St. Louis Star,* May 29, 1917. *Belleville News-Democrat,* May 29, 1917.

11. *East St. Louis Daily Journal,* May 29, 1917.

12. *St. Louis Post-Dispatch,* May 29, 1917.

13. "Congressional Hearings," pp. 1078, 1350.

14. *St. Louis Republic,* May 30, 1917.

15. *East St. Louis Daily Journal,* May 29, 1917. See also "Military Board of Inquiry," p. 523.

16. *St. Louis Argus,* June 1, 1917.

17. *East St. Louis Daily Journal,* May 29, 1917. See also *Belleville Daily Advocate,* May 29, 1917.

18. Whether or not the town actually maintained a racial bar, the 1910 United States Census listed only one Negro resident in Vandalia; according to the 1920 census there were no Negroes.

19. For discussion see the following newspapers on May 30, 1917: *St. Louis Post-Dispatch, St. Louis Globe-Democrat, St. Louis Republic, St. Louis Star, St. Louis Times,* and *East St. Louis Daily Journal.*

20. *St. Louis Republic,* May 30, 1917. *St. Louis Argus,* June 1, 1917.

21. *St. Louis Argus,* June 1 and 8, 1917. For further discussion, see the following newspapers on May 31 and June 1, 1917: *St. Louis Post-Dispatch, St. Louis Republic, St. Louis Globe-Democrat,* and *East St. Louis Daily Journal.*

22.   *St. Louis Globe-Democrat,* May 30 and July 7, 1917. See also *St. Louis Star,* May 30, 1917. *East St. Louis Daily Journal,* May 31, 1917.

23.   *East St. Louis Daily Journal,* June 3, 1917. See also *Journal,* May 29, 1917. *St. Louis Globe-Democrat,* May 30, 31, June 1, and July 7, 1917. *St. Louis Republic,* June 1, 1917. *St. Louis Times,* May 29 and June 3, 1917.

24.   Of course, it could be argued that the enrollment figures remained the same because the exodus in May was replaced by a large immigration of other Negro families in June. Had that situation occurred, the resultant disruption in the colored schools would have been a subject for discussion at the Board of Education's monthly meeting. No such discussion took place. ("Minutes of the Board of Education, East St. Louis," X, [1915–18], 163, 172.)

25.   *St. Louis Argus,* June 8, 1917.

26.   *St. Louis Globe-Democrat,* May 30 and June 3, 1917.

27.   *St. Louis Republic,* June 1, 1917.

28.   *East St. Louis Daily Journal,* May 29, 1917.

29.   *Report of the Labor Committee, Illinois State Council of Defense,* June 30, 1917, pp. 3–4.

30.   *St. Louis Republic,* June 5, 1917. *East St. Louis Daily Journal,* June 10 and 15, 1917.

31.   *East St. Louis Daily Journal,* June 10 and 11, 1917. White strikebreakers were on occasion also assaulted. (*St. Louis Republic,* June 9, 1917.)

32.   "Congressional Hearings," pp. 1138–39. See also "Military Board Hearings," pp. 156–58.

33.   *East St. Louis Daily Journal,* June 22, 25, and 26, 1917.

34.   *Ibid.,* June 8, 1917.

35.   *Ibid.,* June 20, 21, and 26, 1917.

36.   *Ibid.,* June 18, 1917.

37.   *Ibid.,* June 25 and 26, 1917.

38.   *Ibid.,* June 22 and 24, 1917.

39.   "Military Board Hearings," p. 30. See also "Congressional Hearings," p. 317.

40.   "Congressional Hearings," pp. 687, 1078, 1352–54.

41.   *Ibid.,* pp. 2133, 3532, 3631.

42.   *Ibid.,* p. 1354.

43.   *Ibid.,* pp. 1107, 1138–39. See also "Military Board Hearings," p. 155. *St. Louis Argus,* July 6, 1917.

44.   People v. Le Roy Bundy, Circuit Court, (March Term, 1919, pp. 732–45). See also "Congressional Hearings," p. 1107.

45.   *St. Louis Republic,* July 2, 1917. See also *St. Louis Post-Dispatch,* July 2, 1917. *St. Louis Globe-Democrat,* July 2 and 8, 1917. "Military Board Hearings," p. 154.

46.   "Congressional Hearings," p. 561. See also pp. 546–47, 557–60, 562.

47.   Almost all of East St. Louis white citizens may have chosen to believe Albertson's original but improbable description of Detective Coppedge's death. Unaccountably in the final report of the Congressional Committee, at least a majority of the members went along, ignoring Rep. Raker's painstaking interrogation of Albertson. ("The East St. Louis Riots," House of Representative Document, No. 1231, *Congressional Record,* Sixty-fifth Congress, 2nd Session, July 15, 1918, p. 8827. Hereafter referred to as *House Document.*)

It should also be noted that Raker's cross-examination of the journalist was ignored by the major St. Louis newspapers and not fully reported by the *East St. Louis Daily Journal.* Furthermore, as early as July 3rd, the *New York Times* and the *Chicago Daily Tribune* printed a mistaken identity explanation of the shooting—"the negro version"—but not until the following week did the papers in the St. Louis area publish it.

48.   "Congressional Hearings," p. 2039.

49.   *Ibid.,* pp. 251–52.

50.   *Ibid.,* p. 403. See also People v. Evanhoff, *et al.,* Circuit Court (September Term, 1917, pp. 2–3, 15–16).

Chapter Five

1.   "Military Board Hearings," p. 568.

2.   "Congressional Hearings," pp. 3100–3101, 3653.

3.   "Military Board Hearings," pp. 14–15, 627.

4.   *Ibid.,* p. 320.

5.   *Ibid,* p. 468.

6.   *Ibid.,* pp. 394–96.

7.   *Ibid.,* pp. 319–41. See also "Congressional Hearings," pp. 251–56. People v. Evanhoff *et al., op. cit.,* p. 3. East St. Louis Police Department Files: "Report of Officer Key to Chief of Police Ransom Payne," July 2, 1917.

8.   *Belleville News-Democrat,* July 3, 1917.

9.   People v. Evanhoff *et al., op. cit.,* pp. 8–10. See also "Congressional Hearings," p. 619. *St. Louis Republic,* July 3, 1917. *St. Louis Star,* July 3, 1917.

10.   "Congressional Hearings," pp. 109, 215, 218–19.

11.   *Chicago Daily Tribune,* July 3, 1917. *St. Louis Post-Dispatch,* July 3, 1917.

12.   *St. Louis Post-Dispatch,* July 3, 1917. See also "Congressional Hearings," p. 576.

13.   *St. Louis Republic,* July 3, 1917.

14.   "Congressional Hearings," p. 1229.

15.   *East St. Louis Daily Journal,* July 5, 1917.

16.   People v. Evanhoff *et al., op. cit.,* pp. 8–9. See also People v. Richard Brockway, *et al.,* Circuit Court (September Term, 1917, p. 61). "Military Board Hearings," p. 332.

17.   People v. Richard Brockway *et al., op. cit.,* p. 113.
18.   "Military Board Hearings," pp. 352, 491.
19.   *St. Louis Post-Dispatch,* July 3, 1917. See also People v. Richard Brockway *et al., op. cit.,* pp. 94–95.
20.   *East St. Louis Daily Journal,* July 5, 1917.
21.   "Congressional Hearings," p. 384. See also People v. Richard Brockway *et al., op. cit.,* pp. 95–96. *St. Louis Globe-Democrat,* July 3, 1917.
22.   "Congressional Hearings," pp. 1236–37.
23.   Files of the East St. Louis Police Department, "Sergeant Ely to Chief Payne," (July 6, 1917).
24.   *St. Louis Republic,* July 4, 1917.
25.   *Belleville Daily Advocate,* July 3, 1917.
26.   "Military Board Hearings," p. 67.
27.   W. E. B. Du Bois and Martha Gruening, "The Massacre of East St. Louis," *Crisis,* XIV (1917), 228, 231–32.
28.   "Congressional Hearings," pp. 329–30, 4091, 4094–95. See also "Military Board Hearings," pp. 517, 674.
29.   People v. Evanhoff *et al., op. cit.,* pp. 61–88, 101, 113, 121–26, 194–96.
30.   *Belleville Daily Advocate,* July 3, 1917.
31.   Grimshaw, *op. cit.,* p. 222.
32.   "Congressional Hearings," pp. 1280, 3713. See also *Congressional Record,* LVI (1918), 1654. *St. Louis Republic,* July 4, 1917. *St. Louis Globe-Democrat,* July 3, 1917. *New York Times,* July 3, 1917.
33.   *Eighth and Ninth Annual Reports of the N.A.A.C.P., 1917–18* (New York: 1919), p. 90. *N.A.A.C.P. Branch Bulletin,* I (1917), 53. Du Bois and Gruening, *op. cit.,* p. 219. *Chicago Defender,* July 7, 1917.
34.   *House Document,* p. 8828.
35.   "Congressional Hearings," p. 1229. See also *St. Louis Globe-Democrat,* July 18, 1917. *Belleville News-Democrat,* July 18, 1917.
36.   "Congressional Hearings," pp. 252–53, 288. *St. Louis Post-Dispatch,* July 15, 1917.
37.   "Congressional Hearings," p. 498.
38.   *Ibid.,* pp. 1248, 1250.
39.   *Ibid.,* pp. 1230–50.
40.   "Military Board Hearings," p. 632.
41.   *St. Louis Globe-Democrat,* July 5 and August 15, 1917. "St. Clair County Grand Jury Report," *op. cit.,* pp. 333–39. *Illinois Attorney General's Report, 1917–18* (Springfield: 1918), pp. 16–18.
42.   "Congressional Hearings," pp. 271, 1230. See also, East St. Louis Police Department Files, "Report from Sergeant Ely to Chief of Police Payne," July 4, 1917. "Military Board Hearings," p. 393. *East St. Louis Daily Journal,* July 5, 1917. *St.*

Louis Globe-Democrat, July 5, 1917. In the *Belleville Daily Advocate* of July 3, 1917, there was a report that hundreds of corpses were thrown into Cahokia Creek and the Mississippi River.

43. *St. Louis Globe-Democrat,* July 3, 1917.

44. "Congressional Hearings," p. 271. See also Leonard, *op. cit.,* pp. 331–33.

45. "Congressional Hearings," p. 3713.

46. *Ibid.,* pp. 343–44. See also *Belleville Daily Advocate,* July 5, 1917.

47. "Congressional Hearings," p. 1244.

48. Interviews with Mr. and Mrs. J. A. Gladden, April, 1962.

49. *House Document,* p. 8828. See also "Congressional Hearings," pp. 1744–54. East St. Louis Police Department Files, "East St. Louis Police Department Memorandum," July 3, 1917. "Memorandum from Sergeant Ely to Chief Payne," July 5, 1917. *East St. Louis Daily Journal,* July 3, 1917. *St. Louis Times,* July 3, 1917. *St. Louis Post-Dispatch,* July 3, 1917. *New York Times,* July 3, 1917.

50. "St. Clair County Grand Jury Report," *op. cit.,* pp. 333–39.

51. "Congressional Hearings," pp. 117, 2230. See also People v. Richard Brockway, *op. cit.,* pp. 115–16, 1087.

52. "Military Board Hearings," p. 432.

53. "Congressional Hearings," pp. 1424–28, 1691–94, 1785–87. See also *St. Louis Post-Dispatch,* July 3, 1917. *East St. Louis Daily Journal,* July 3, 1917.

54. *St. Louis Republic,* July 3, 1917.

55. "Military Board Hearings," pp. 78, 471, 556, 560–61.

56. *Ibid.,* pp. 471–474.

57. W. E. B. Du Bois, *Darkwater* (New York: Harcourt, Brace, 1920), pp. 94–95.

58. *Cleveland Gazette,* July 7, 14, and November 10, 1917.

59. *Chicago Defender,* July 7, 1917.

60. However late in June, 1917, some Negroes asked the East St. Louis police chief to return their weapons. He claimed that his department complied with their request before the July riot. (*St. Louis Post-Dispatch,* July 2, 1917.) On the day of the riot the Illinois militia again confiscated Negro weapons, but only after the owners of these guns were rescued and transported to the City Hall or to St. Louis. A Norfolk Negro newspaper inaccurately mentioned the July 2 confiscation as an important reason why many Negroes did not defend themselves. (*Norfolk Journal and Guide,* July 7, 1917.)

Chapter Six

1. Reprinted in *Crisis,* XIV (1917), 300.

2. Leonard, *op. cit.,* pp. 331–33.

3. This sketch also appeared on a banner which New York City Negroes intended to carry in the Fifth Avenue "Silent Parade" of protest in July, 1917. According to the press, because officials of the police department considered the banner objectionable, it was removed before the demonstration began. (*New York Times,* July 29, 1917.)

4. "The Illinois Race War and Its Brutal Aftermath," *Current Opinion,* LXIII (1917), 75–77.

5. *Chicago Daily Tribune,* July 4, 1917. See also *Tribune,* July 5 and 6, 1917.

6. *Chicago Daily News,* July 3, 1917. See also *Daily News,* July 5 and 6, 1917.

7. *St. Louis Globe-Democrat,* July 4, 1917. *St. Louis Post-Dispatch,* July 4, 1917.

8. Reprinted in *Outlook,* CXVI (July 18, 1917), 436.

9. Printed in *Crisis,* XIV (1917), 300.

10. Reprinted in *Congressional Record,* Sixty-fifth Congress, LV (1917), 5152.

11. *Tampa Morning Tribune,* July 4, 1917.

12. *Chicago Daily News,* July 3, 1917.

13. *Congressional Record,* 65th Congress, LV (1917), 6061. See also *New York Times,* July 17, 1917.

14. *Tampa Morning Tribune,* July 4, 1917. *Atlanta Constitution,* reprinted in *St. Louis Globe-Democrat,* July 5, 1917. *Nashville Tennesseean,* reprinted *Current Opinion, op. cit.,* pp. 75–77.

15. Reprinted in *Chicago Daily News,* July 3, 1917.

16. Reprinted in *Current Opinion, op. cit.,* pp. 75–77.

17. Reprinted in *St. Louis Globe-Democrat,* July 5, 1917.

18. Reprinted in *Norfolk Journal and Guide,* July 14 and 28, 1917.

19. R. H. Leavell, *et al., Negro Migration in 1916–17, op. cit.,* p. 30. *Congressional Record,* Sixty-fifth Congress, LV (1917), 5152.

20. *Cleveland Gazette,* July 7 and 14, 1917.

21. *Ninth Report of the N.A.A.C.P.,* 1918, p. 10.

22. *Norfolk Journal and Guide,* July 14 and 28, 1917. *Chicago Defender,* July 28, 1917. *Cleveland Gazette,* July 7, 1917. *New York Age,* July 12, 1917.

23. *New York Age,* July 26, 1917.

24. *St. Louis Republic,* July 4, 1917.

25. Jessie Fauset, "A Negro on East St. Louis," *Survey,* XXXVIII (August 18, 1917), 448.

26. *Cleveland Gazette,* July 21, 1917.

27.   Crisis, XIV (1917), 112, 219–39. See also *St. Louis Argus,* July 27, 1917. *Norfolk Journal and Guide,* July 7, 1917.

*28.   * Reprinted in *New York Age,* July 12, 1917.

29.   Washington Bee, July 14, 1917.

*30.   * Chandler Owen and A. Philip Randolph, "The Cause and Remedy for Race Riots," *Messenger* (September, 1919), pp. 14–17.

31.   Washington Bee, July 14, 1917. See also *California Eagle,* July 21, 1917. *Messenger* (July, 1918), pp. 9–10.

32.   Chicago Defender, July 14. 1917.

*33.   * Fauset, *op. cit.,* p. 448.

34.   Norfolk Journal and Guide, July 7, 1917. See also *New York Age,* July 12 and 19, 1917. *St. Louis Argus,* July 6, 1917. *Chicago Daily Tribune,* July 4, 1917.

35.   Crisis, XIV (1917), 216–17. See also *California Eagle,* July 21, 1917. *New York Age,* July 12, 1917.

36.   California Eagle, July 7, 1917.

37.   St. Louis Republic, July 4, 1917.

38.   Cleveland Gazette, July 7, 1917.

39.   Chicago Defender, July 14, 1917. See also *St. Louis Argus,* July 6, 1917.

40.   Chicago Daily Tribune, July 7 and 10, 1917.

41.   New York Age, July 12, 1917.

42.   East St. Louis Daily Journal, July 6, 1917.

43.   St. Louis Globe-Democrat, July 4, 1917. *Belleville Daily Advocate,* July 3, 1917. "Congressional Hearings," p. 414.

44.   St. Louis Post-Dispatch, July 3, 1917. See also *Chicago Daily Tribune,* July 3, 1917. *St. Louis Republic,* July 4, 1917. *St. Louis Globe-Democrat,* July 4, 1917. *Crisis,* XIV (1917), 175–78.

45.   Belleville, the county seat, allowed few Negro refugees to enter. After one truckload arrived, police informed the driver that if he returned with any more he would be arrested. (*Belleville News-Democrat,* July 3, 4, 1917).

46.   East St. Louis Daily Journal, July 5, 1917. *St. Louis Republic,* July 4, 1917.

47.   St. Louis Globe-Democrat, July 5 and 6, 1917. *Chicago Daily Tribune,* July 5 and 6, 1917.

48.   St. Louis Globe-Democrat, July 4, 1917. *St. Louis Post-Dispatch,* July 8, 1917.

49.   Belleville Daily Advocate, July 5, 1917.

50.   St. Louis Globe-Democrat, July 9, 1917. *St. Louis Republic,* July 5, 1917.

51.   St. Louis Argus, July 6, 1917.

*52.   * "Congressional Hearings," pp. 65, 100, 146. For further discussion of refugees, see *East St. Louis Daily Journal,* July 5 and 9, 1917. *St. Louis Globe-Democrat,* July 4 and 6, 1917. *St. Louis Post-Dispatch,* July 3, 5, and 6, 1917. *St. Louis Republic,*

July 5 and 10, 1917. *Belleville Daily Advocate,* July 5 and 6, 1917. *Belleville News-Democrat,* July 5 and 6, 1917. *Chicago Daily Tribune,* July 7, 1917. *Chicago Defender,* September 22, 1917. *Crisis,* XIV (1917), 238.

53. *St. Louis Globe-Democrat,* July 4, 1917. See also *St. Louis Post-Dispatch,* July 7, 1917.

54. *Crisis,* XIV (1917), 238.

55. *Belleville News-Democrat,* July 5, 1917.

56. *Belleville Daily Advocate,* July 5, 1917.

57. *St. Louis Globe-Democrat,* July 6, 1917.

58. *Belleville News-Democrat,* July 11, 1917. *East St. Louis Daily Journal,* July 12, 1917.

59. *St. Louis Argus,* July 20, 1917. See also *Chicago Defender,* August 11, 1917. East St. Louis Police Department Files, "Memorandum from Sergeant Ely to Chief of Police Payne, July 5, 1917." "G. F. Bond to Chief of Police Keating, July 31, 1917."

60. *St. Louis Globe-Democrat,* July 5 and August 29, 1917. *Belleville News-Democrat,* August 29, 1917.

61. *East St. Louis Daily Journal,* July 15, 1917.

62. *Ibid.,* July 5, 1917. *St. Louis Republic,* July 5, 1917.

63. *St. Louis Republic,* July 5, 1917. *East St. Louis Daily Journal,* July 5, 9, 1917.

64. *East St. Louis Daily Journal,* July 5, 9, and 10, 1917.

65. *St. Louis Republic,* July 5, 1917.

66. *Ibid.,* July 5 and 7, 1917. *East St. Louis Daily Journal,* July 5 and 8, 1917. See also *Belleville News-Democrat,* July 7, 1917. *Belleville Daily Advocate,* July 7 and August 14, 1917.

67. *St. Louis Post-Dispatch,* July 8, 1917. Efforts to locate a copy of the inquest transcript were unsuccessful. It is not on file at the county courthouse or in the coroner's office. In a recent conversation, former Coroner Renner stated that the document is not among his personal papers.

68. U.S. Attorney Charles Karch, who kept Attorney General Gregory apprised of East St. Louis developments, apparently believed there was a black army plot, or at least he wanted his superior to believe it. In a letter to Gregory, he wrote, ". . . the blacks organized clandestinely and armed themselves in their houses not only to resist any further outbreak, but to lead an attack upon the white citizens on the 4th of July. When the police discovered that movement, they visited the headquarters of the negroes" [which ended in the killings of Detectives Coppedge and Wadley]. (National Archives, Washington, D.C., U.S. Department of Justice. Charles Karch to Thomas Gregory, [July 23, 1917]).

69. *St. Louis Post-Dispatch,* July 14, 1917.

70. *Belleville Daily Advocate,* July 9, 1917. See also *East St. Louis Daily Journal,* July 5 and 10, 1917. *St. Louis Globe-Democrat,* July 5, 1917.

71.   *East St. Louis Journal,* July 8 and 13, 1917. See also *St. Louis Globe-Democrat,* July 6, 12, 13, 14, 15, 16, 19, August 4, 9, and 21, 1917. *St. Louis Republic,* July 13, 1917. *Belleville News-Democrat,* July 13, 1917. "Congressional Hearings," p. 2671. East St. Louis Police Department Files, "M. A. Lowry to East St. Louis Chief of Police," (July 19, 1917). "H. L. Walker to Mr. Neville, Chief of Detectives," (August 8, 1917).

72.   *St. Louis Post-Dispatch,* July 3, 1917. See also *St. Louis Globe-Democrat,* July 4, 5, 6, and 12, 1917. *St. Louis Republic,* July 4, 1917. *Belleville Daily Advocate,* July 5, 1917. *Chicago Daily Tribune,* July 4 and 5, 1917.

Chapter Seven

1.   "Congressional Hearings," p. 511. See also *St. Louis Post-Dispatch,* July 11 and 16, 1917. *Belleville Daily Advocate,* October 9, 1917.

2.   "Military Board Hearings," p. 456.

3.   *Ibid.,* p. 206.

4.   *Ibid.,* p. 264.

5.   Board of Inquiry, "Report upon the Conduct of Officers and Men, Illinois National Guard on Duty at East St. Louis, July 2, 1917," p. 14. (This report was unpublished and submitted to the Adjutant General, Illinois National Guard, August 2, 1917.)

6.   "Congressional Hearings," pp. 1250, 1258.

7.   "Military Board Hearings," pp. 491–92.

8.   *Ibid.,* p. 309.

9.   *Ibid.,* pp. 221–22.

10.   *Ibid.,* pp. 672–73.

11.   *Ibid.,* p. 425. See also pp. 191–92.

12.   *Ibid.,* pp. 448–49.

13.   *Ibid.,* p. 261.

14.   *Ibid.,* p. 351. See also p. 395.

15.   *Ibid.,* p. 355. See also, pp. 196, 261, 322.

16.   *Ibid.,* pp. 183, 213, 219–20, 262, 456.

17.   *Ibid.,* pp. 216, 258.

18.   *Ibid.,* pp. 323, 344.

19.   *Ibid.,* pp. 634–37. Du Bois and Gruening, *op. cit.,* pp. 225–26.

20.   "Military Board Hearings," pp. 495–96.

21.   Although the Military Board was clearly concerned with justifying the conduct of the soldiers, it was also true that on occasion it was unfairly attacked by critics. For example, a reporter told the Congressional Investigating Committee that the Military Board did not allow him to identify soldiers who shot down two Negroes during the race riot. However, in the journalist's actual appearance before the Board, he had mentioned

nothing about the shooting incident. ("Military Board Hearings," pp. 349–58. "Congressional Hearings," pp. 396–97).

22. "Congressional Hearings," pp. 108–17, 389, 395, 506, 594–95. See also *St. Louis Republic,* October 19, 1917. *St. Louis Globe-Democrat,* October 23, 1917. *St. Louis Post-Dispatch,* October 26, 1917. *East St. Louis Daily Journal,* October 23, 1917.

23. For examples see "Military Board Hearings," pp. 394–407, 415–42, 464–84, 131.

24. Report of Military Board of Inquiry, *op. cit.,* p. 15.

25. For examples see "Military Board Hearings," pp. 76, 78–79, 345, 353–54.

26. *Ibid.,* p. 192.

27. Some Negro newspapers apparently did not know about these illustrations of good conduct. For example, the *Baltimore American* unfairly condemned every member of the Illinois National Guard, reporting that there was "not one single act of bravery on the part of the guardsmen." (Reprinted in *Crisis,* XIV, [1917], 176.)

28. "Military Board Hearings," pp. 78–80, 559–60.

29. Board of Inquiry, *op. cit.,* p. 14.

30. "Military Board Hearings," pp. 14–15. See also "Congressional Hearings," p. 485.

31. "Military Board Hearings," pp. 255, 534.

32. Board of Inquiry, *op. cit.,* p. 12.

33. *Ibid.,* p. 13.

34. "Military Board Hearings," pp. 530–31.

35. *Ibid.,* pp. 215–16.

36. *Ibid.,* pp. 545–46, 607–12.

37. "Congressional Hearings," p. 505.

38. *Ibid.,* p. 774.

39. *Ibid.,* p. 924. See also "Military Board Hearings," pp. 552–53, 608.

40. "Military Board Hearings," pp. 415, 694–95.

41. *Ibid.,* p. 240.

42. "Congressional Hearings," p. 830.

43. "Military Board Hearings," p. 72.

44. *Ibid.,* pp. 74–75.

45. *Ibid.,* pp. 564, 607.

46. "Congressional Hearings," pp. 761, 833, 835.

47. *Ibid.,* p. 836.

48. Board of Inquiry, *op. cit.,* p. 15.

49. *Belleville News-Democrat,* July 10, 1917. See also *East St. Louis Daily Journal,* July 9, 1917. *St. Louis Globe-Democrat,* July 9, 1917. *St. Louis Republic,* July 9, 1917. *Chicago Daily Tribune,* July 8 and 12, 1917. *St. Louis Post-Dispatch,* July 9, 1917.

50. *St. Louis Post-Dispatch,* July 11, 1917.

51. In his interrogation before the Congressional Committee several months afterwards, Tripp said that because the first troops had very little ammunition, he asked militiamen arriving later to bring extra cartridges. Evidently he was not aware that the two companies of soldiers guarding the war plants had ammunition. ("Congressional Hearings," pp. 408–9, 761).

52. Board of Inquiry, *op. cit.*, p. 14.

53. "Congressional Hearings," pp. 4449–50.

54. *Ibid.*, p. 489.

55. "Military Board Hearings," pp. 43–44.

56. *Ibid.*, pp. 43, 176, 188.

57. *Ibid.*, pp. 307–308, 554. See also "Congressional Hearings," pp. 771, 1061.

58. "Congressional Hearings," pp. 322–23.

59. "Military Board Hearings," p. 38.

60. "Congressional Hearings," p. 3655.

61. *Ibid.*, p. 916. See also Lindsay Cooper, "Congressional Investigation of the East St. Louis Riots," *Crisis* XV (January, 1918), 116–21.

62. Board of Inquiry, *op. cit.*, pp. 9–10.

63. "Military Board Hearings," pp. 47–48.

64. *House Document*, p. 8833. See also "Congressional Hearings," pp. 753–932.

65. "Congressional Hearings," pp. 757–59, 787–90.

66. *Ibid.*, pp. 486–87. "Military Board Hearings," p. 73.

67. *House Document*, p. 8833. Although Tripp was criticized, the legislators commended Lt. Colonel Clayton: "Had it not been for his promptness and determination the mob certainly would have committed many more atrocities."

68. "Military Board Hearings," p. 140.

69. *Ibid.*, pp. 132, 140–41, 143, 224, 626–27. See also "Congressional Hearings," pp. 117, 403–04, 406, 411, 525–26, 611. *House Document*, p. 8829. "St. Clair County Grand Jury Report," *op. cit.*, pp. 333–39.

70. *St. Louis Globe-Democrat*, July 3, 1917. See also *St. Louis Post-Dispatch*, July 6, 1917.

71. "Military Board Hearings," pp. 166–67, 169.

72. *Ibid.*, p. 337. "Congressional Hearings," pp. 309–12, 495–97. See also *St. Louis Post-Dispatch*, July 13, 1917. *St. Louis Globe-Democrat*, October 21, 1917. *East St. Louis Daily Journal*, October 22, 1917.

73. "Military Board Hearings," p. 76.

74. *Ibid.*, pp. 80–81. See also *St. Louis Republic*, July 4, 1917. *New York Times*, July 4, 1917.

75. "Congressional Hearings," p. 2353.

76. *Belleville Daily Advocate*, July 9, 1917.

77. *St. Louis Post-Dispatch*, October 21, 1917.

78. *Ibid.*, July 7, 8, and 14, 1917. See also *St. Louis Globe-*

Democrat, July 10 and 11, 1917. *St. Louis Republic,* July 10, 1917.

79.   *East St. Louis Daily Journal,* July 5, 6, and 10, 1917. See also *St. Louis Globe-Democrat,* July 6, 1917. *Chicago Daily Tribune,* July 6, 1917.

80.   See the following in East St. Louis Police Department Files, "Note from Sergeant Ely to Chief of Police Payne, July 5, 1917." "Memorandum from Ely to Payne, July 5, 1917." "Ely to Payne, July 9, 1917." "Green and Mill to Payne, July 2, 1917."

81.   "Military Board Hearings," pp. 9–10. The figures exclude supervisory personnel. Many newspapers reported that the police department employed seventy persons. That statement is accurate, if it is recognized that the number included janitors, office clerks, and chauffeurs, as well as administrative personnel.

82.   *Ibid.,* pp. 174–75. See also "Congressional Hearings," pp. 1110–11, 1122, 1151.

83.   *East St. Louis Daily Journal,* April 14, 1916.

84.   "Proceedings of the East St. Louis City Council," September 13, 1912, pp. 48–49, 68–69.

85.   See *East St. Louis Daily Journal,* May 10, 1917.

86.   "Military Board Hearings," p. 145.

87.   "Congressional Hearings," p. 636.

88.   *St. Louis Post-Dispatch,* October 24, 1917.

89.   "Congressional Hearings," p. 523.

90.   *East St. Louis Daily Journal,* March 29 and 30, 1911. See also *Journal* March 9, 13, 21, 27, 28, and 31, 1913.

91.   *St. Louis Times,* March 22, 1917. For earlier illustrations see *East St. Louis Daily Journal,* January 18, 20, March 2 and 19, 1911.

92.   "Military Board Hearings," p. 135.

93.   *East St. Louis Daily Journal,* July 9, 1917. *Belleville Daily Advocate,* July 10, 1917. *St. Louis Post-Dispatch,* October 24, 1917.

94.   *East St. Louis Daily Journal,* August 10, 1915.

95.   *East St. Louis Daily Journal,* March 16, 1913. See also "Congressional Hearings," p. 3211. *House Document,* p. 8829.

96.   "Congressional Hearings," pp. 4079–81.

97.   *Ibid.,* pp. 3554–55. See also *House Document,* pp. 8831–32. *East St. Louis Daily Journal,* November 17, 18, 26, and 28, 1916. September 30, 1917.

98.   *East St. Louis Daily Journal,* May 13, 1914.

99.   "Congressional Hearings," pp. 2606, 2615.

100.   *St. Louis Post-Dispatch,* July 5, 6, and 11, 1917. See also *St. Louis Globe-Democrat,* July 7, 10, and 12, 1917. *East St. Louis Daily Journal,* July 7 and 8, 1917. *Belleville Daily Advocate,* July 5, 1917.

101.   *St. Louis Globe-Democrat,* July 12, 1917.

102.   *St. Louis Globe-Democrat,* July 8, 12, 20, and 21, 1917. See also *St. Louis Post-Dispatch,* July 15, 1917. *East St. Louis Daily Journal,* July 9 and 12, 1917.

103.   "Congressional Hearings," p. 2625.

104.   *Ibid.,* pp. 2623, 2681. See also "Military Board Hearings," pp. 625–26.

105.   *East St. Louis Daily Journal,* February 23, 1918.

106.   *Ibid.,* February 20 and 23, 1918. See also "St. Clair County Grand Jury Report," *op. cit.,* pp. 333–39. *St. Louis Globe-Democrat,* September 9, 1917.

107.   "Congressional Hearings," pp. 3576, 3662, 4301.

108.   *East St. Louis Daily Journal,* February 15, 18, 20, 21, and 23, 1918.

109.   *St. Louis Post-Dispatch,* February 15 and 20, 1918. See also *St. Louis Republic,* February 9, 15, 16, 22, and March 1, 1918.

110.   "Proceedings of the East St. Louis City Council," *op. cit.,* February 21, 1918, p. 602.

Chapter Eight

1.   *St. Louis Post-Dispatch,* July 9, 1917. See also *St. Louis Republic,* July 4, 1917. *East St. Louis Daily Journal,* July 10 and 11, 1917.

2.   "Military Board Hearings," pp. 116–17.

3.   "Congressional Hearings," p. 2629. See also "Illinois Attorney General's Report, 1917–1918," *op. cit.,* pp. 16–18. *St. Louis Globe-Democrat,* July 5, 7, 8, and 12, 1917. *St. Louis Republic,* July 6 and 7, 1917.

4.   *Belleville News-Democrat,* July 12, 1917. See also *Belleville Daily Advocate,* July 14, 1917.

5.   *St. Louis Globe-Democrat,* July 17, 1917. See also *East St. Louis Daily Journal,* July 11 and 12, 1917. *St. Louis Post-Dispatch,* July 11, 1917. *Belleville Daily Advocate,* July 9, 1917.

6.   Of the twenty-three man panel, only two were East St. Louis residents.

7.   "St. Clair County Grand Jury Report," *op. cit.,* pp. 333–39. "Proceedings of East St. Louis City Council," September 11, 1917, pp. 577–78.

8.   *St. Louis Globe-Democrat,* September 9, 1917. *Belleville Daily Advocate,* September 14, 1917. *East St. Louis Daily Journal,* February 4, 1918.

9.   *St. Louis Post-Dispatch,* August 16, 1917. See also *Post-Dispatch,* September 9 and 12, 1917. *East St. Louis Daily Journal,* October 15, 1917. *St. Louis Republic,* September 3, 11, and December 8, 1917. *St. Louis Globe-Democrat,* September 9, 11, and 12, 1917. *Belleville Daily Advocate,* August 17, 1917. *Chi-*

cago Defender, September 15, 1917 and February 16, 1918.
Norfolk Journal and Guide, October 6, 1917.

10. *Belleville News-Democrat,* September 4, 1917.

11. *St. Louis Globe-Democrat,* August 19, 1917.

12. The twelfth Negro went to the penitentiary for setting fire
to his own house during the rioting. (*Belleville News-Democrat,*
October 26, 1917.)

13. *Chicago Defender,* November 3, 1917 and April 20, 1918.
See also *Messenger,* July, 1918, pp. 9–10.

14. For examples see *East St. Louis Daily Journal,* December 4 and 10, 1917. *Belleville Daily Advocate,* December 3, 1917.

15. "Congressional Hearings," pp. 3648–49.

16. *St. Louis Post-Dispatch,* March 29, 1919. *House Document,* p. 8834.

17. *East St. Louis Daily Journal,* February 6 and 8, 1918.

18. *St. Louis Argus,* February 8, 1918.

19. *House Document,* pp. 8830–31. See also "Congressional
Hearings," pp. 2641–46, 2982–3109.

20. "Congressional Hearings," pp. 1259–71, 1373–79. See also
House Document, p. 8829. *East St. Louis Daily Journal,* July 20,
1917. *St. Louis Post-Dispatch,* July 10, 13, and 18, 1917. *St.
Louis Globe-Democrat,* July 18 and August 16, 1917. *Belleville
News-Democrat,* July 18 and 19, 1917.

21. For Press accounts of this trial see *East St. Louis Daily
Journal,* October 8, 9, 10, 11, 12, 15, and 16, 1917. *St. Louis
Post-Dispatch,* October 8, 10, 11, 12, 13, and 15, 1917. *St. Louis
Globe-Democrat,* October 8, 9, 10, 11, 12, and 13, 1917. *St. Louis
Republic,* October 8, 9, 11, and 13, 1917. *Belleville Daily Advocate,* October 10, 11, 12, and 13, 1917. *Belleville News-Democrat,*
October 8, 9, 10, 11, and 12, 1917.

22. *St. Louis Times,* October 10, 11, and 12, 1917.

23. *Belleville Daily Advocate,* October 12, 1917.

24. *St. Louis Post-Dispatch,* October 12, 1917.

25. *Chicago Defender,* October 20, 1917.

26. Reprinted in *East St. Louis Daily Journal,* October 19,
1917.

27. *Ibid.,* October 9 and 11, 1917. In Belleville where the
trials of the whites were held, the *News-Democrat* on occasion did
not resist the temptation to act as jury. For example, in the midst
of one case, the newspaper's column head was, "Conviction in
Trial Seems Near." (*Belleville News-Democrat,* November 15,
1917).

28. *St. Louis Post-Dispatch,* October 18, 1917. See also People v. Brockway *et al., op. cit.,* pp. 102–6.

29. *St. Louis Post-Dispatch,* October 19, 1917.

30. For Press accounts of the trial see *East St. Louis Daily
Journal,* October 14, 15, 16, 17, 18, 19, 21, 22, and 23, 1917.
St. Louis Globe-Democrat, October 13, 18, 19, 20, 22, and 23,

1917. *St. Louis Post-Dispatch,* October 12, 16, 17, 18, 19, 21, 22, and 23, 1917. *Belleville News-Democrat,* October 18, 1917. *Belleville Daily Advocate,* October 18, 19, and 22, 1917. *Chicago Defender,* October 20 and 27, 1917.

31.   People v. Brockway, *et al., op. cit.,* pp. 134–202, 225, 281–82, 290, 298–9, 309–10.

32.   *Ibid.,* pp. 206, 252–53, 268.

33.   *Ibid.,* pp. 1101, 1105.

34.   *Ibid.,* pp. 927–1015, 1136.

35.   *Ibid.,* pp. 1105, 1177.

36.   *Ibid.,* pp. 52–63, 91–92, 94–96, 115–16.

37.   *Ibid.,* p. 1087.

38.   For Press accounts of the trial see *St. Louis Globe-Democrat,* October 13, November 14, 15, and 25, 1917. *St. Louis Republic,* November 13, 14, 15, and 20, 1917. *St. Louis Post-Dispatch,* November 14, 15, 17, 19, 20, and 21, 1917. *East St. Louis Daily Journal,* November 6, 13, 14, 21, 22, 23, and 25, 1917. *Belleville News-Democrat,* November 13 and 14, 1917. *Belleville Daily Advocate,* November 14 and 24, 1917.

39.   People v. Brockway *et al., op. cit.,* pp. 404–6, 415, 429, 495, 599, 623–40. See also "Congressional Hearings," p. 1164.

40.   People v. Brockway *et al., op. cit.,* pp. 508–18, 659–73.

41.   People v. Mike Evanhoff *et al., op. cit.,* pp. 59–60, 78, 87, 158.

42.   *Ibid.,* pp. 137, 180–89.

43.   *Ibid.,* pp. 101–3, 126.

44.   *Ibid.,* pp. 142–43, 194–95, 211, 381–82, 424–28, 450. See also *St. Louis Republic,* November 28 and 30, 1917. *East St. Louis Daily Journal,* November 26, 27, 28, 29, and 30, 1917.

Chapter Nine

1.   *St. Louis Argus,* October 5, 1917.

2.   *East St. Louis Daily Journal,* October 4, 1917. See also *St. Louis Globe-Democrat,* October 2 and 3, 1917.

3.   *Chicago Defender,* October 20, 1917.

4.   People v. Fayette Parker *et al., op. cit.,* pp. 186–91.

5.   *Ibid.,* pp. 274–77.

6.   *Ibid.,* pp. 107–12, 120–22, 245–46.

7.   *Ibid.,* pp. 196–224.

8.   *Ibid.,* pp. 197–98.

9.   *Ibid.,* pp. 12, 123.

10.   For example see *Ibid.,* p. 78.

11.   In view of the poor lighting on the streets, it is difficult to understand how Wilson could have seen anything from that distance. However, the point was not brought up at the trial. Wilson testified that the gunshots were fired at approximately 11 o'clock. Actually the murder occurred at 12:10 A.M. on July 2. The witness did not have a watch and fixed the time by a factory whistle which blew at eleven o'clock each evening. Defense attorneys used the time discrepancy to discredit him, but the prosecution contended that he was simply mistaken about which whistle he heard since another one was sounded daily shortly after midnight.

12. *Ibid.,* pp. 138–54.

13. "Congressional Hearings," pp. 1109, 1121.

14. People v. Fayette Parker *et al., op. cit.,* pp. 161–62, 590–93.

15. *Ibid.,* p. 163.

16. *Ibid.,* pp. 172–75.

17. *Ibid.,* pp. 552–63.

18. In a recent conversation on January 24, 1963, Renner stated that he did not remember why he was not asked to testify.

19. People v. Le Roy Bundy, *op. cit.,* pp. 770–71, 791–93.

20. People v. Parker *et al., op. cit.,* pp. 289–93.

21. *Ibid.,* pp. 295, 351–52, 372, 383, 390. See also pp. 346, 368–69, 436.

22. However, one alibi witness appeared to strengthen the prosecution's position since he claimed he was awakened when the bell sounded "to get out of the way . . . of the shooting." (*Ibid.,* pp. 336–39.)

23. *East St. Louis Daily Journal,* October 5, 1917.

24. Through executive clemency the men were released from Menard Penitentiary in November, 1924. Two whites were also freed at the same time. (Interview with Fayette Parker, January, 1963. See also *East St. Louis Daily Journal,* November 6 and 7, 1924.)

25. People v. Parker *et al.,* No. 11972, "Reports of Cases at Law and in Chancery, Argued and Determined in Supreme Court of Illinois—Illinois Reports," (CCLXXXIV 1918, 272).

26. *St. Louis Post-Dispatch,* October 3, 1917.

27. *East St. Louis Daily Journal,* October 4, 1917.

28. *St. Louis Republic,* October 5 and 6, 1917.

29. *St. Louis Globe-Democrat,* October 8, 1917.

30. *St. Louis Argus,* July 13, 1917. See also *N.A.A.C.P. Branch Bulletin,* I (August, 1917), 57.

31. "Minutes of the Board of Directors of the N.A.A.C.P." (July 9, September 17, 1917, Unpublished). See also *N.A.A.C.P. Branch Bulletin,* I (October, 1917), 65.

32. *East St. Louis Daily Journal,* October 4, 1917.

33. *St. Louis Post-Dispatch,* October 4, 1917. See also *St. Louis Republic,* October 5, 1917. *St. Louis Globe-Democrat,* October 13, 1917.

34. People v. Parker, *op. cit.,* pp. 260–66.

35. *St. Louis Post-Dispatch,* October 4, 1917.

36. People v. Parker, *op. cit.,* pp. 266–73.

37. *St. Louis Republic,* October 5, 1917.

38. People v. Parker, *op. cit.,* pp. 226–27.

39. The *Republic* also brought Bundy's red automobile into the testimony of other prosecution witnesses, despite the fact that the trial transcript of their remarks indicated no mention of that vehicle. *St. Louis Republic,* October 4, 1917. See testimony of Barbara Stapp and Edward Wilson in People v. Parker, *op. cit.,* pp. 119–75.

40. *St. Louis Republic,* October 4, 1917.

41. *St. Louis Post-Dispatch,* October 4, 1917.

42. People v. Parker, *op. cit.,* pp. 186–90.

43. *St. Louis Republic,* October 4, 1917.

44. *East St. Louis Daily Journal,* October 3, 1917. *St. Louis Post-Dispatch,* October 4, 1917.

45. People v. Parker, *op. cit.,* pp. 50–51.

46. *St. Louis Republic,* October 6, 1917. See also *St. Louis Globe-Democrat,* October 5, 1917. *Belleville News-Democrat,* October 5, 1917.

47. Wilson denied being a practicing numbers writer although he admitted formerly selling them. The Illinois Supreme Court, in reviewing the trial transcript when the case was appealed, conferred upon him a degree of respectability which local Negroes disputed. The jurists identified Wilson as a "colored man who had resided in the city of East St. Louis for seventeen or eighteen years and had been in business there." Over two years later, however, in considering the Bundy appeal, the Court noted, "A part, at least, of the business of Wilson was selling to colored people tickets which he called policies, connected with some sort of wheel game." (People v. Parker, *op. cit.,* p. 159. The People v. Parker *et al.,* No. 11972, opinion filed June 20, 1918, in "Reports of Cases at Law and in Chancery Argued and Determined in Supreme Court of Illinois—Illinois Reports," [CCXVIC 272–86]. People v. Bundy, No. 13366, opinion filed December 21, 1920, in "Reports of Cases at Law and in Chancery Argued and Determined in Supreme Court of Illinois—Illinois Reports," [CCVC 322–31]).

48. *Chicago Defender,* October 20, November 24, 1917 and January 19, 1918. See also *Cleveland Gazette,* November 10, 1917. *St. Louis Argus,* February 8, 1918.

49. See *St. Louis Post-Dispatch,* October 7, 1917. *St. Louis Globe-Democrat,* October 15, 1917. *East St. Louis Daily Journal,* October 4, 1917.

50. *East St. Louis Daily Journal,* July 6, 1917. *St. Louis Republic,* August 14, 1917. *Belleville Daily Advocate,* August 14, 1917.

51. *East St. Louis Daily Journal,* July 5, 6, 7, and 8, 1917. See also *St. Louis Globe-Democrat,* July 6, 1917. *Belleville News-Democrat,* July 7, 1917. *St. Louis Republic,* July 3, 5, 7, 1917.

52. People v. Bundy, *op. cit.,* (pp. a. to e.).

53. "Congressional Hearings," p. 3873.

54. *Chicago Defender,* October 20, 1917. See also interview notes with Mr. James A. Gladden, April, 1962. East St. Louis Police Department Files, "Memorandum from Chief of Police Payne to Cleveland Chief of Police, July 7, 1917."

55. "Council of Defense Hearings," pp. 82–83.

56. *Ibid.,* pp. 68–83. See also "Congressional Hearings," pp. 2037, 2046–47, 4339.

57. The *Chicago Tribune* reported that many whites threatened to lynch him when he was arrested. (*Chicago Daily Tribune,* July 6, 1917.)

58. *St. Louis Globe-Democrat,* October 12 and 13, 1917. See also *St. Louis Post-Dispatch,* October 12, 1917. *St. Louis Republic,* October 5, 1917. *Chicago Defender,* August 25, October 20, 1917. *Cleveland Gazette,* August 25, 1917.

59. *St. Louis Post-Dispatch,* March 20, 1919.

60. *New York Age,* November 29, 1917. *Washington Bee,* December 1, 1917.

61. *Belleville Daily Advocate,* November 19, 1917. See also *St. Louis Republic,* November 20, 1917. *St. Louis Post-Dispatch,* March 29, 1919. *East St. Louis Daily Journal,* November 14, 1918.

62. "Minutes of the N.A.A.C.P. Board of Directors," June 10, 1918.

63. *Loc. cit.*

64. *Ibid.,* July 8, 1918.

65. *Ibid.,* September 9, 1918. See also *Crisis, XV* (1917–18), 62. *Crisis,* XVI (1918), 224–25. *Crisis,* XXV (1922–23), 16–21. *Chicago Defender,* October 27, November 3, 1917, and August 17, 1918. *Chicago Broadax,* November 3, 1917. *Cleveland Gazette,* November 10 and December 29, 1917.

66. *Chicago Defender,* July 20, 27, August 17, and November 2, 1918.

67. *Ibid.,* September, 14, 1918.

68. *Cleveland Gazette,* July 27, August 3, 17, 1918; April 5 and May 17, 1919.

69. *St. Louis Republic,* March 21, 1919.

70. The witness was a sister-in-law of the deceased detective, Frank Wadley, who spelled the family name differently.

71. People v. Bundy, *op. cit.,* pp. 229–46. See also *St. Louis Post-Dispatch,* March 21, 1919. *St. Louis Globe-Democrat,* March 22, 1919. *East St. Louis Daily Journal,* March 21, and 27, 1919.

72. People v. Bundy, *op. cit.,* (pp. 816–17).

73. *Ibid.,* pp. 162–88. See also *St. Louis Post-Dispatch,* March 21, 1919.

74. People v. Bundy, *op. cit.,* pp. 14–24. See also People v. Parker, *op. cit.,* (p. 46).

75. *St. Louis Globe-Democrat,* March 21, 1919.

76. People v. Bundy, *op. cit.,* (pp. 648–49, 825).

77. *East St. Louis Daily Journal,* June 3, 1917. See also *St. Louis Republic,* May 30, 1917.

78. People v. Bundy, *op. cit.,* (pp. 655–66).

79. *Ibid.,* p. 819.

80. *Ibid.,* pp. 648–53, 690–99, 713–28.

81. *Ibid.,* pp. 5–9.

82. *Ibid.,* pp. 303–7.

83. *Ibid.,* pp. 135–50.

84. *St. Louis Post-Dispatch,* March 21, 1919.

85. *Ibid.,* March 22 and 26, 1919.

86. People v. Bundy, *op. cit.,* pp. 252, 487, 589.

87. "Congressional Hearings," pp. 3545–46. See also *East St. Louis Daily Journal,* August 17, 1917. East St. Louis Police Department Files, "Memorandum from Sergeant Ely to Chief of Police Payne, July 1, 1917."

88. People v. Bundy, *op. cit.,* pp. 251–303.

89. *Ibid.,* pp. 436–40, 457–58.

90. People v. Parker, *op. cit.,* pp. 240, 249, 255.

91. People v. Bundy, *op. cit.,* p. 845.

92. *Ibid.,* pp. 32–61, 68–73.

93. *East St. Louis Daily Journal,* March 20, 1919. See also *St. Louis Globe-Democrat,* March 21, 1919. *St. Louis Post-Dispatch,* March 20, 1919.

94. At the 1917 trial, Mrs. Stapp had indeed sworn she observed the automobiles leaving Bundy's place. At the 1919 trial, however, vigorous cross-examination brought modifications of her original testimony. Despite this illustration (and others) of journalistic unfairness, there is no doubt that the coverage of the press was far more objective at Bundy's trial than in the Parker case.

95. People v. Bundy, *op. cit.,* pp. 567–78.

96. *St. Louis Globe-Democrat,* March 22, 1919.

97. People v. Bundy, *op. cit.,* pp. 395–435.

98. *Ibid.,* pp. 851, 857, 899–905.

99. *Ibid.,* pp. 883, 963–64.

100. *Ibid.,* pp. 732–45, 763–65, 793.

101. *Ibid.,* pp. 21, 764–65, 842.

102. *Ibid.,* pp. 1010–18.

103. *Ibid.,* pp. 1198–99.

104. *Ibid.,* pp. 205, 861–69.

105. *Ibid.,* p. 777.

106. *Chicago Defender,* April 5, 12, May 3 and 10, 1919. *St. Louis Argus,* April 4, 1919. *New York Age,* April 5, 1919. Although some N.A.A.C.P. board members disliked Bundy, they were also surprised by his conviction. As early as December of 1917, lawyer Arthur Springarn told the N.A.A.C.P. board that it was probable Bundy would be acquitted or the case even allowed to drop. ("Minutes of the N.A.A.C.P. Board of Directors," December 10, 1917).

107.   People v. Bundy, No. 13366, "Reports of Cases at Law and in Chancery Argued and Determined in Supreme Court of Illinois, Illinois Reports," CCVC (1921), 322–31. *Criminal Record, Monroe County,* XXX, October 8, 1921, 113. See also *East St. Louis Daily Journal,* December 22, 1920. *St. Louis Post-Dispatch,* December 22, 1920. *St. Louis Globe-Democrat,* December 22, 1920. *Belleville Daily Advocate,* December 21, 1920.

108.   After his victory, secured without help of the N.A.A.C.P., Bundy joined the black nationalist Garvey movement. Marcus Garvey, who was also at war with the Association, made the Negro dentist a "Knight Commander of the Distinguished Service Order of Ethiopia," and within a short time, Sir Le Roy Bundy became Garvey's "First Assistant." (W. E. B. Du Bois, "Le Roy Bundy," *Crisis,* XXV, 1922–23, 16–21. See also Rudwick, *W. E. B. Du Bois: A Study in Minority Group Leadership, op. cit.,* pp. 216–21).

109.   Grimshaw, *op. cit.,* p. 288.

Chapter Ten

1.   *St. Louis Globe-Democrat,* July 4, 1917.

2.   Reprinted in *Crisis,* XIV (1917), 305.

3.   *St. Louis Post-Dispatch,* July 7, 1917. See also *New York Times,* July 7, 1917. "Riots in East St. Louis," *Pan-American Magazine,* XXV (1917), 173–74.

4.   *Crisis,* XIV (1917), 164. *New York Age,* July 12, 1917.

5.   *New York Age,* July 12 and 19, 1917. *St. Louis Argus,* July 27, 1917.

6.   *Cleveland Gazette,* July 21, 1917.

7.   *Norfolk Journal and Guide,* July 21, 1917. *California Eagle,* July 21, 1917. See also Arthur S. Link, *The New Freedom* (Princeton: Princeton University Press, 1956), pp. 457–59.

8.   "Minutes of the N.A.A.C.P. Board of Directors," (September 17, 1917). See also *Norfolk Journal and Guide,* August 11, 1917. *New York Age,* July 26 and August 2, 1917. *St. Louis Argus,* August 10, 1917. *Cleveland Gazette,* August 18, 1917. *Chicago Defender,* July 28, 1917. *New York Times,* July 29, 1917. *Crisis,* XIV (1917), 241, 244.

9.   *New York Age,* August 9, 1917.

10.   *Norfolk Journal and Guide,* July 21 and August 18, 1917. See also Kelly Miller's open letter to Woodrow Wilson, August 4, 1917, reprinted in *Congressional Record,* Sixty-fifth Congress, LV (1917), 6990–93.

11.   "Congressional Hearings," p. 2639. See also letter from Charles Karch to Thomas W. Gregory, July 8, 1917, in unsigned memorandum to Gregory, July 20, 1917. (In United States Department of Justice files on East St. Louis riots, National Archives, Washington, D.C. Hereafter referred to as Department of Justice Files).

12.   *St. Louis Post-Dispatch,* July 8 and 10, 1917.

13.   Telegram from Citizens Committee of One Hundred to Congressman Rodenberg, July 19, 1917. See also following communications—Congressman Rodenberg to Thomas W. Gregory, July 20, 1917. Charles Karch to Gregory, July 6, 1917. Congressman Dyer to Woodrow Wilson, July 20, 1917, Department of Justice Files.

14.   Memorandum for Mr. Fitts from "Herron," July 20, 1917, Department of Justice Files.

15.   Charles Karch to Thomas W. Gregory, July 23, 1917, Department of Justice Files.

16.   *Belleville News-Democrat,* July 28, 1917.

17.   *New York Times,* July 17, 1917.

18.   See following communications, Woodrow Wilson to Thomas W. Gregory, July 23, 1917. Thomas W. Gregory to Woodrow Wilson, July 27, 1917. Thomas W. Gregory to Charles Karch, July 27, 1917, Department of Justice Files.

19.   Charles Karch to Thomas W. Gregory, July 23, 1917: Department of Justice Files.

20.   *New York Times,* August 4, 1917. See also *St. Louis Globe-Democrat,* August 4, 1917.

21.   The St. Louis Congressman did not want the public to be confused between his city and the Illinois community across the Mississippi River. Out of apparent seriousness and an undoubted desire for publicity, he asked East St. Louis to change its name. Postmaster-General Burleson was requested to take charge of the renaming rites. (*St. Louis Globe-Democrat,* July 12, 1917).

22.   H. J. Resolution #118, Sixty-fifth Congress, 1st Session, in House of Representatives, July 9, 1917. See also *St. Louis Post-Dispatch,* July 9, 1917. *St. Louis Globe-Democrat,* July 10, 1917.

23.   *Congressional Record,* LV (1917), 5150–51. See also *St. Louis Post-Dispatch,* July 15, 1917. *St. Louis Globe-Democrat,* July 17, 1917. *Cleveland Gazette,* July 21, 1917.

24.   The N.A.A.C.P. took the position that there were no legal barriers to a federal investigation because the race riots had interfered with the U.S. Mails. Furthermore, because Negro males fled East St. Louis after the violence, their registration under the conscription law was "confused and aborted." (*N.A.A.C.P. Branch Bulletin,* I, 1917, 57).

25.   *St. Louis Argus,* October 26, 1917.

26.   *New York Age,* July 19, 1917.

27.   House Resolution #128, Sixty-fifth Congress, 1st Session, 1917.

28.   "Congressional Hearings," pp. 64, 429–31.

29. *Ibid.,* p. 7.
30. *Ibid.,* pp. 19–20, 28–30.
31. *Ibid.,* p. 72
32. *Ibid.,* p. 129.
33. *Ibid.,* pp. 31, 105, 570.
34. Letter from Thomas W. Gregory to Congressman Ben Johnson, October 10, 1917, Department of Justice Files.
35. *East St. Louis Daily Journal,* November 19, 1917.
36. *St. Louis Globe-Democrat,* November 19, 1917.
37. *Belleville News-Democrat,* November 17, 1917. *East St. Louis Daily Journal,* November 20, 1917.

Chapter Eleven

1. "Congressional Hearings," pp. 4312–15. One week after the riot on July 2, a *Globe-Democrat* columnist recalled the May 28 gathering at City Hall, and charged that union leaders on that occasion had counseled "mob law." However, on May 29, the *Globe-Democrat* as well as other newspapers reporting the meeting mentioned nothing about incendiary speeches by labor leaders. (*St. Louis Globe-Democrat,* May 29, July 8, 1917. See also *St. Louis Post-Dispatch,* May 29, 1917. *East St. Louis Daily Journal,* May 29, 1917.)
2. "Congressional Hearings," pp. 282–83.
3. *Ibid.,* pp. 280, 417.
4. *Ibid.,* pp. 439, 2375.
5. *Ibid.,* p. 3154. In an historical study of the Chicago meat-packing industry, Clark examined the destruction of the Amalgamated Meatcutters and Butcher Workers Union of North America after an unsuccessful national strike in 1904—an event which had its parallel in East St. Louis. The author's comments on wages were also applicable to the East St. Louis stockyard workers during the period under discussion: "The period from 1904 to 1916 was marked by little union activity on the part of the union organizers. It was a period during which the employers were in absolute control. True to the general characteristics of such a situation it was marked by a gradual decrease in wages. During this entire period there were no wage increases, in fact, the wages of the common laborer actually decreased, although the cost of living increased about sixty percent." (Edna L. Clark, "History of the Controversy Between Labor And Capital In The Slaughtering And Meat Packing Industries In Chicago," [Master's thesis, University of Chicago, 1922] pp. 130, 139, 143).
6. "Congressional Hearings," p. 2374.
7. *Ibid.,* p. 435.
8. *Ibid.,* p. 2071.
9. *East St. Louis Daily Journal,* December 17, 1914.

10.   *Ibid.*, January 21, 1915. "Congressional Hearings," pp. 3177–78.

11.   Emmett J. Scott, *Negro Migration During the War*, (New York: 1920), p. 100.

12.   "Congressional Hearings," pp. 1913, 2078, 2374.

13.   *Ibid.*, pp. 2415–24.

14.   *Ibid.*, pp. 431, 436, 2433, 2448–49.

15.   *Ibid.*, pp. 2433, 3180–81.

16.   Spero and Harris, *op. cit.*, p. 406. This quotation appeared originally in *Proceedings of the Socialist Party Convention, 1919,* p. 45.

17.   *Ibid.*, pp. 104–6, 110–12. See also A. M. Dieckmann, "The Effect of Common Interests on Race Relations in Certain Northern Cities, (Master's thesis, Columbia University, 1923), pp. 38–41. *The Negro in Chicago, op. cit.,* p. 406. *East St. Louis Daily Journal,* October 21 and November 20, 1917. *St. Louis Post-Dispatch,* July 6, 1917. *St. Louis Globe-Democrat,* July 6, 1917. *Norfolk Journal and Guide,* September 29, 1917. *New York Age,* November 22, 1917 and May 4, 1918. Herbert Hill, "Labor Unions and the Negro," *Commentary,* XXVIII (1959), 479–88.

18.   W. E. B. Du Bois, *Darkwater* (New York: Harcourt, Brace, 1920), pp. 92–93.

19.   "Congressional Hearings," pp. 1187–88.

20.   *Ibid.*, p. 3153.

21.   *Ibid.*, p. 2373.

22.   *Ibid.*, pp. 2391–92. Some East St. Louis white laborers were not enthusiastic about going off to war—"Why don't they send these black curs to France instead of us fellows?" Concern about job security was rationalized in terms of the need to protect white women from Negroes. (*St. Louis Globe-Democrat,* July 3, 1917.)

23.   "Congressional Hearings," pp. 2434–35.

24.   *New York Age,* July 19, 1917. *St. Louis Argus,* June 1, 1917.

25.   "Congressional Hearings," pp. 3174, 4339.

26.   *St. Louis Post-Dispatch,* July 30, 1916.

27.   "Congressional Hearings," pp. 3153, 3187–93, 3358. See also *East St. Louis Daily Journal,* April 24, 1917.

28.   "Congressional Hearings," pp. 1901, 1911, 2011, 3195–96, 4339.

29.   *Ibid.*, pp. 1355–56, 2060–61, 2077.

30.   *St. Louis Republic,* July 4, 1917. See also "Congressional Hearings," p. 446.

31.   "Congressional Hearings," pp. 66, 73, 125, 715, 1048, 1829.

32.   *East St. Louis Daily Journal,* January 25 and December 12, 1916.

33. "Congressional Hearings," p. 1549.

34. *Ibid.,* pp. 1551, 1585, 1629, 1648.

35. *Ibid.,* pp. 1683–90.

36. *Ibid.,* pp. 1019, 1510, 1627, 3628.

37. *Ibid.,* p. 3611. See also "Council of Defense Hearings," pp. 91–92, 128–29.

38. "Congressional Hearings," pp. 3610–11.

39. *Ibid.,* p. 1544. See also "Council of Defense Hearings," p. 31.

40. Irwin Raut, "Report to Advisory Board, Industrial Branch, YMCA," April 18, 1917, *Y.M.C.A. Minute Book, 1915–18,* p. 45.

41. *Ibid.,* June 1, 1917, p. 47.

42. *Ibid.,* April 18, 1917, p. 45. Attached is *Survey on Conditions Among Colored People,* April, 1917.

43. "Congressional Hearings," pp. 1472–73, 1905, 3612–14. See also *St. Louis Post-Dispatch,* May 29 and October 28, 1917.

44. "Council of Defense Hearings," pp. 16–17.

45. *Ibid.,* pp. 28–31, 43. See "Congressional Hearings," pp. 1044, 1509–10.

46. "Congressional Hearings," pp. 1606, 1683.

47. "Council of Defense Hearings," pp. 14–20. See also "Minutes of the East St. Louis Chamber of Commerce," May 22 and June 15, 1917.

48. "Congressional Hearings," pp. 2061–63.

49. Department of Justice Files, From Major Cavanaugh, Commanding Officer, Detachment 6th Regiment, Illinois Infantry National Guard to Commanding General, Central Department, Chicago, July 26, 1917. From Flour Mills Company to Adjutant General Edward T. Donnelly, War Department, Washington, July 16, 1917. From "McCain" to Commanding General, Central Department, Chicago, July 21, 1917.

50. "Congressional Hearings," p. 2631. "Minutes of the East St. Louis Chamber of Commerce," October 24, 1917. See also *St. Louis Post-Dispatch,* August 15, 1917.

51. "Congressional Hearings," pp. 2672–73, 2687, 2718–20.

52. *House Document,* p. 8828.

53. East St. Louis Chamber of Commerce Files, "Letter from J. Lionberger Davis to East St. Louis Chamber of Commerce," December 18, 1917.

54. *Loc. cit.*

55. *East St. Louis Daily Journal,* July 4, 27, 1918; August 17, 1919.

56. *Ibid.,* June 24, 1919. See also "Proceedings of the East St. Louis City Council," (Meetings of June 23, 30, and July 7, 1919), pp. 687, 689, 693.

57. *East St. Louis Daily Journal,* December 30, 1920 and January 4, 1921. Some sources thought that the social service plan of the War Civics Committee was budgeted at $350,000. (Annual Report of the National Urban League, 1917–18, excerpt contained in a letter to the author from Mrs. Enid C. Baird, August 23, 1961.) For other material on the War Civics Committee in East St. Louis see Margaret Long, "Coordinating a Community," *Conference on Americanization Proceedings,* Washington, 1919, pp. 95–100. "Community Leadership," *Survey,* XLIII (February 14, 1920), 588. "East St. Louis," *Survey,* XLIV (August 16, 1920), 631–33.

58.   East St. Louis YMCA Files, "Letter from Irwin Raut to R. F. Rucker," January 17, 1917, in "Minutes of the Industrial Y.M.C.A.," pp. 36–37. See also pp. 40–41, for Annual Report of Raut to Industrial Branch Advisory Committee, February 1, 1917.

59.   *Ibid.,* p. 63 for Raut's report to advisory committee, September 9, 1918. See also p. 67 for Raut's report to advisory committee, December 1, 1918.

60.   East St. Louis YMCA Files, "Y.M.C.A. of East St. Louis, Report of 1923," mimeographed, pages not numbered.

61.   *East St. Louis YWCA Files.* Clipping from *Southern Illinois Press,* December 10, 1921, in "Interracial Volume, Y.W.C.A., 1921–43." Subsequently, colored women continued to be excluded from the white YWCA. As late as 1940, the YWCA's Board of Directors rejected an application for membership from the Mary Bethune Business and Professional Women's Club: ". . . it has been the policy of the local YWCA since its establishment nearly thirty years ago to maintain its building and facilities for the use not only of members but of all white women in the community. . . . Although the purpose of the Young Women's Christian Association is to build fellowship of women and girls regardless of race, religion, or political opinion, that purpose does not necessarily mean mutual participation of all groups under the same roof. . . . We as a Board of Directors deem it unwise to open our membership to negro women at this time. . . . We suggest . . . that you encourage members of your club to affiliate with the Phyllis Wheatley [Negro] branch in St. Louis. . . ." Within a few years following this exchange of letters, the East St. Louis YWCA opened its membership rolls to all without regard to race. (Letter from Beatrice Hunter to East St. Louis YWCA Board of Directors, May 23, 1940. Letter from President of "Y" to Beatrice Hunter, June 13, 1940. Interview with Mary T. Biggerstaff, October, 1962).

62.   Although the League died in East St. Louis, the race riot was the stimulus for the establishment of a branch in St. Louis, which served Negroes of that city. (Interviews with Leo Bohanon and Frank Campbell, February and June, 1962. See also "Minutes of the St. Louis Urban League," I, 1919–1925.)

Chapter Twelve

1. "Council of Defense Hearings," p. 20.
2. "Report of the Illinois State Council of Defense Labor Committee," June 30, 1917, p. 2.
3. "St. Clair County Grand Jury Report," pp. 333–39.
4. *House Document*, p. 8827.
5. The wildest estimate appeared in the *St. Louis Star*, July 3, 1917. According to this source, 40,000 Negroes and 45,000 whites lived in East St. Louis.
6. *New Orleans Times-Picayune*, April 27, 1917.
7. *St. Louis Post-Dispatch*, May 29, 1917.
8. "Military Board Hearings," p. 16.
9. "Council of Defense Hearings," p. 7.
10. "Congressional Hearings," p. 139.
11. Although F. A. Hunter told the Council of Defense that 2000 to 3000 Negroes migrated to East St. Louis during the year before the riot, he informed the Congressional Committee that there were 4000 additional Negro "heads of families" in 1917 compared to 1915. "Council of Defense Hearings," p. 88. "Congressional Hearings," pp. 91–92.
12. "Congressional Hearings," pp. 2057, 3150.
13. *Ibid.*, pp. 2045, 2058, 3120, 3136. "Council of Defense Hearings," p. 63. See also *St. Louis Star*, May 10, 1917. *St. Louis Post-Dispatch*, July 5, 1917. Victor Olander, Secretary of the Illinois Federation of Labor, estimated the migration at 6800 to 15,000 in addition to the 10,000 or more Negroes who lived in East St. Louis before 1917.
14. "Council of Defense Hearings," pp. 119–23. See also "Congressional Hearings," pp. 199–200, 234–36.
15. "Congressional Hearings," pp. 422–24.
16. *Ibid.*, p. 424.
17. *Ibid.*, pp. 68, 90, 134, 150, 437, 640, 690–91. See also "Council of Defense Hearings," pp. 88, 97.
18. "Congressional Hearings," p. 652.
19. R. H. Leavell, *op. cit.*, p. 7.
20. Thomas J. Woofter, Jr., *Negro Migration* (New York: W. D. Gray, 1920), p. 14. See also *St. Louis Star*, February 15, 1917. *St. Louis Times*, February 15, 1917. *St. Louis Argus*, March 9 and June 29, 1917.
21. No one has been able to discover how great this movement was in size. W. E. B. Du Bois thought that during 1916–17, a quarter of a million Negroes left the South, while the Urban League believed the number was closer to 350,000. Other figures ranged from 150,000 to 750,000. The Labor Department sponsored an investigation concluding that few reliable figures were available. Estimates were made on the basis of many sources, e.g.,

watching the railroad stations, guessing the number of train tickets Negroes purchased. The researcher who wrote the Mississippi report for the Department of Labor maintained that the data were so scanty that they had no scientific value; the Alabama researcher reported that his statistics possessed no scientific accuracy. (Henderson H. Donald, "The Negro Migration of 1916–1918," *Journal of Negro History*, VI [1921], 399–407. R. H. Leavell, *et al.*, *Negro Migration in 1916–17*, (Washington: U.S. Department of Labor, Division of Labor Economics, 1919) pp. 5, 15, 52, 97. W. E. B. Du Bois, "The Migration of Negroes," *Crisis*, XIV [1917], 63–66. See also Emmett J. Scott, *Negro Migration During the War*, [New York: Oxford University Press, 1920], Chicago Commission on Race Relations, *The Negro in Chicago*, [University of Chicago Press, 1922], p. 79).

22.   "Report of the Illinois State Council of Defense Labor Committee," June 30, 1917, p. 3. "Council of Defense Hearings," p. 129. See also *Cleveland Gazette*, July 7 and 14, 1917.

23.   "Congressional Hearings," p. 3202.

24.   Department of Justice Files, "Charles Karch to Thomas W. Gregory, July 23, 1917."

25.   *St. Louis Star*, May 10, 1917. See also "Congressional Hearings," p. 1476.

26.   "Congressional Hearings," pp. 1413, 1497, 3202.

27.   *Ibid.*, pp. 1115, 1117, 1757–65. "Council of Defense Hearings," pp. 72, 79–80. See also *Chicago Daily Tribune*, July 5, 1917.

28.   "Congressional Hearings," pp. 1876–78.

29.   *Ibid.*, pp. 1765–66.

30.   *Ibid.*, p. 1766.

31.   Nor did the Congressional Committee use the resources of the U.S. Census Bureau which in 1918 published two estimates of the East St. Louis population. However, the failure to consult these resulted in no loss. According to the Bureau's calculations, as of July 1, 1917, there had been 68,152 whites and 9,160 Negroes in the city, but this inaccurate information was an arithmetical projection based upon the 1900–10 population growth. The second Census estimate had been made at the request of the Provost Marshal General of the War Department solely for use as a basis for the apportionment for the forthcoming draft. It was based on the June 5, 1917 draft registration of men 21–30 years of age. According to the Census Bureau's national calculations, males in that age category constituted slightly more than 9 per cent of the total population. Since 9,011 persons registered in East St. Louis, the projected population for the city was given at 92,983, of whom about 24,500 would have been Negroes. However, East St. Louis as a highly industrial community attracted an over-average number of young men. Since that fact was not taken into account, the Census projection was inaccurate for

whites and particularly inaccurate for Negroes. (*Estimates of Population of the United States,* U.S. Department of Commerce, Bureau of the Census, Bulletin Number 138, 1918, p. 46. *United States Senate Documents,* XI, Sixty-fifth Congress, First Session, 1918, p. 13. See also communication from Fred W. Warriner, Jr. to the writer, May 11, 1962.)

32.   Jean D. Grambs, *Education in a Transition Community,* undated publication of the National Conference of Christians and Jews, pp. 91–97.

33.   Reports of the Superintendent of Schools inserted in "Minutes of the East St. Louis Board of Education" VIII: December 4, 1911, 206. April 1, 1912, 242. July 1, 1912, 272. October 7, 1912, 290. IX: February 3, 1913, 14. March 3, 1913, 22. April 7, 1913, 28. May 12, 1913, 44. June 2, 1913, 50. July 7, 1913, 56. October 6, 1913, 74. November 3, 1913, 85. December 1, 1913, 90. January 5, 1914, 97. February 2, 1914, 107. March 2, 1914, 114. April 6, 1914, 128. May 4, 1914, 143. June 1, 1914, 150. July 6, 1914, 159. October 5, 1914, 180. November 2, 1914, 186. December 7, 1914, 191. January 4, 1915, 202. February 1, 1915, 211. March 1, 1915, 219. April 5, 1915, 234. May 3, 1915, 253. June 7, 1915, 274. July 13, 1915, 285. X: October 4, 1915, 12. November 1, 1915, 20. December 6, 1915, 26. January 3, 1916, 30. February 7, 1916, 37. March 6, 1916, 44. April 3, 1916, 51. May 1, 1916, 63. June 5, 1916, 70. July 3, 1916, 84. October 2, 1916, 105. November 6, 1916, 113. December 4, 1916, 120. January 2, 1917, 126. February 5, 1917, 130. March 5, 1917, 134. April 2, 1917, 141. May 7, 1917, 153. June 4, 1917, 163. July 2, 1917, 172. October 1, 1917, 198. November 5, 1917, 205. December 3, 1917, 211. January 7, 1918, 219. February 4, 1918, 224. March 4, 1918, 228. April 1, 1918, 235. May 6, 1918, 249. June 3, 1918, 257. July 1, 1918, 268. XI: October 7, 1918, 15. November 4, 1918, 25. December 2, 1918, 32. January 6, 1919, 39. February 3, 1919, 44. March 3, 1919, 50. April 7, 1919, 58. May 4, 1919, 70. June 2, 1919, 81. July 7, 1919, 89. October 6, 1919, 108. November 3, 1919, 114. December 1, 1919, 119. January 5, 1920, 125. February 2, 1920, 131. March 1, 1920, 137. April 5, 1920, 146. May 3, 1920, 159. June 7, 1920, 167. July 6, 1920, 178.

34.   The arithmetical progression method of estimation involves several steps: 1) Divide the total Negro school population at the close of the 1909–10 school year by the 1910 U.S. Census enumeration of East St. Louis Negroes. 2) Follow the same procedure for the 1920 data. This results in two ratios of Negro school children to total Negro population. Since these ratios differ somewhat, an arithmetical interpolation is needed to get an estimate for 1917. 3) The assumption is that $7/10$ of the difference of ratio would have occurred by the seventh year following 1910.

$$\frac{(1910 \text{ Negro school population})}{(1910 \text{ total Negro population})} \quad \frac{1011}{5882} = .172$$

$$\frac{(1920 \text{ Negro school population})}{(1920 \text{ total Negro population})} \quad \frac{1515}{7437} = .204$$

Since the change in ratio of Negro school children to total Negro population between 1910 and 1920 was .032 (.204 — .172), the change for each year in the decade was .0032. Thus for 1916, the expected ratio was $6 \times .0032 + .172$ (which is the 1910 ratio) $= .1912$. At the close of the 1916 school year, there were 1575 Negro students.

$$\frac{1575}{.1912} = 8,237 \text{ (total Negro population estimate in East St. Louis, 1916)}$$

In 1917, the corresponding figures were:

$$\frac{2064}{.1944} = 10,617 \text{ (total Negro population estimate in East St. Louis, 1917)}$$

35.   *St. Louis Star,* May 10 and 29, 1917. See also *Chicago Daily Tribune,* July 10, 1917. *St. Louis Post-Dispatch,* December 10, 1916. Donald, *op. cit.,* p. 407.

36.   Henderson H. Donald, "The Urbanization of the American Negro," G. P. Murdock, Ed., *Studies in the Science of Society* (New Haven: Yale University Press, 1937), pp. 196–97. Lyonel C. Florant, "Negro Internal Migration," *American Sociological Review,* VII (1942), 787–88. T. Lynn Smith, *Fundamentals of Population Study* (Philadelphia: Lippincott Company, 1960), pp. 203–04, 483–86. Dorothy S. Thomas, *Research Memorandum on Migration Differentials,* Bulletin 43 (New York: Social Science Research Council, 1938), p. 11. C. A. McMahan, "Selectivity of Rural-to-Urban Migration," T. Lynn Smith and C. A. McMahan, Eds., *The Sociology of Urban Life* (New York: Dryden Press, 1951), p. 337. Homer L. Hitt, "Migration and Southern Cities," Smith and McMahan, *ibid.,* pp. 334–37.

37.   The writer gratefully acknowledges the generous co-operation of Mr. Fred W. Warriner, Jr., Acting Chief, Federal Records Center, East Point, Georgia. Mr. Warriner authorized his staff to make an age-race breakdown of the June 5, 1917 registration cards. Until now, the only published official source on 1917 East St. Louis registrants contained no information by race. (Communication from Fred W. Warriner, Jr. to the writer, May 11, 1962. See also, *United States Senate Documents,* XI, Sixty-fifth Congress, First Session, 1918, p. 13.)

38.   "Report of the Illinois State Council of Defense Labor Committee," June 30, 1917, p. 5.

39.   *House Document,* p. 8827.

40.   "Council of Defense Hearings," p. 14.
41.   *Ibid.,* pp. 20–26, 110–12.
42.   *Ibid.,* pp. 100–01.
43.   *Ibid.,* pp. 146, 152, 158, 163.
44.   *Ibid.,* pp. 137, 142, 150.
45.   "Congressional Hearings," pp. 692, 1015–16, 1025–26.
46.   *Belleville News-Democrat,* May 31, 1917.
47.   "Congressional Hearings," pp. 3248–78.
48.   *Ibid.,* pp. 3306–07.
49.   *Ibid.,* p. 3311.
50.   Spero and Harris, *op. cit.,* p. 162.
51.   "Council of Defense Hearings," pp. 121–22.
52.   *House Document,* p. 8827.
53.   After the Chicago Race Riot of 1919, the Commission on Race Relations made a "thorough investigation" of the importation rumors and found "no evidence of any value . . . to support them." (*The Negro in Chicago, op. cit.,* pp. 363–64, 577).
54.   Donald, *op. cit.,* pp. 410–11. Leavell, *op. cit.,* p. 11.
55.   John Hope Franklin, *op. cit.,* p. 464.
56.   Donald, *op. cit.,* pp. 399–400. See also *New York Times,* November 12, 1916.
57.   *Negro Population, 1790–1915* (Washington: U.S. Department of Commerce, 1918), p. 74.
58.   The 1920 census enumeration of 66,767 East St. Louisans demonstrated that for years residents had also been exaggerating the size of the white population as well as the Negro population. Local boosters fully expected the 1920 census to show a total of 80,000 to 90,000 residents. (*East St. Louis Daily Journal,* February 10 and May 26, 1920. See also *Report of the Illinois State Council of Defense Labor Committee,* June 30, 1917, p. 2. "Military Board Hearings," p. 629. "Congressional Hearings," p. 3543).
59.   "Congressional Hearings," p. 3179. See also pp. 2388–89. *St. Clair County Grand Jury Report, op. cit.,* pp. 333–39. *St. Louis Post-Dispatch,* May 29 and July 3, 1917. *East St. Louis Daily Journal,* May 4 and July 5, 1917. "East St. Louis Race Riots," *Literary Digest,* LV (1917), 10–11.
60.   "Council of Defense Hearings," pp. 27–28, 93–95, 102. "Congressional Hearings," 71, 1027, 1043. However, some representatives of industry maintained there was a scarcity of Negro labor shortly before the riots. See "Council of Defense Hearings," p. 186. "Military Board Hearings," p. 524. "Congressional Hearings," p. 1766.

Chapter Thirteen

1.   *St. Louis Times,* July 5, 1917. See also *East St. Louis Daily Journal,* July 8, 1917.

2.   St. Clair County Grand Jury Report, op. cit., pp. 333–39.

3.   Belleville Daily Advocate, December 5, 1917. See also *New York Age,* September 13, 1917. *East St. Louis Daily Journal,* November 19, 1917.

4.   St. Louis Post-Dispatch, July 3, 1917. *Chicago Daily Tribune,* July 4, 1917.

5.   East St. Louis Daily Journal, September 7, 1913 and April 11, 1915.

6.   East St. Louis Daily Journal, May 21, 1961.

7.   House Document, p. 8833.

*8.   For discussion of these cases see *East St. Louis Daily Journal,* November 27, 1916; March 30, 1917; December 4, 5, 28, 1917; July 21, December 26, 27, 1918; December 7, 1919. *St. Louis Post-Dispatch,* December 4, 1917. *Belleville Daily Advocate,* December 27, 1917.

9.   East St. Louis Daily Journal, August 21, 1912. See also *Journal,* August 25, 1912; April 3, June 20 and 22, 1913. "Proceedings of the East St. Louis City Council," (March 3 and August 18, 1913), pp. 155, 253.

10.   East St. Louis Daily Journal, April 3, 1914. According to the *Journal* of April 3, 1916, "for the first time in the history of the schools in East St. Louis," the school treasurer intended to turn over bank interest to the city.

11.   St. Louis Post-Dispatch, June 27 and 29, 1913. See also *East St. Louis Daily Journal,* June 27, July 1, and October 22, 1913. "Proceedings of the East St. Louis City Council," *op. cit.,* (June 30 and July 7, 1913), pp. 232–34.

12.   East St. Louis Daily Journal, October 22 and 23, 1913.

13.   Ibid., February 25 and June 23, 1913. "Proceedings of the East St. Louis City Council," *op. cit.,* (February 24, 1913), pp. 151–52.

14.   St. Louis Post-Dispatch, September 5, 1913. *East St. Louis Daily Journal,* September 5, 1913.

15.   East St. Louis Daily Journal, September 26, 1913. See also *Journal,* July 22, August 12, August 25, 1913. "Proceedings of the East St. Louis City Council," *op. cit.,* (August 18, 1913), p. 249.

16.   East St. Louis Daily Journal, July 22, 1913. See also *Journal,* July 15, 1913.

17.   Ibid., August 28, 1913.

18.   Loc. cit.

19.   Ibid., August 26 and 27, 1913.

20.   Ibid., March 5 and 22, 1914.

21.   Ibid., March 29, 1914.

22.   Ibid., December 7, 1913. See also *Journal,* March 26, 1915.

23.   Ibid., December 7, 1913.

24.   Ibid., November 9, 1913 and February 19, 1914.

25.   Of the $50,000, about $20,000 represented money which Gerold, upon leaving office in 1913, had attempted to transfer to his successor. The new treasurer, Frank Keating, demanded that Gerold indicate to which separate city accounts the funds should be applied. Since the latter was unable to comply, a stalemate resulted, and he was not permitted to return the $20,000 until his trial.

26.   *East St. Louis Daily Journal,* March 24 and 27, 1914.

27.   The Court also acted on technical grounds, e.g., the State's Attorney, in impounding several treasurer's account books, had erred in refusing to allow Gerold to examine them until the trial. (People v. Gerold, Reports of Cases at Law and in Chancery, Argued and Determined in Supreme Court of Illinois—Illinois Reports. [CCLXV, 1915, 448–86.] Interview with Fred Gerold, December 1962. For newspaper discussion of the case see *East St. Louis Daily Journal,* March 11, 15 to 29, 1914; April 28, 29, 1914; December 9, 17, and 20, 1914. *St. Louis Post-Dispatch,* December 17, 1914.)

28.   For newspaper discussion of proceedings see *East St. Louis Daily Journal,* February 2, 5, 8, 10, 11, 12, 14, 15, and 16, 1915. *St. Louis Post-Dispatch,* February 3, 10, 12, and 16, 1915.

29.   "Congressional Hearings," pp. 3539, 4349.

30.   *House Document,* p. 8829.

31.   "Congressional Hearings," p. 4565.

32.   *House Document,* pp. 8829–30.

33.   "Congressional Hearings," pp. 4439–40.

34.   *House Document,* p. 8830.

35.   "Congressional Hearings," pp. 3812–23, 4596–99.

36.   *House Document,* p. 8830.

37.   *Loc. cit.*

38.   *Loc. cit.*

39.   *East St. Louis Daily Journal,* July 5 and 6, 1917. See also *St. Louis Times,* July 5, 1917. *St. Louis Globe-Democrat,* October 20, 1917. "Congressional Hearings," p. 168.

40.   *East St. Louis Daily Journal,* March 22, 1915.

41.   *Ibid.,* February 28, March 23, and March 28, 1915.

42.   *Ibid.,* March 30, 1915. See also *Journal,* March 21, 22, 23, 24, 25, 31, April 1, 2, 4, and 7, 1915.

43.   *Ibid.,* November 26 and 27, 1917. See also *St. Louis Republic,* November 26, 1917. *St. Louis Post-Dispatch,* November 25, 1917. *St. Louis Globe-Democrat,* November 26 and 27, 1917.

44.   *St. Louis Post-Dispatch,* November 9, 1916. See also "Congressional Hearings," pp. 3836–37.

45.   *East St. Louis Daily Journal,* October 13, 1916.

46.   *Chicago Daily News,* October 17, 18, and 19, 1916. *East St. Louis Daily Journal,* October 19 and 20, 1916. See also *Chicago Herald,* October 18 and 19, 1916. *Chicago Evening Post,*

October 18, 1916. *Belleville Daily Advocate,* October 20, 1916. *St. Louis Republic,* October 18, 1916 and November 26, 1917.

47. *East St. Louis Daily Journal,* March 6, 30, and April 14, 1917.

48. *House Document,* p. 8830.

49. *East St. Louis Daily Journal,* March 23, 1917.

50. *Ibid.,* March 25, 1917.

51. The Chicago Commission on Race Relations, terming the East St. Louis epidemic of smallpox "imaginary," considered it simply as one of the many rumors or myths circulated in periods of racial tension. The present writer disagrees and accepts the outbreak as a fact. During January, 1917, the Department of Health was alerted when several Negro employees at the Swift and Armour meat packing plants were believed to have contracted smallpox. By the end of the month, the Deputy Health Commissioner ordered ten persons to the Pest House. In late February forty-one persons were in the county hospital with the disease. The *Journal* noted that "East St. Louis is experiencing one of the severest attacks of smallpox in its history." The Board of Education showed its concern by temporarily closing the largest white school in the city and more than 1500 pupils were ordered vaccinated. On March 22, more than forty persons were patients in the hospital and several weeks later there were "about twenty" at the institution.

Most of the published reports prior to that time did not list the race of the victims, but many, if not the majority, were whites. For example, on February 12, "there are now 25 persons suffering from the disease at the hospital. Thirteen of the patients are men; six being negroes." In March, the *Journal* noted several new cases which "were distributed in all parts of the city and the disease seems to be generally prevalent." However, about the time of the mayoralty election, and especially when the Aluminum Ore strike began a few weeks later, the epidemic was used in another propaganda effort to attack the Negro migrants. In April, the newspaper reported that "most cases in the contagion hospital seem to be among the negroes who came to the city within the last two months from the south." A week after the May race riot, readers were told that "practically all" the cases then at the hospital were colored migrants. The statement was obviously exaggerated and probably made to inflame the populace. Nevertheless, Negroes, sharing unhygienic living conditions, must have constituted a sizable portion of the smallpox victims. (Chicago Commission on Race Relations, *The Negro in Chicago, op. cit.,* p. 572. *East St. Louis Journal,* January 11, 14, 21, 23, February 2, 12, 20, 22, 26, March 6, 13, 14, 15, 22, April 23, May 3, 17, and June 5, 1917. *Belleville News-Democrat,* January 12, 20, May 8, 19, 25, 28, and 30. "Report of the Superintendent of Schools, to East St. Louis Board of Education," March 5, 1917 in "Minutes of the East St. Louis Board of Education," X, 1915–18, 134. ("Congressional Hearings," pp. 1870, 2045, 2393, 2400.)

52.   *East St. Louis Daily Journal,* March 28 and 29, 1917.

53.   *Chicago Broadax,* December 8, 1917. *St. Louis Argus,* November 30, 1917.

54.   *East St. Louis Daily Journal,* November 26, 1917. In view of the outcome of Bundy's trial, it is scarcely possible that any deals had been made in exchange for his confession of political fraud. Several months before the Bundy case was heard in court, the N.A.A.C.P. Board of Directors—keeping in touch with East St. Louis developments—had no evidence that the Negro dentist had made any sort of bargain with the Illinois Attorney General's office. ("Minutes of the N.A.A.C.P. Board of Directors," October 14, 1918.)

55.   *St. Louis Republic,* November 27 and 30, 1917. See also *East St. Louis Daily Journal,* November 27, 1917.

56.   *St. Louis Republic,* November 26, 1917.

57.   *Ibid.,* November 27, 1917.

58.   *Ibid.,* December 1, 2, and 3, 1917.

59.   *Ibid.,* November 18, 1917.

60.   *Ibid.,* December 14, 1917. See also *East St. Louis Daily Journal,* February 20, 1918.

61.   *St. Louis Republic,* December 22, 1917.

62.   *Ibid.,* December 25, 1917.

63.   *Belleville News-Democrat,* November 26, 27, and 28, 1917.

64.   *St. Louis Republic,* November 27 and December 1, 1917.

65.   *St. Louis Globe-Democrat,* November 27, 1917. See also *St. Louis Argus,* November 30, 1917.

66.   *St. Louis Post-Dispatch,* November 26, 1917. See also *Belleville Daily Advocate,* December 5, 1917, which asked Illinois Attorney General Brundage to make a full-scale inquiry into voting fraud.

67.   *East St. Louis Daily Journal,* November 27, 1917.

68.   *St. Louis Globe-Democrat,* November 27, 1917.

69.   "Board of Inquiry's Report upon the Conduct of Officers and Men, Illinois National Guard on Duty at East St. Louis, July 2, 1917," p. 2.

70.   "Military Board Hearings," p. 632.

71.   *Ibid.,* p. 629. See also "Congressional Hearings," p. 2813.

72.   "Congressional Hearings," pp. 2882, 2896–97, 3470–71.

73.   *Ibid.,* p. 3465.

74.   The value of these warrants, issued in the last months of a year, was limited by law to seventy percent of the anticipated revenue (collected in the first quarter of the following year). After East St. Louis floated all of the anticipation warrants allowable, "comptroller warrants" were printed. At the end of 1912, for example, $155,000 of these comptroller warrants had been issued, "making a total indebtedness much bigger than next year's revenue will be." (*St. Louis Post-Dispatch,* November 26, 1912.)

75. "Congressional Hearings," pp. 2957–60, 3460, 4423. See also *East St. Louis Daily Journal,* November 27, 1912; January 2, June 24, October 23, 1913; May 19, June 13, 1915.

76. "Congressional Hearings," p. 2778.

77. *Ibid.,* p. 1052.

78. *East St. Louis Daily Journal,* June 20 and 24, 1913.

79. "Congressional Hearings," pp. 2778, 2816.

80. *Ibid.,* p. 2816. See also "Military Board Hearings," p. 628.

81. After the race riot, Mr. Warning was convicted of embezzlement of county funds.

82. "Proceedings of the St. Clair County Board of Supervisors," XI (1915–17), 327–28.

83. "Congressional Hearings," p. 2790.

84. *Ibid.,* pp. 3798–99.

85. *Ibid.,* p. 2822. According to the U.S. Census, National City had 253 residents in 1910 and 426 in 1920.

86. *Ibid.,* pp. 457, 3806–7.

87. *East St. Louis Daily Journal,* October 25, 1914. The *Journal's* own editorial columns were sometimes enlisted in serving the corporations: "We hope that our Board of Assessment Review will be fair and just to our industries and manufactures, and not permit the imposition of malicious and exorbitant taxation to drive them away and prevent additional ones from coming here." (*East St. Louis Daily Journal,* August 3, 1915.)

88. *House Document,* p. 8831. See also "Congressional Hearings," pp. 4484–85.

89. "Congressional Hearings," p. 460.

90. *Ibid.,* pp. 364, 463, 2790–91.

91. *Ibid.,* pp. 2962, 2979.

92. *Ibid.,* pp. 729–730, 2778.

93. *Ibid.,* pp. 2891–92, 4261–64. See also *East St. Louis Daily Journal,* August 26, 1913.

94. "Military Board Hearings," p. 629. *East St. Louis Daily Journal,* November 22, 1916. In 1916 State's Attorney Charles Webb also complained about the low corporation assessments and his aggressive attempt to raise valuations was perhaps one more reason for his defeat in the fall election. (*East St. Louis Daily Journal,* July 25 and 26, 1916. *Belleville News-Democrat,* July 25, 1916.)

95. *East St. Louis Daily Journal,* December 27, 31, 1916 and May 18, 1917.

96. "Congressional Hearings," p. 2817.

97. "Proceedings of the St. Clair County Board of Supervisors," XII (1917–19), 467, 581. See also *Belleville Daily Advocate,* December 19, 1917. *East St. Louis Daily Journal,* December 18, 1917.

98. *St. Louis Globe-Democrat,* November 7, 1917. See also

Globe-Democrat, August 15, September 11, October 31, 1917. *St. Louis Post-Dispatch,* August 15, September 11, October 19, 23, 30, and November 2, 1917. *St. Louis Republic,* November 6 and 7, 1917. *East St. Louis Daily Journal,* November 1, 1917.

99. *St. Louis Republic,* November 7, 1917. See also *St. Louis Globe-Democrat,* November 7, 1917. *East St. Louis Daily Journal,* November 7, 1917.

100. *East St. Louis Daily Journal,* February 26, 1919. *St. Louis Argus,* February 28, 1919.

101. *East St. Louis Daily Journal,* December 1, 1920. "Proceedings of the East St. Louis City Council," (1919–1923), meeting of December 2, 1920, p. 203.

Chapter Fourteen

1. The Valley was an area with somewhat indefinite boundaries. Many East St. Louisans considered that the neighborhood extended for about one mile north from Railroad Avenue across Broadway to St. Clair Avenue, and along Second and Third Streets. In this section were the notorious Black and White Valleys. However, when other citizens referred to the Valley, they also seemed to have meant a broader geographical area in the South End of the city, and it was in this latter neighborhood where many burnings occurred on July 2.

2. "Congressional Hearings," p. 4118.

3. *St. Louis Star,* July 5, 6, and 7, 1911. See also *East St. Louis Daily Journal,* July 7, 1911.

4. *East St. Louis Daily Journal,* September 19, 1921 and May 21, 1961.

5. *St. Louis Star,* March 11 and 12, 1912.

6. *Ibid.,* July 5, 1911. See also *East St. Louis Daily Journal,* August 14 and 22, 1911; February 15, 1912; February 11, 1913. *East St. Louis Gazette,* April 1, 1911 and March 14, 1913.

7. *East St. Louis Gazette,* May 27, August 5, September 2, 23, November 25, December 2, 16 and 30, 1911; March 7, October 25, 1912. See also *East St. Louis Daily Journal,* December 5, 1911; February 13, 14, 15, October 27, November 25 and 26, 1912. *St. Louis Post-Dispatch,* October 27, 1912.

8. *East St. Louis Daily Journal,* February 13 and 14, 1912.

9. *Ibid.,* December 5, 1911. See also *East St. Louis Gazette,* December 9, 1911.

10. *East St. Louis Gazette,* March 20, 1912. See *East St. Louis Daily Journal,* October 19, 1911 for previous announcement.

11. *East St. Louis Daily Journal,* June 23, 1912.

12. *Ibid.,* December 30, 1912. See *Journal,* January 28, February 18, and December 31, 1912.

13. *Ibid.,* December 3, 1912; January 31 and February 2,

1913. *East St. Louis Gazette,* January 24 and February 14, 1913. *St. Louis Post-Dispatch,* November 29 and 30, 1912; January 19, 20, 21, 27 and 30, 1913.

14.   *East St. Louis Daily Journal,* January 19, February 10, 28, March 6, April 7, 13 and 17, 1913. *East St. Louis Gazette,* January 24 and February 14, 1913. Earlier a police commissioner was indicted for gambling. (See *Journal,* January 11, 19, and February 16, 1911.)

15.   *East St. Louis Daily Journal,* April 7, 1913.

16.   *Ibid.,* August 4, 1913. See *Journal,* July 3, August 3, 6, 11, and December 2, 1913.

17.   *Ibid.,* December 20, 1914; January 22, 1915; May 21, 1961.

18.   *Ibid.,* August 18, 1914.

19.   Lucrative rents were also obtained from saloonkeepers. See "Congressional Hearings," pp. 2736, 3279–80, 3533–42. *East St. Louis Daily Journal,* January 29, 1914; March 22, 1915. *St. Louis Globe-Democrat,* July 7, 1917. *St. Louis Post-Dispatch,* October 24, 1917.

20.   "Congressional Hearings," pp. 3569–74, 3603, 3607.

21.   *Ibid.,* pp. 3516, 3519, 3524. See also *East St. Louis Daily Journal,* August 2, September 28, October 23, 29, November 1, 15, 1915; January 3, 5, 11, 24, and May 31, 1916.

22.   *East St. Louis Daily Journal,* November 19, 1915.

23.   *Ibid.,* January 6, 1916.

24.   *Ibid.,* June 18, 1916.

25.   *Ibid.,* January 6, February 9, June 27 and 28, 1916.

26.   "Congressional Hearings," pp. 3500, 3835–36. *St. Louis Post-Dispatch,* August 1, 1916.

27.   "Congressional Hearings," pp. 296–97, 318.

28.   *East St. Louis Daily Journal,* September 9, 1915.

29.   *Ibid.,* September 3, 1916. See also *Journal,* June 2, July 30, September 22, 28, October 24, 1915; August 6, 1916. *Belleville News-Democrat,* January 24, 1917.

30.   *House Document,* p. 8830.

31.   "Congressional Hearings," p. 369.

32.   *Ibid.,* pp. 4282–83. See also *East St. Louis Daily Journal,* July 2 and 9, 1915.

33.   *East St. Louis Daily Journal,* April 18, 1917.

34.   "Congressional Hearings," pp. 3451, 3841.

35.   *East St. Louis Daily Journal,* October 26, 1915 and September 3, 1916.

36.   "Congressional Hearings," pp. 321, 3443, 3849–55. See also *Chicago Defender,* October 27, 1917. *East St. Louis Daily Journal,* June 13, 22, 29, July 7, 1915; August 17, 1916.

37.   *House Document,* p. 8832.

38.   "Congressional Hearings," pp. 3556–57.

39.   *Ibid.,* pp. 3424–28, 3522–23.

40.   *House Document,* p. 8832. See also *East St. Louis Daily Journal,* July 20, 1915; June 6, 1916; January 21, February 11, 13 and 16, 1917. *Belleville Daily Advocate,* October 3, 1916.

41.   "Congressional Hearings," p. 3519.

42.   *House Document,* p. 8832. *East St. Louis Daily Journal,* July 1, October 2, 1913; May 21, 1961. For situation in county see "Proceedings of the St. Clair County Board of Supervisors," XI, *op. cit.,* 393.

43.   *House Document,* p. 8833.

44.   *East St. Louis Daily Journal,* October 15, 1915. See also *Journal,* October 17, 18, 20, 26, 1915; August 17 and September 3, 1916.

45.   *St. Louis Times,* January 4 and 6, 1917.

46.   *East St. Louis Daily Journal,* June 14, 1914. See also *Journal,* May 12 and June 2, 1914.

47.   *Ibid.,* October 30, 1913.

48.   *Ibid.,* January 4 and December 1, 1916. See also *Journal,* July 29, December 3, 7, 8, 12, 13 and 19, 1915; January 14 and 24, 1916.

49.   *Ibid.,* December 1 and 5, 1916.

50.   "Congressional Hearings," p. 3512.

51.   *Belleville News-Democrat,* January 4, 1917. *East St. Louis Daily Journal,* December 29, 1916.

52.   *East St. Louis Daily Journal,* January 3, 1917. See also *Journal,* December 31, 1916; January 3, 4, 10, 11, 14, 15, 16, 23, 30, and February 11, 1917.

53.   *Belleville News-Democrat,* May 26, 1917. See *News-Democrat,* January 4, 1917. *East St. Louis Daily Journal,* January 30, 1917.

54.   *East St. Louis Daily Journal,* December 31, 1916.

55.   "Congressional Hearings," p. 3529. See also *East St. Louis Daily Journal,* March 26, 1917.

56.   *East St. Louis Daily Journal,* February 15, 1917.

57.   "Congressional Hearings," p. 4065.

58.   *East St. Louis Daily Journal,* February 15, 1917.

59.   *Ibid.,* February 15, 18, 22, 26, March 26, and April 2, 1917.

60.   *Ibid.,* March 5, 1917. See also *Journal,* March 26, April 1 and 2, 1917.

61.   "Congressional Hearings," p. 4074.

62.   As previously indicated, Allison was aggressively interested in social welfare projects which would improve the living conditions of factory workers. In that respect he seemed unlike many East St. Louis ministers who generally ignored political and especially economic problems in the community and saw vice as the only devil. In their sermons the Valley was regularly discussed: "I expect to see the day when . . . the Valley will be a park filled with trees and blooming flowers. . . ." Allison did a great deal to combat vice but his view of social reform encompassed other problems as well. (*East St. Louis Daily Journal*, February 5, 1913. *Belleville News-Democrat*, July 5, 1917.)

63. "Congressional Hearings," pp. 3500–9, 3515. See also *House Document*, pp. 8831–32.

64. *East St. Louis Daily Journal*, April 9, 1917.

65. "Congressional Hearings," pp. 3717–18.

66. *East St. Louis Daily Journal*, May 21 and 27, 1917.

67. "Congressional Hearings," pp. 3518–19, 3524.

68. *Ibid.*, p. 3548.

69. *St. Louis Post-Dispatch*, October 28, 1917. *St. Louis Republic*, November 10, 1917.

70. "Congressional Hearings," p. 3549.

71. *Ibid.*, p. 4075.

72. *Ibid.*, pp. 1434, 1467.

73. *Ibid.*, pp. 3509–12, 3527–30.

74. *Ibid.*, p. 3530.

75. *Ibid.*, pp. 4075, 4078.

76. *Belleville Daily Advocate*, June 29, 1917. *East St. Louis Daily Journal*, June 29, 1917.

77. "St. Clair County Grand Jury Report," *op. cit.*, pp. 333–39.

78. *House Document*, p. 8830. See also *East St. Louis Daily Journal*, November 21 and 23, 1916; January 17 and April 2, 1917. *St. Louis Star*, April 24 and 30, 1917.

79. For discussion of "lid-tilting" in the vicinity of East St. Louis see *St. Louis Times*, May 4, 1917. *St. Louis Star*, May 5, 9, 10, 12, 21, 28, 30, and June 11, 1917. *East St. Louis Daily Journal*, May 4, 8, 9, 10, 11, 13, 15, 21, 28, 31, June 3, 11, 15, 17, 18, 20 and 28, 1917.

80. "Congressional Hearings," pp. 3582, 3991–4003, 4145–47, 4151–85. See also *St. Louis Star*, April 24, 30, and May 5, 1917. *St. Louis Republic*, October 22, 1916.

81. *St. Louis Star*, March 13, 1917.

82. "Congressional Hearings," pp. 4140–43, 4149, 4412–20. See also *St. Louis Star*, March 12, 13, 14, 26, April 5, 10, May 5, and May 10, 1917.

83. *House Document*, p. 8830.

84. "Congressional Hearings," pp. 3102, 3183. See also *East St. Louis Daily Journal*, July 5, 6, October 8 and 23, 1917. *Chicago Daily Tribune*, July 5, 1917. *St. Louis Times*, July 5, 1917.

85. "Congressional Hearings," pp. 2095, 3183, 3432, 3550–52, 3873.

86. *House Document*, p. 8832.

87. *The Negro in Chicago*, *op. cit.*, pp. 328–29.

88. "Congressional Hearings," p. 3525.

89. *East St. Louis Daily Journal*, November 27, December 10,

1916; October 23, 1917. *Belleville News-Democrat,* January 3 and May 14, 1917. See also Letter from Department of Justice Files, "Charles Karch to Thomas W. Gregory, July 23, 1917."
90.   "Congressional Hearings," p. 3121. The Congressional Investigating Committee erred in accepting the statement as a fact. See *House Document,* p. 8832. For other comments of labor leaders who were the most vocal in accusing migrants of lawbreaking, see "Congressional Hearings," pp. 1867, 1988–89, 2123, 2505, 3150, 3181. *St. Louis Post-Dispatch,* July 3, November 1 and 2, 1917. Spero and Harris, *op. cit.,* p. 162.
91.   "Board of Inquiry Report upon the Conduct of Officers and Men, Illinois National Guard on Duty at East St. Louis, July 2, 1917," p. 5.
92.   "Military Board Hearings," p. 21.

Chapter Fifteen

1.   Alfred M. Lee and Norman D. Humphrey, *Race Riot* (New York: Dryden Press, 1943), p. 117. Allen D. Grimshaw, "A Study in Social Violence: Urban Race Riots in the U.S.," (Doctoral dissertation, University of Pennsylvania, 1959, pp. 83, 292).
2.   Grimshaw, *op. cit.,* p. 175. See also Alma Herbst, *The Negro in the Slaughtering and Meat-Packing Industry in Chicago* (Boston: Houghton Mifflin, 1932), p. 24. Chicago Commission on Race Relations, *The Negro in Chicago* (Chicago: University of Chicago Press, 1922), pp. 2, 404. Lee and Humphrey, *op. cit.,* pp. 25, 90.
3.   Lee and Humphrey, *op. cit.,* pp. 92–94. Chicago Commission on Race Relations, *op. cit.,* p. 596.
4.   Chicago Commission on Race Relations, *op. cit.,* pp. 271–95. Grimshaw, *op. cit.,* p. 170.
5.   Chicago Commission on Race Relations, *op. cit.,* pp. 301–8. Grimshaw, *op. cit.,* pp. 88–90.
6.   Chicago Commission on Race Relations, *op. cit.,* p. 3. See also St. Clair Drake and Horace Cayton, *Black Metropolis* (New York: Harcourt, Brace, 1945), pp. 69, 110.
7.   Drake and Cayton, *op. cit.,* pp. 110, 294–95.
8.   *Ibid.,* pp. 362–63. Chicago Commission on Race Relations, *op. cit.,* pp. 342–44.
9.   Grimshaw, *op. cit.,* p. 21. Lee and Humphrey, *op. cit.,* pp. 102–3.
10.   Chicago Commission on Race Relations, *op. cit.,* pp. 3, 288–95, 595–96.
11.   Gunnar Myrdal, *An American Dilemma* (New York: Harper and Bros., 1944), p. 568. See also Lee and Humphrey, *op. cit.,* pp. 25, 90, 111. Grimshaw, *op. cit.,* p. 170.
12.   Lee and Humphrey, *op. cit.,* p. 111.

13.   Alfred M. Lee, *Race Riots Aren't Necessary,* Public Affairs Pamphlet, No. 107, n. p., n. d., p. 8.

14.   Grimshaw, *op. cit.,* p. 161.

15.   Chicago Commission on Race Relations, *op. cit.,* pp. 4–5, 596.

16.   Lee and Humphrey, *op. cit.,* pp. 21, 27–28. Grimshaw, *op. cit.,* p. 170

17.   S. H. Britt, *Social Psychology of Modern Life* (New York: Rinehart, 1949), pp. 184–87.

18.   Grimshaw, *op. cit.,* pp. 114–15.

19.   Chicago Commission on Race Relations, *op. cit.,* pp. 363, 577.

20.   *Ibid.,* p. 29. Alfred M. Lee, *op. cit.,* p. 8.

21.   Lee and Humphrey, *op. cit.,* p. 38.

22.   Chicago Commission on Race Relations, *op. cit.,* pp. 571, 576.

23.   *Ibid.,* pp. 29–31. Lee and Humphrey, *op. cit.,* p. 27.

24.   Lee and Humphrey, *op. cit.,* p. 32.

25.   *Ibid.,* pp. 26–27, 102–3. Chicago Commission on Race Relations, *op. cit.,* pp. 11, 22–24. Grimshaw, *op. cit.,* pp. 186–88.

26.   Grimshaw, *op. cit.,* pp. 272–73. Chicago Commission on Race Relations, *op. cit.,* pp. 6–7, Lee and Humphrey, *op. cit.,* pp. 36–37.

27.   Chicago Commission on Race Relations, *op. cit.,* p. 6. Lee and Humphrey, *op. cit.,* pp. 28, 33–34. Grimshaw, pp. 195–200, 217.

28.   Chicago Commission on Race Relations, *op. cit.,* pp. 8–12, 601. Lee and Humphrey, *op. cit.,* pp. 28–33, 39. Grimshaw, *op. cit.,* p. 212.

29.   Grimshaw, *op. cit.,* pp. 222–24.

30.   *Ibid.,* pp. 223–24, 288. Chicago Commission on Race Relations, *op. cit.,* pp. 35–36.

31.   Chicago Commission on Race Relations, *op. cit.,* p. 39. Lee and Humphrey, *op. cit.,* pp. 32–33, 39, 76–78.

32.   Lee and Humphrey, *op. cit.,* pp. 40–41, 84. Grimshaw, *op. cit.,* pp. 222–23.

33.   Lee and Humphrey, *op. cit.,* p. 115. Chicago Commission on Race Relations, *op. cit.,* p. 34.

34.   Chicago Commission on Race Relations, *op. cit.,* p. 278.

35.   Myrdal, *op. cit.,* p. 568. Lee and Humphrey, *op cit.,* p. 74.

36.   Grimshaw, *op. cit.,* pp. 83, 292.

37.   Chicago Commission on Race Relations, *op. cit.,* p. 40.

38.   Lee and Humphrey, *op. cit.,* pp. 29–30, 35–36, 42–43, 78. Grimshaw, *op. cit.,* pp. 286–87.

39.   Chicago Commission on Race Relations, *op. cit.,* pp. 48, 600. Grimshaw, *op. cit.,* p. 372.

40.   Grimshaw, *op. cit.,* p. 315.

41.   Chicago Commission on Race Relations, *op. cit.,* p. 46.

42.   *Detroit Hearings Before the United States Commission on Civil Rights,* Washington, 1961, p. 26. See also Chicago Commission on Race Relations, *op. cit.,* pp. xix, 48, 600. Lee and Humphrey, *op. cit.,* pp. 51–52. Grimshaw, *op. cit.,* pp. 293–305.

43.   Lee and Humphrey, *op. cit.,* pp. 64–65, 68–69. Grimshaw, *op. cit.,* pp. 301–4.

44.   The Congressional Committee's 24 page report, "Report of the Special Committee Authorized by Congress to Investigate the East St. Louis Riots," was published in 1918 as *House Document* No. 1231. It was also read into the *Congressional Record* on July 6, 1918. Supposedly because of economy, the full testimony of the hearings was never printed; apparently only one copy of the transcript presently exists and it is on file at the National Archives. In the House of Representatives, Congressman L. C. Dyer of Missouri was the leading voice favoring the publication of the full testimony. Since he considered the riot so important, he objected to the printing of only a brief report about it. In a letter to the N.A.A.C.P. he complained that the Riot Investigating Committee's Chairman, Rep. Ben Johnson, and the Democrats of the House were satisfied with the publication of only a relatively short summary of the riot's background. (For a discussion of the House debate on the printing of the report see *Congressional Record,* LVI [1918], 1653–55. See also Minutes of the Board of Directors of the N.A.A.C.P., March 11, 1918.)

45.   Grimshaw, *op. cit.,* p. 299.

46.   *Ibid.,* pp. 293, 317–18.

47.   Letter from East St. Louis YWCA General Secretary to Esther M. Clark, October 2, 1937, in "Interracial Volume, 1921–43," YWCA files.

48.   Myrdal, *op. cit.,* pp. 568–69.

I. *Books and Articles*

Anderson, Sherwood. "Nobody's Home," *Today,* (March 30, 1935), pp. 6–7, 20–21.

Angle, Paul. *Bloody Williamson,* New York: 1952.

Baldwin, Roger. "East St. Louis—Why?" *Survey,* XXXVIII (August 18, 1917), 447–48.

Bontemps, Arna and Jack Conroy. *They Seek a City,* New York: 1945.

Britt, S. H. *Social Psychology of Modern Life,* New York: 1949.

Budenz, Louis F. "The East St. Louis Riots," *National Municipal Review,* VI (September, 1917), 622.

Chicago Commission on Race Relations. *The Negro in Chicago,* Chicago: 1922.

Clark, Edna L. "History of the Controversy Between Labor and Capital in the Slaughtering and Meat Packing Industries in Chicago." Unpublished Master's thesis, University of Chicago, 1922.

"Community Leadership," *Survey,* XLIII (February 14, 1920), 588.

Cooper, Lindsay. "The Congressional Investigation of the East St. Louis Riots," *Crisis,* XV (January, 1918), 116–21.

Crouthamel, James L. "The Springfield Race Riot of 1908," *Journal of Negro History,* XLV (1960), 164–81.

Davie, Maurice R. *Negroes in American Society,* New York: 1949.

Dieckmann, A. M. "The Effect of Common Interests on Race Relations in Certain Northern Cities." Master's thesis, Columbia University, 1923.

Diehm, Margaret G. *Through the Years,* St. Louis: 1944.

Donald, Henderson H. "The Negro Migration of 1916–1918," *Journal of Negro History,* VI (1921), 383–498.

———. "The Urbanization of the American Negro," in *Studies in the Science of Society,* ed. G. P. Murdock, New Haven: 1937, pp. 181–99.

Drake, St. Clair and Horace Cayton. *Black Metropolis,* New York: 1945.

Du Bois, W. E. B. "The Migration of Negroes," *Crisis,* XIV (1917), 63–66.

———— and Martha Gruening. "The Massacre of East St. Louis," *Crisis,* XIV (1917), 219–38.

————. *Darkwater,* New York: 1920.

————. "Le Roy Bundy," *Crisis,* XXV (1922–23), 16–21.

"East St. Louis," *Survey,* XLIV (August 16, 1920), 631–33.

"East St. Louis Race Riots," *Literary Digest,* LV (1917), 10–11.

Fauset, Jessie. "A Negro on East St. Louis," *Survey,* XXXVIII (August 18, 1917), 448.

Fifty Golden Years: The Story of a City and a Business, St. Louis: 1944.

Florant, Lyonel C. "Negro Internal Migration," *American Sociological Review,* VII (1942), 782–91.

Franklin, John H. *From Slavery to Freedom,* 2nd ed. New York: 1956.

Frazier, E. Franklin. *The Negro in the United States,* New York: 1951.

Grambs, Jean D. *Education in a Transition Community,* n. p., n. d.

Grimshaw, Allen D. "A Study in Social Violence: Urban Race Riots in the U.S.," Unpublished Ph.D. dissertation, University of Pennsylvania, 1959.

Haynes, George E. "Conditions among Negroes in the Cities," *Annals of the American Academy of Political and Social Science,* LIX (1913), 105–19.

Herbst, Alma. *The Negro in the Slaughtering and Meat-Packing Industry in Chicago,* Boston: 1932.

Hill, Herbert. "Labor Unions and the Negro," *Commentary,* XXVIII (1959), 479–88.

Hitt, Homer L. "Migration and Southern Cities," in *The Sociology of Urban Life,* eds. T. Lynn Smith and C. A. McMahan, New York: 1951, pp. 319–34.

Illinois Attorney General's Report, 1917–1918, Springfield: 1918.

"Illinois Race War and Its Brutal Aftermath," *Current Opinion,* LXIII (1917), 75–77.

Illustrated Art Souvenir of East St. Louis, Chicago: 1900.

Jenison, M. E. *The Wartime Organization of Illinois,* Springfield: 1923.

————. (ed.). *War Documents and Addresses,* Springfield: 1923.

Jones, Thomas J. "Negro Population in the United States," *Annals of the American Academy of Political and Social Science,* LIX (1913), 1–9.

Kirschten, Ernest. *Catfish and Crystal,* New York: 1960.

Lee, Alfred M. and Norman D. Humphrey. *Race Riot,* New York: 1943.

Lee, Alfred M. *Race Riots Aren't Necessary*, Public Affairs Pamphlet No. 107, n. p., n. d.

Leonard, Oscar, "The East St. Louis Pogrom," *Survey*, XXXVIII (July 14, 1917), 331–33.

Lewis, Edward E. *The Mobility of the Negro*, New York: 1931.

Link, Arthur S. *The New Freedom*, Princeton: 1956.

Long, Margaret. "Coordinating a Community," *Conference on Americanization Proceedings*, Washington: 1919.

McMahan, C. A. "Selectivity of Rural-to-Urban Migration," *The Sociology of Urban Life*, T. Lynn Smith and C. A. McMahan (eds.) New York, 1951, pp. 334–40.

Myrdal, Gunnar. *An American Dilemma*, New York: 1944.

NAACP Eighth and Ninth Annual Reports, New York: 1919.

Ovington, Mary White. *How the National Association for the Advancement of Colored People Began*, New York: 1914.

Owen, Chandler and A. Philip Randolph. "The Cause and Remedy for Race Riots," *Messenger*, (September, 1919), pp. 14–17.

"Riots in East St. Louis," *Pan American Magazine*, XXV (August, 1917), 173–74.

Ross, Frank A. and Louise V. Kennedy. *A Bibliography of Negro Migration*, New York: 1934.

Rudwick, Elliott M. *W. E. B. Du Bois: A Study of Minority Group Leadership*, Philadelphia: 1960.

Schwendemann, Glen. "St. Louis and the 'Exodusters' of 1879," *Journal of Negro History*, LIV (1961), 32–46.

Scott, Emmett J. *Negro Migration During the War*, New York: 1920.

"Senate Report on the Exodus of 1879," *Journal of Negro History*, IV (1919), 57–92.

Smith, T. Lynn. *Fundamentals of Population Study*, Philadelphia: 1960.

Spero, Sterling and Abram Harris. *The Black Worker*, New York: 1931.

Thomas, Dorothy S. *Research Memorandum on Migration Differentials*, New York: 1938.

Thornthwaite, C. Warren. *Internal Migration in the United States*, Philadelphia: 1934.

Turner, Lucy Mae. *History of Lincoln High School*, unpublished ms., 1962.

Tyson, Robert A. *History of East St. Louis*, East St. Louis: 1875.

"What Some Americans Think of East St. Louis," *Outlook*, CXVI (July 18, 1917), 435–36.

Woofter, Thomas J., Jr. *Negro Migration*, New York: 1920.

YMCA of East St. Louis Report of 1923, unpublished ms., n. d.

II. *Newspapers and Periodicals*

American Industry in War Time, I, 1917.
Belleville Daily Advocate, 1915–18.
Belleville News-Democrat, 1915–18, 1935–36.
California Eagle, 1916–17.
Chicago Broadax, 1915–19.
Chicago Daily News, 1916–17.
Chicago Daily Tribune, 1916–17.
Chicago Defender, 1915–19.
Chicago Evening Post, 1916.
Chicago Herald, 1916–17.
Cleveland Gazette, 1915–19.
Crisis, XIV, XV, XVI, 1917–18.
East St. Louis Gazette, 1910–13.
East St. Louis Daily Journal, 1900–21, 1924, 1949, 1961.
Messenger, 1917–20.
N.A.A.C.P. Branch Bulletin, I, 1917.
New Orleans Times-Picayune, 1917.
New York Age, 1915–19.
New York Times, 1916–18.
Norfolk Journal and Guide, 1916–19.
St. Louis Argus, 1915–19.
St. Louis Globe-Democrat, 1915–19.
St. Louis Post-Dispatch, 1911–19.
St. Louis Republic, 1915–19.
St. Louis Star, 1911–12, 1917–19.
St. Louis Times, 1917–19.
Tampa Morning Tribune, 1917.
Washington Bee, 1915–19.

III. *United States Government Publications*

Congressional Record. First Session, Sixty-fifth Congress, LV, Washington, 1917.
————. Second Session, Sixty-fifth Congress, LVI, Washington, 1918.
United States Bureau of the Census. *Thirteenth Census of the United States,* II, Washington, 1910.
————. *Estimates of Population of the United States,* Washington, 1918.
————. *Negro Population, 1790–1915,* Washington, 1918.
————. *Fourteenth Census of the United States,* III, Washington, 1920.
United States Commission on Civil Rights. *Detroit Hearings Be-*

fore the *United States Commission on Civil Rights,* Washington, 1961.

United States Department of Labor. *Negro Migration in 1916–1917,* Washington, 1919.

United States House of Representatives. "Report of the Special Committee Authorized by Congress to Investigate the East St. Louis Riots," *House Documents,* CXIV, Document No. 1231, (Sixty-fifth Congress, 1918). Also reprinted in *Congressional Record,* Second Session, Sixty-fifth Congress, LVI, Washington, 1918, pp. 8826–34.

United States Senate. *United States Senate Documents,* First Session, (Sixty-fifth Congress), XI, Washington, 1918.

IV. *Unpublished Minutes*

"East St. Louis Board of Education," 1909–21.
"East St. Louis Chamber of Commerce," 1917–18.
"East St. Louis City Council," 1912–20.
"East St. Louis Industrial YMCA," 1915–18.
"East St. Louis YWCA," 1915–18.
"N.A.A.C.P. (New York City)," 1917–18.
"St. Clair County Board of Supervisors," 1915–19.
"St. Louis Urban League," 1919–25.

V. *Investigations*

"Hearings Before Illinois State Council of Defense Labor Committee," unpublished volume, June, 1917. (This is the investigation of the May, 1917 riots. The only copy of this transcript that the writer found is now in the National Archives, Washington, D. C.)

Report of the Labor Committee, Illinois State Council of Defense, 1917. (This report was based on the hearings and published June 30, 1917. A copy is on file at the National Archives.)

"Proceedings Before the Board of Inquiry," two unpublished volumes, July, 1917. (This is the inquiry into the conduct of the Illinois guardsmen. The transcript is on file at the National Archives.)

"Report Upon The Conduct Of Officers And Men, Illinois National Guard on Duty At East St. Louis July 2, 1917." (This report, dated August 2, 1917, was submitted by the Board of Inquiry to the Adjutant General of the Illinois

National Guard. A copy is on file at the National Archives.)

"St. Clair County Grand Jury Report," in *Circuit Court Record, Criminal*, April Term, 1917, pp. 333–39. (This brief report was made several weeks after the July riot, and was based on the grand jury investigation. This record was found at the St. Clair County Courthouse, Belleville, Illinois; unfortunately, the writer could not find the transcript of testimony presented by the witnesses.)

"Select Committee to Investigate Conditions in Illinois and Missouri Interfering with Interstate Commerce between these States," 23 unpublished volumes, October-November, 1917. (This transcript is in the National Archives and contains the testimony presented by witnesses appearing before the Congressional committee investigating the riots.)

VI. *Court Cases*

People v. Richard Brockway, *et al.*, in Circuit Court, September Term, 1917. Unpublished trial transcript, St. Clair County Courthouse.

People v. Le Roy Bundy, in Circuit Court, March Term, 1919. Unpublished trial transcript. (The Bundy case was tried at the Monroe County Courthouse, Waterloo, Illinois. The transcript at Waterloo has been lost or destroyed, but since the case was appealed to the Illinois Supreme Court, a copy was found at Springfield).

People v. Le Roy Bundy: In the Supreme Court of the State of Illinois. Statement, Brief and Argument for Plaintiff in Error. T. M. Webb, *et al.*, Attorneys, privately published, 1920.

People v. Le Roy Bundy: In the Supreme Court of the State of Illinois. Statement, Brief and Argument for Defendant in Error. Edward J. Brundage, *et al.*, Attorney General's Office, 1920.

People v. Le Roy Bundy, No. 13366, opinion filed December 21, 1920, in Reports of Cases at Law and in Chancery Argued and Determined in Supreme Court of Illinois—Illinois Reports (CCVC, 1921, pp. 322–31).

People v. Mike Evanhoff *et al.*, in Circuit Court, September Term, 1917. Unpublished trial transcript, St. Clair County Courthouse.

People v. Fred Gerold, in Reports of Cases at Law and in Chancery Argued and Determined in Supreme Court of Illinois —Illinois Reports (CCLXV, 1915, pp. 448–86).

People v. Fayette Parker, *et al.,* in Circuit Court, September Term, 1917. Unpublished trial transcript, St. Clair County Courthouse.

People v. Fayette Parker, *et al.,* No. 11972, opinion filed June 20, 1918, in Reports of Cases at Law and in Chancery Argued and Determined in Supreme Court of Illinois—Illinois Reports (CCLXXXIV, 1919, pp. 272–86).

VII. *Miscellaneous*

"Criminal Record, Monroe County," XXX, 1921.

"East St. Louis Race Riot," File of correspondence, East St. Louis Police Department, 1917.

"East St. Louis Race Riot," File of correspondence, United States Department of Justice, 1917. (Located at National Archives, Washington, D. C.).

Lincoln School (East St. Louis) "Attendance Record Book," 1917.

Young Women's Christian Association of East St. Louis, "Interracial Volume," 1921–43, unpublished.

INDEX

Ahearn, Maurice: 93; involvement in city government, 203–4
Albertson, Roy: reporting and testimony concerning July riot, 38–40, 244
Alexander, Marshall, 112
Allison, George W.: and social reform in East St. Louis, 150, 208–9, 214, 279–80
Alton and Southern Railway, 177
Altrogge, John B.: and the influx of Negroes, 168–69
Aluminum Ore Company, 5, 33, 149–50, 152, 177, 193, 239. *See also* Strikes
Aluminum Ore Employees Protective Association, 17–19, 31
Amalgamated Meatcuters and Butcher Workers Union of North America, 263
American Federation of Labor, 17, 19, 23, 121, 134, 144–46, 162
American Steel Foundries Company, 152, 160, 162, 193
Anderson, Paul Y., 46, 101, 202
Anderson, Sherwood, 190
Anti-Saloon League, 206
Armour meat packing plant, 5, 139, 152, 158, 168–69, 192–93, 274. *See also* Strikes
Atlanta Constitution, 62
Atlanta Independent, 64
Augusta Chronicle, 62
Augustus, Rosa, 109–10

Bagley, William, 147
Bailbondsmen, 203–5
Baker, Newton D., 239
Barrett, Thomas, 127
Bateman, Earl, 128
Baxter, Samuel W., 114, 123, 125, 128–31

Bayles, James, 117, 124, 127
Belleville Daily Advocate, 71, 102, 246
Belleville News-Democrat, 9–10, 71, 169, 189–90, 207, 255
Belleville Police Department, 248
Bluitt, Lyman B., 37, 88, 147
Boston Equal Rights League, 64
Boston Journal, 59
Brockway, Richard, 106–10
Brooklyn (Ill.), 11, 54–55, 130
Brundage, Edward, 89, 92, 174, 189, 209–10
Bundy, Charles, 119–20
Bundy, Le Roy: and colonization controversy, 10, 187, 190; complains of anti-Negro violence, 37; home searched, 54; tried as riot leader, 111, 119–32, 258, 260, 275; in Parker trial, 112–17, 127, 258, 260; supports Mollman administration, 120, 185, 187–88; favors unionization of Negroes, 121, 147; testifies at Council of Defense investigation, 121, 157; quarrels with N.A.A.C.P., 122–23; confesses to voting frauds, 185, 188–90, 275; establishes St. Clair County Republican League, 186–87; joins Garvey Movement, 261
Burleson, Albert S., 262

California Eagle, 66
Campbell, Martha, 130
Canavan, Thomas, 181–82, 184–85, 194, 203, 209, 213
Cannon, Joe, 138
Cary, Rachel, 109
Cashel, Stephen J., 194
Cavanaugh, R. W., 29, 35–36
Central Trades and Labor Union, 23–24, 27, 35, 159

REPRINT EDITIONS

King: A Biography *David Levering Lewis* Second edition

The Death and Life of Malcolm X *Peter Goldman* Second edition

Race Relations in the Urban South, 1865–1890 *Howard Rabinowitz*, with a Foreword by C. Vann Woodward

W. E. B. Du Bois: Voice of the Black Protest Movement *Elliott Rudwick*

Race Riot at East St. Louis, July 2, 1917 *Elliott Rudwick*